ROMANS

NCCS | New Covenant Commentary Series

The New Covenant Commentary Series (NCCS) is designed for ministers and students who require a commentary that interacts with the text and context of each New Testament book and pays specific attention to the impact of the text upon the faith and praxis of contemporary faith communities.

The NCCS has a number of distinguishing features. First, the contributors come from a diverse array of backgrounds in regards to their Christian denominations and countries of origin. Unlike many commentary series that tout themselves as international the NCCS can truly boast of a genuinely international cast of contributors with authors drawn from every continent of the world (except Antarctica) including countries such as the United States, Australia, the United Kingdom, Kenya, India, Singapore, and Korea. We intend the NCCS to engage in the task of biblical interpretation and theological reflection from the perspective of the global church. Second, the volumes in this series are not verse-by-verse commentaries, but they focus on larger units of text in order to explicate and interpret the story in the text as opposed to some often atomistic approaches. Third, a further aim of these volumes is to provide an occasion for authors to reflect on how the New Testament impacts the life, faith, ministry, and witness of the New Covenant Community today. This occurs periodically under the heading of "Fusing the Horizons." Here authors provide windows into community formation (how the text shapes the mission and character of the believing community) and ministerial formation (how the text shapes the ministry of Christian leaders).

It is our hope that these volumes will represent serious engagements with the New Testament writings, done in the context of faith, in service of the church, and for the glorification of God.

Series Editors:
Michael F. Bird (Highland Theological
 College, Dingwall, Scotland)
Craig Keener (Palmer Seminary,
 Philadelphia, USA)

Titles in this series:
Colossians and Philemon Michael F. Bird

Confirmed forthcoming titles (in order of projected publication):

Revelation Gordon Fee

Luke Jeannine Brown

Ephesians Lynn Cohick

2 Peter and Jude Andrew Mbuvi

James Pablo Jimenez

Matthew Joel Willits

1–3 John Sam Ngewa

1 Peter Eric Greaux

John Jey Kanagaraj

Philippians Linda Belleville

Pastoral Epistles Aída Besançon-Spencer

Hebrews Tom Thatcher

Mark Kim Huat Tan

Galatians Brian Vickers

Acts Youngmo Cho

2 Corinthians David deSilva

ROMANS

A New Covenant Commentary

Craig S. Keener

CASCADE *Books* · Eugene, Oregon

ROMANS
A New Covenant Commentary

New Covenant Commentary Series 6

Copyright © 2009 by Craig S. Keener.

Cascade Books
A Division of Wipf and Stock Publishers
199 W. 8th Ave., Suite 3
Eugene, OR 97401

www.wipfandstock.com

ISBN: 978-1-60608-156-3

Cataloging-in-Publication data:

Keener, Craig S.

Romans : a new covenant commentary / Craig S. Keener

xxvi + 274 p. ; 23 cm. Includes bibliographical references and indexes.

New Covenant Commentary Series 6

ISBN: 978-1-60608-156-3

1. Bible. N.T. Romans—Commentaries. I. Title. II. Series.

BS2665.53 K3 2009

Manufactured in the United States of America

To my siblings and siblings-in-law:
Thérèse, Emmanuel, Chris and Minglan, Eliser, Brett and Sally,
Aimé and Ornella, Gracia, and Jennifer

Contents

Outline of Romans

Preface

Romans is well-served with strong academic commentaries, but sparser on the end of concise, academically informed commentaries for a general audience. I hope that this brief commentary will contribute to that niche. I trust that readers will recognize that I could not cover every point in a commentary this size. I have covered what I could, but retain research notes to produce a much larger commentary on Romans if time permits. I am grateful to my co-editor for allowing me more space than some shorter volumes in the series, so that I did not need to end my comments, like some early manuscripts of Romans, with chapter 14 (or at least to omit the cover).

I have included only a fraction of my research documentation in the notes for interested readers to follow up, endeavouring at the same time to avoid distracting readers who choose such a volume for its conciseness.[1] Less technical readers should not feel intimidated by the footnotes, but should simply feel free to ignore them. Use of footnotes allowed me to keep the main text more readable, focused on the points that seemed most central to Paul's case.

To keep the series balanced, the editors' first two choices for a Romans commentator offered perspectives and backgrounds different from mine; I have offered mine here only because our first choices' other commitments precluded their participation. I am grateful to E. P. Sanders for conversation in the fall of 2008 about my understanding of the rhetoric of Paul's argument, and editorial feedback from my Palmer colleague Julia Pizzuto-Pomaco regarding Romans 16. Thanks to Chris Spinks and Heather Carraher at Wipf and Stock. Special thanks go to Michael Bird, my co-editor for the series, hence the only objective editor for this volume. Michael is the series' original designer, but having invited my participation, negotiated very flexibly both with respect to the series as a whole and with regard to my own volume (while reminding me of the series constraints where necessary).

1. Because I treated the background for some topics in Romans in greater detail in other works, I refer readers there at appropriate points to conserve space here. Nevertheless, readers will find many of my primary references new to Romans research.

Abbreviations

AB	Anchor Bible
ABR	*Australian Biblical Review*
ACCS	Ancient Christian Commentary on Scripture
ACNT	Augsburg Commentaries on the New Testament
AJP	*American Journal of Philology*
AUSS	*Andrews University Seminary Studies*
BA	*Biblical Archaeologist*
BBR	*Bulletin for Biblical Research*
BDAG	W. Bauer, F. W. Danker, W. F. Arndt, and F. W. Gingrich, *A Greek-English Lexicon of the New Testament and Other Early Christian Literature* (3rd ed.; Chicago: University of Chicago Press, 2000)
BDF	F. Blass, A. Debrunner, and R. W. Funk, *A Greek Grammar of the New Testament and Other Early Christian Literature* (Chicago: University of Chicago Press, 1961)
BECNT	Baker Exegetical Commentary on the New Testament
Bib	*Biblica*
BK	*Bibel und Kirche*
BZ	*Biblische Zeitschrift*
BZNW	Beihefte zur Zeitschrift für die neutestamentliche Wissenschaft
CBET	Contributions to Biblical Exegesis and Theology
CBQ	*Catholic Biblical Quarterly*
CJ	*Classical Journal*
ConBNT	Coniectanea biblica: New Testament Series
ConBOT	Coniectanea biblica: Old Testament Series
CSEL	Corpus scriptorum ecclesiasticorum latinorum
DNTB	*Dictionary of New Testament Background*, edited by Craig A. Evans and Stanley E. Porter (Downers Grove: InterVarsity, 2000)
DSD	*Dead Sea Discoveries*
ETL	*Ephemerides theologicae lovanienses*
ETS	Evangelical Theological Society
EvQ	*Evangelical Quarterly*

ExpTim	*Expository Times*
FBBS	Facet Books, Biblical Series
GRBS	*Greek, Roman, and Byzantine Studies*
HNTC	Harper's New Testament Commentaries
HTR	*Harvard Theological Review*
HTS	Harvard Theological Studies
IRT	Issues in Religion and Theology
ITQ	*Irish Theological Quarterly*
JANESCU	*Journal of the Ancient Near Eastern Society of Columbia University*
JBL	*Journal of Biblical Literature*
JBQ	*Jewish Bible Quarterly*
JGRChJ	*Journal of Greco-Roman Christianity and Judaism*
JJS	*Journal of Jewish Studies*
JRS	*Journal of Roman Studies*
JSJ	*Journal for the Study of Judaism in the Persian, Hellenistic, and Roman Periods*
JSNT	*Journal for the Study of the New Testament*
JSNTSup	JSNT Supplement Series
JSP	*Journal for the Study of the Pseudopigrapha*
JSQ	*Jewish Studies Quarterly*
JTS	*Journal of Theological Studies*
LCL	Loeb Classical Library
LEC	Library of Early Christianity
LXX	Septuagint
MScRel	*Mélanges de science religieuse*
NASB	New American Standard Bible
NICNT	New International Commentary on the New Testament
NIGTC	New International Greek Testament Commentary
NovT	*Novum Testamentum*
NovTSup	Supplements to Novum Testamentum
NIV	New International Version
NLT	New Living Translation
NRSV	New Revised Standard Version
NT	New Testament
NTL	New Testament Library
NTS	*New Testament Studies*
OBT	Overtures to Biblical Theology
OCD	*Oxford Classical Dictionary*, edited by S. Hornblower and A. Spawforth (3rd ed.; Oxford, 1996)

PGM	*Papyri graecae magicae: Die griechischen Zauberpapyri*, edited by K. Preisendanz (Berlin: B.G. Teubner, 1928)
PIBA	Proceedings of the Irish Biblical Association
PRSt	*Perspectives in Religious Studies*
RevQ	*Revue de Qumran*
RHR	*Revue de l'histoire des religions*
RQ	*Römische Quartalschrift für christliche Altertumskunde und Kirchengeschichte*
RSR	*Recherches de science religieuse*
SBLDS	Society of Biblical Literature Dissertation Series
SBLMS	Society of Biblical Literature Monograph Series
SBLSBS	Society of Biblical Literature Sources for Biblical Study
SBT	Studies in Biblical Theology
ScrTh	*Scripta theological*
SD	Studies and Documents
SJT	*Scottish Journal of Theology*
SNTSMS	Society for New Testament Studies Monograph Series
SP	Sacra pagina
SPhilo	*Studia philonica*
TBC	Torch Bible Commentaries
TNIV	Today's New International Version
TS	*Theological Studies*
TSAJ	Texte und Studien zum antiken Judentum
TynBul	*Tyndale Bulletin*
VE	*Vox evangelica*
WBC	Word Biblical Commentary
WUNT	Wissenschaftliche Untersuchungen zum Neuen Testament
ZAW	*Zeitschrift für die alttestamentliche Wissenschaft*
ZKG	*Zeitschrift für Kirchengeschichte*
ZNW	*Zeitschrift für die neutestamentliche Wissenschaft und die Kunde der älteren Kirche*

ANCIENT SOURCES

Jewish Sources

Apocrypha

Bar	Baruch
1 Esd	1 Esdras
Jdt	Judith

1–2 Macc	1–2 Maccabees
Pr Man	Prayer of Manasseh
Sir	Sirach
Tob	Tobit
Wis	Wisdom of Solomon

Dead Sea Scrolls

CD	Cairo Genizah copy of the *Damascus Document*
1QH	*Thanksgiving Hymns*
1QM	*War Scroll*
1QpHab	*Pesher Habakkuk*
1QS	*Rule of the Community*
4Q158	*Reworked Pentateuch*[a]
4Q174	*Eschatological Midrash*[a]
4Q403	*Songs of the Sabbath Sacrifice*[d]
4Q416	*Instruction*[b]
4Q417	*Instruction*[c]
4Q418	*Instruction*[d]
4Q436	*Bless, Oh my Soul*[c]
4Q504	*Words of the Luminaries*[a]
4QMMT	*Some Precepts of the Law*

Josephus

Ag. Ap.	*Against Apion*
Ant.	*Jewish Antiquities*
J.W.	*Jewish War*
Life	*The Life*

Philo of Alexandria

Abraham	*On the Life of Abraham*
Alleg. Interp.	*Allegorical Interpretation*
Cherubim	*On the Cherubim*
Creation	*On the Creation of the World*
Decalogue	*On the Decalogue*
Dreams	*On Dreams*
Embassy	*On the Embassy to Gaius*
Giants	*On Giants*
Good Person	*That Every Good Person is Free*
Heir	*Who Is the Heir?*
Migration	*On the Migration of Abraham*
Moses	*On the Life of Moses*
Planting	*On Planting*

Philo of Alexandria (*continued*)

Posterity	*On the Posterity of Cain*
Providence	*On Providence*
Sacrifices	*On the Sacrifices of Cain and Abel*
Spec. Laws	*On the Special Laws*
Unchangeable	*That God is Unchangeable*

Pseudepigrapha

Apoc. Mos.	*Apocalypse of Moses*
2 Bar.	*2 Baruch (Syriac Apocalypse)*
3 Bar.	*3 Baruch (Greek Apocalypse)*
1 En.	*1 Enoch (Ethiopic Apocalypse)*
2 En.	*2 Enoch (Slavonic Apocalypse)*
3 En.	*3 Enoch (Hebrew Apocalypse)*
Gk. Apoc. Ezra	*Greek Apocalypse of Ezra*
Jos. Asen.	*Joseph and Asenath*
Jub.	*Jubilees*
L.A.B.	*Liber antiquitatum biblicarum* (Pseudo-Philo)
L.A.E.	*Life of Adam and Eve*
Let. Aris.	*Letter of Aristeas*
3–4 Macc.	3–4 Maccabees
Pss. Sol.	*Psalms of Solomon*
Ps.-Phoc.	Pseudo-Phocylides
Sib. Or.	*Sibylline Oracles*
T. Ab.	*Testament of Abraham*
T. Ash.	*Testament of Asher*
T. Benj.	*Testament of Benjamin*
T. Dan	*Testament of Dan*
T. Iss.	*Testament of Issachar*
T. Job	*Testament of Job*
T. Jos.	*Testament of Joseph*
T. Jud.	*Testament of Judah*
T. Levi	*Testament of Levi*
T. Mos.	*Testament of Moses*
T. Naph.	*Testament of Naphtali*
T. Reub.	*Testament of Reuben*
T. Sim.	*Testament of Simeon*
T. Zeb.	*Testament of Zebulon*

Rabbinic Literature

'Abod. Zar.	*'Abodah Zarah*
'Abot R. Nat.	*'Abot de Rabbi Nathan*

A.M.	'Ahare Mot
b.	Babylonion Talmud
Bah.	Bahodesh
Behuq.	Behuqotai
Bek.	Bekhorot
Ber.	Berakhot
Besh.	Beshallah
Git.	Gittin
Hag.	Hagigah
Hor.	Horayot
Hul.	Hullin
Mek.	Mekilta
m.	Mishnah
Pesah.	Pesahim
Pesiq. Rab.	Pesiqta Rabbati
Pesiq. Rab Kah.	Pesiqta of Rab Kahana
Pesiq. Rab Kah. Sup.	Pesiqta of Rab Kahana Supplement
Qed.	Qedoshim
Qidd.	Qiddushin
Rab.	Rabbah
Ros. Has.	Ros HaShanah
Sanh.	Sanhedrin
Seqal.	Sheqalim
Shab.	Shabbat
Shir.	Shirata
t.	Tosefta
Tg. Neof.	Targum Neofiti
Tg. Ps.-J.	Targum Pseudo-Jonathan
Tg. Qoh.	Targum Qoheleth
VDDeho.	Vayyiqra Dibura Dehobah
y.	Jerusalem Talmud
Yebam.	Yebamot

Early Christian Sources

Apos. Con.	Apostolic Constitutions

Apostolic Fathers

Barn.	Barnabas
1 Clem.	1 Clement
Did.	Didache

Apostolic Fathers (*continued*)

Herm.	*Shepherd of Hermas*
Ign. *Eph.*	Ignatius, *To the Ephesians*
Ign. *Magn.*	Ignatius, *To the Magnesians*
Ign. *Smyrn.*	Ignatius, *To the Smyrnaeans*

Augustine

Contin.	*Continence*
Doctr. chr.	*Christian Instruction*
Exp. prop. Rom.	*Commentary on Statements in the Letter to the Romans*
Simpl.	*To Simplicianus*

Cyril of Alexandria

Expl. Rom.	*Explanation into the Letter to the Romans*

Gregory of Nazianzus

Or. Bas.	*Oration in Praise of Basil*
Theo. Or.	*Theological Orations*

Jerome

Pelag.	*Against Pelagius*

John Chrysostom

Hom. Cor.	*Homilies on Corinthians*
Hom. Rom.	*Homilies on Romans*

Justin

Dial.	*Dialogue with Trypho*

Origen

Comm. Rom.	*Commentary on Romans*

Pelagius

Comm. Rom.	*Commentary on Romans*

Theordoret of Cyr

Interp. Rom.	*Interpretation of the Letter to the Romans*

Other Greco-Roman Sources

Achilles Tatius

Leuc. Clit.	*The Adventures of Leucippe and Cleitophon*

Aelian

Nat. an.	*Nature of Animals*

Aeschines
    Tim.   *Against Timarchus*

Aeschylus
    Ag.   *Agamemnon*
    Suppl.   *Suppliant Women*

Apuleius
    Metam.   *Metamorphoses (The Golden Ass)*

Aristotle
    Eth. eud.   *Eudemian Ethics*
    Eth. nic.   *Nichomachean Ethics*
    Pol.   *Politics*
    Rhet.   *Rhetoric*

Arius Didymus
    Epit.   *Epitome of Stoic Ethics*

Arrian
    Alex.   *Anabasis of Alexander*

Artemidorus Daldianus
    Onir.   *Onirocritica*

Athenaeus
    Deipn.   *Deipnosophists*

Aulus Gellius
    Noct. att.   *Attic Nights*

Caesar
    Bell. civ.   *Civil War*
    Bell. gall.   *Gallic War*

Chariton
    Chaer.   *Chaereas and Callirhoe*

Cicero
    Amic.   *De amicitia*
    Att.   *Epistulae ad Atticum*
    Cael.   *Pro Caelio*
    Cat.   *In Catalinam*
    De or.   *De oratore*
    Fam.   *Epistulae ad familiares*
    Fin.   *De finibus*
    Font.   *Pro fonteio*
    Inv.   *De inventione rhetorica*

Cicero (*continued*)

Leg.	*De legibus*
Mil.	*Pro Milone*
Mur.	*Pro Murena*
Nat. d.	*De natura deorum*
Off.	*De officiis*
Or. Brut.	*Orator ad M. Brutum*
Phil.	*Orationes philippicae*
Pis.	*In Pisonem*
Quinct.	*Pro Quinctio*
Quint. fratr.	*Epistulae ad Quintum fratrem*
Rep.	*De republica*
Rosc. Amer.	*Pro Sexto Roscio Amerino*
Scaur.	*Pro Scauro*
Sull.	*Pro Sulla*
Tusc.	*Tusculanae disputationes*

Cynic Epistles

Ps.-Crates *Ep.*	Pseudo-Crates, *Epistles*
Ps.-Diogenes *Ep.*	Pseudo-Diogenes, *Epistles*
Ps.-Heraclitus *Ep.*	Pseudo-Heraclitus, *Epistles*

Demetrius

Eloc.	*Style*

Demosthenes

Aristog.	*Against Aristogeiton*
Con.	*Against Conon*
Epitaph.	*Funeral Oration*

Dio Chrysostom

Ep.	*Epistles*
Or.	*Orations*

Dionysius of Halicarnassus

Ant. rom.	*Roman Antiquities*
Dem.	*Demosthenes*
Epid.	*Epideictic* (Pseudo-Dionysius)
Lys.	*Lysias*
Thuc.	*Thucydides*

Epictetus

Disc.	*Discourses*
Ench.	*Enchiridion*

Euripides
    Alc.   *Alcestis*
    El.   *Electra*
    Med.   *Medea*

Fronto
    Ad Amic.   *Ad amicos*
    Ad M. Caes.   *Ad Marcus Caesarem et invicem*
    Eloq.   *Ad Antonium Imperator de eloquentia*
    Verum Imp.   *Ad Verum Imperator et invicem*

Gaius
    Inst.   *Institutes*

Heraclitus
    Hom. Prob.   *Homeric Problems*

Hermogenes
    Progymn.   *Progymnasmata*

Herodotus
    Hist.   *Histories*

Hesiod
    Op.   *Works and Days*

Homer
    Il.   *Iliad*
    Od.   *Odyssey*

Horace
    Ep.   *Epistles*
    Sat.   *Satires*

Iamblichus
    Myst.   *Mysteries*
    V.P.   *Pythagorean Life*

Isaeus
    Cleon.   *Cleonymus*

Isocrates
    Ad Nic.   *To Nicocles (Oration 2)*
    Demon.   *To Demonicus (Oration 1)*
    Nic.   *Nicocles (Oration 3)*

Juvenal
    Sat.   *Satires*

Lucian
  Alex.   Alexander the False Prophet
  Am.   Affairs of the Heart
  Demon.   Demonax
  Deor. conc.   Parliament of the Gods
  Dial. d.   Dialogues of the Gods
  Gall.   The Dream, or the Cock
  Hermot.   Hermotimus, or Sects
  Imag.   Essays in Portraiture
  Philops.   The Lover of Lies
  Prom.   Prometheus
  Sacr.   Sacrifices
  Syr. d.   The Goddess of Syria
  Tim.   Timon, or Misanthrope
  Tyr.   The Tyrannicide
  Ver. hist.   A True Story
  Vit. auct.   Philosophies for Sale

Lysias
  Or.   Orations

Marcus Aurelius
  Med.   Meditations

Maximus of Tyre
  Or.   Orations

Ovid
  Fast.   Fasti
  Metam.   Metamorphoses

Petronius
  Sat.   Satyricon

Philostratus
  Ep. Apoll.   Epistles of Appolonius
  Hrk.   Heroikos
  Vit. Apoll.   Life of Appolonius

Plato
  Alcib.   Alcibiades
  Charm.   Charmides

Pliny the Elder
  Nat.   Natural History

Pliny the Younger
    Ep.   *Epistles*

Plotinus
    Enn.   *Ennead*

Plutarch
    Alc.   *Alcibiades*
    Alex.   *Alexander*
    Cam.   *Camillus*
    Cic.   *Cicero*
    Cor.   *Marcus Coriolanus*
    De esu   *Eating Flesh*
    De laude   *Boasting Inoffensively*
    Frat. amor.   *On Brotherly Love*
    Isis   *Isis and Osiris*
    Ought not Borrow   *That We Ought Not Borrow*
    Quaest. conv.   *Table-Talk*
    Quaest. rom.   *Roman Questions*
    Superst.   *Superstition*
    Thes.   *Theseus*

Poryphyry
    Ar. Cat.   *On Aristotle's Categories*
    Marc.   *To Marcella*

Pseudo-Callisthenes
    Alex.   *Alexander Romance*

Pyth. Sent.   *Pythogorean Sentences*

Quintilian
    Inst.   *Institutes of Oratory*

Rhet. Alex.   *Rhetorica ad Alexandrum*

Rhet. Her.   *Rhetorica ad Herennium*

Sallust
    Bell. Cat.   *War with Cataline*
    Rep.   *Letters to Caesar on the State*

Seneca the Elder
    Controv.   *Controversiae*
    Suas.   *Suasoriae*

Seneca the Younger
   Ben.   *On Benefits*
   Dial.   *Dialogues*
   Ep. Lucil.   *Epistles to Lucilius*
   Med.   *Medea*
   Nat.   *Natural Questions*

Sextus Empiricus
   Pyr.   *Outlines of Pyrrhonism*

Sophocles
   Phil.   *Philoctetes*

Suetonius
   Aug.   *Divus Augustus*
   Claud.   *Divus Cladius*
   Dom.   *Domitian*
   Jul.   *Divus Julius*
   Tib.   *Tiberius*

Tacitus
   Ann.   *Annals*
   Hist.   *Histories*

Terence
   Andr.   *Andria*

Theon
   Progymn.   *Progymnasmata*

Virgil
   Aen.   *Aeneid*

   Vit. Aes.   *Life of Aesop*

Xenophon
   Anab.   *Anabasis*
   Apol.   *Apologia Socratis*
   Cyn.   *Cynegeticus*
   Cyr.   *Cyropaedia*
   Hell.   *Hellinica*
   Mem.   *Memorabilia*

Inscriptions, Papyri, and Other

*ANET*²	*Ancient Near Eastern Texts Relating to the Old Testament*, edited by J. B. Pritchard (2nd ed.; Princeton: Princeton University Press, 1955)
CIJ	*Corpus inscriptionum judaicarum*
CPJ	*Corpus papyrorum judaicarum*, edited by V. Tcherikover (3 vols.; Cambridge: Magnes Press, Hebrew University, 1957–64)
P. Giess.	*Griechische Papyri im Museum des oberhessischen Geschichtsvereins zu Giessen*, edited by E. Kornemann, O. Eger, and P. M. Meyer (Leipzig-Berlin, 1910–12)
PGM	*Papyri graecae magicae: Die griechischen Zauberpapyri*, edited by K. Preisendanz (Berlin: B.G. Teubner, 1928)
P. Lond.	*Greek Papyri in the British Museum*, edited by F. S. Kenyon and H. I. Bell (London, 1903–17)
P. Oxy.	*The Oxyrhynchus Papyri*, edited by B. P. Grenfell and A. S. Hunt (17 vols.; 1896–1927)

Introduction

Because Romans is the first Pauline letter in our NT canon, I begin with an introduction that may shed some light on the letters in general, although it is designed with Romans particularly in mind.

READING LETTERS

In the past, some scholars made much of the difference between "letters" and "epistles," placing Paul's in the former category to show their proximity to most surviving ancient letters (from Egyptian papyri) rather than literary letters. While Paul did not belong to the elite circles of leisured letter writers like Cicero or Pliny, he did not simply compose his major letters, like Romans, off the top of his head. Given the time necessary to take normal dictation in antiquity (shorthand being unavailable), Paul may have taken over eleven hours to dictate this letter to Tertius, its scribe (Rom 16:22).[1] Since such a major undertaking probably involved more than one draft (and Paul could draw on his preaching experience), the final draft may have taken less than this estimate, but the total time invested in the letter was probably greater. Given the cost of papyrus and of the labor required (though Tertius, a believer, might have donated his services), one scholar estimates the cost of Romans at 20.68 denarii, which he calculates as roughly $2275 in recent US currency.[2] In other words, Paul did not simply offer this project as an afterthought; Romans is a carefully premeditated work.

As we shall note below, Romans is no ordinary letter; it is a sophisticated argument. The average ancient papyrus letter was 87 words; the orator Cicero was more long-winded, averaging 295 words (with as many as 2530 words); and the philosopher Seneca averaged 995 words (with as many as 4134). The extant letters attributed to Paul average 2495 words,

---

1. Richards 2004: 165.
2. Richards 2004: 169.

while Romans, his longest, has 7114 words.[3] Because ancient urban argumentation typically involved rhetoric, we shall explore possible connections with rhetoric below.

One characteristic of letters that is surely relevant here is that authors expected the specified audience of their letters to understand them. Whether authors always communicated adequately or readers always understood adequately is another question, but most authors at least tried to communicate so as to be clearly understood. Paul thus writes to his audience in Greek. (Greek was the first language of many non-Italians in Rome, including the majority of Jews and of Christian ministers who had come from the east; only in the second century is it clear that many lower-class, Latin-speaking Romans joined the church.) Paul also apparently writes with what he assumes will be shared cultural assumptions regarding language and concepts that he uses without detailed explanation. Informing ourselves about these shared cultural assumptions will help us understand his language; this objective is one of the primary purposes of this commentary (like many others). Better understanding the local situation in Rome does not mean that Paul would expect the principles he articulates there to be applicable there only; he does, after all, apply many of the same principles to other situations in other congregations. But noting these situations will help us better understand his argument and better identify the principles he is applying.

PAUL AND RHETORIC

Scholars today often read Paul's letters in light of ancient rhetoric, a mostly positive development. Although some scholars have carried rhetorical analysis too far, as we shall observe, the development is mostly positive because ancient rhetoric offers a much more concrete basis for analyzing Paul's arguments than modern guesses would.

Two forms of advanced education existed in the Greco-Roman world: philosophy and rhetoric. The former concerned itself especially with truth and reality, and the latter with communication and persuasion. Despite traditional, stereotypical hostility between the two disciplines, most educated people recognized the value in and made use of both. Nevertheless, rhetoric was the dominant discipline, being considered more practical for

---

3. Anderson 1999: 113, noting that Paul departed from conventional epistolary expectations here (cf. also Malherbe 1977: 16; Demetrius *Eloc.* 4.228).

public life (politics, speeches in the courts, and so forth). Although only a small minority of people had advanced training of any kind, rhetoric pervaded society and shaped the way urban people thought and argued. Not only could passersby listen to speakers practicing in the marketplace, but oratory dominated civic assemblies and was even the subject of some public competitions.

Because such oratorical training became even more dominant in the second century, church fathers often read Paul in light of rhetoric, and Renaissance and Reformation interpreters like Melanchthon continued this practice. By the higher rhetorical standards of the second century, Paul was not an expert rhetorician, but he probably fared better by the standards of his era. Despite objections to his delivery (cf. 1 Cor 2:3; 2 Cor 10:10; 11:6), Paul's letters include numerous rhetorical devices that would have been familiar to his contemporaries. In fact, Paul might have over-compensated to silence his critics; rhetoricians (such as Cicero) tended to limit rhetorical devices in letters, which were intended to be more like conversation than public speech.

Where scholars have overplayed rhetoric is in seeking to structure Paul's letters as if they were speeches. Rhetorical handbooks in this period do not address letters, but when they later do, they do not treat them like speeches. Most genuine speeches do not fit the precise outlines we find in rhetorical handbooks, and we should expect such outlines to prove even less relevant to letters. They do not even fit the letters of rhetorically sophisticated letter writers like Cicero, Pliny, or Fronto.

Nevertheless, Paul's extant letters are not normal letters (though they are comparable in some ways to some letter-essays, e.g., by Seneca).[4] While Paul often includes conversational elements, many of his letters include substantial *argumentation*—which was characteristically the do-main of rhetoric rather than of letters. While rhetoric may rarely provide us detailed outlines for his letters, therefore, it does provide abundant insights into how Paul argues his case.[5]

Scholars differ as to whether Paul had any rhetorical training or sim-ply absorbed practices dominant in his environment.[6] Certainly Paul did

4. The comparison is limited; see Elliott 2008: 17.

5. For some recent nuanced discussions of Paul and rhetoric, see e.g., Porter 1997: 561–67, 584–85; Reed 1997: 182–91; Anderson 1999: 114–26, 280–81; Bird 2008; Keener 2008b: 221.

6. For Paul having more training than many suppose, see Hock 2003.

not have advanced (tertiary) training in a Greek rhetorical school with the goal of becoming a Greek orator; orators exhibited their skills by lavishly citing classical Greek texts, which appear in Paul only very rarely. By contrast, many of Paul's letters (notably including Romans) lavishly display the Jewish Scriptures, typically in the forms dominant in the Greek Diaspora. Paul's display of biblical knowledge suggests the combination of a brilliant mind with the best of training in the Scriptures, probably in the ancient world's best center for such training, namely Jerusalem. If Paul, presumably from a well-off family who could afford such training, studied with Gamaliel in Greek (as suggested in Acts 22:3; cf. *t. Sotah* 15:8), he probably also had some additional training in delivering sermons in acceptable Greek style. Today's equivalent might be advanced study in Bible with a few homiletics courses. If so, Paul masterfully developed the basic skills he received at this level of training.

If Paul used Greek techniques because they were a part of the milieu in which he and Diaspora Judaism (and to a somewhat reduced extent, Palestinian Judaism) moved, Paul's more specifically "Jewish" context informs what he would have viewed as the core of his cultural identity (cf. Rom 9:1–5; 11:1).

Paul, Judaism, and the Law

When we speak of Paul and "Judaism," we are usually thinking in anachronistic terms. Paul, like most of the earliest Christian movement even in the Diaspora, was Jewish. Modern Western readers distinguish "Judaism" and "Christianity" as distinct religions, but the Christian movement, as it came to be called, viewed itself as carrying on the biblical faith of patriarchs and prophets in view of end-time fulfillment in Christ, demonstrated by the eschatological gift of the Spirit.

As scholars today emphasize, first-century Judaism was itself highly diverse; some even speak of "Judaisms" (though emphasizing the wide variation in Jewish practice should make the point sufficiently). Its rabbinic form (which evolved into traditional Orthodox Judaism as we know it today) evolved from Pharisaism, but that evolution postdates Paul's ministry. Paul's faith is, in a sense, an earlier development of Pharisaism (albeit a minority one) than rabbinic Judaism is, as some Jewish scholars have recently pointed out. Jews as a people affirmed circumcision, the temple, the Torah, and other traits (many of these, like distinctive food customs, highlighted over the previous two centuries as costly marks of distinctive Jewish identity). Yet some (more often in the Holy Land) expected the imminent end of the age, whereas others denied it. The degree of Jewish Diaspora assimilation to the surrounding culture varied from one place to another and according to the attitudes of their host cultures.[7] Views about messianic figures varied more widely than we have space to narrate here. Paul has been compared to apocalyptic, mystic, and Pharisaic streams of Judaism, among others.

E. P. Sanders on "the Law"

The dominant current arguments surrounding Paul's relationship with his Jewish context most relevant to Romans, however, involve his own approach to the law versus that of his contemporaries. Views of Paul's relationship to what we call Judaism have varied widely over the centuries, from Marcion's proto-gnostic Paul (who rejected anything Jewish) to W. D. Davies' Paul (who was a Pharisee who believed that the messianic era had dawned). Most scholars today would agree more with Davies than Marcion, but some aspects of Paul's relation to Judaism—and the character of ancient Judaism—remain debated.

E. P. Sanders's work *Paul and Palestinian Judaism*, published in 1977, shook New Testament scholarship in general and Pauline studies in particular. Many New Testament scholars (particularly in the German scholarly tradition—at least according to Anglophone scholars), depicted Judaism as legalistic and seeking to be justified by works. (This grid for reading the sources persisted from debates at the time of the Reformation.) Scholars of Judaism had long challenged the sufficiency of such a paradigm (which pervaded works like Strack-Billerbeck's widely-used rabbinic commentary on the New Testament),[8] but it was Sanders's forceful polemic that shook the old paradigm. He argued that nearly all of ancient Judaism affirmed that Israelites as a whole were graciously chosen as part of the covenant, and remained members of the covenant unless

---

7. For one typology regarding assimilation, accommodation, and acculturation, see Barclay 1995.

8. Earlier scholars with more nuanced views include Moore (1971) and Bonsirven (1964); in Pauline scholarship, Longenecker (1976) also showed analogies in a covenant nomist pattern in Paul's and other early Jewish thought.

cutting themselves off through apostasy. Judaism was thus a religion of grace, and works confirmed rather than earned a place in the covenant.

One complication of revisiting ancient Judaism's approach to works and grace is that one must then revisit Paul's approach to the views of his contemporaries on these matters. Paul does in fact sound like he regards his contemporaries' approach as based on human effort rather than grace, so New Testament scholars set out to reinterpret Paul based on this new interpretation of ancient Judaism. Many found Sanders's reconstruction of ancient Judaism more plausible than his interpretation of Paul, but James D. G. Dunn, Hans Hübner, Heikki Räisänen, Francis Watson, N. T. Wright, and others also offered new readings of Paul in his Jewish setting.[9] Some of these new interpretations became known as the "New Perspective," but the new perspectives are in fact so diverse on various points of detail that the main characteristic of their newness is that they reject the older caricature of Judaism.

While Sanders's challenge to caricatures of Judaism proved to be an important watershed, many of the details of his approach have come under increasing challenge. Sanders's primary thesis, the prevalence of grace in Judaism (and perhaps especially rabbinic Judaism, where it was often least appreciated), won the day, and there is little likelihood, barring a nuclear holocaust or other cataclysmic event that wipes out the current generation of scholars and our work, that the bulk of NT scholarship will backtrack on that point. Yet scholars have increasingly noticed that another side of the picture, "works righteousness," remains in the Jewish sources. A number of scholars argue that Sanders's way of framing the questions (in response to more traditional ways of framing them) and arranging the data downplayed the sources' emphasis on earning merit or even eschatological salvation.[10]

---

9. See e.g., Räisänen 1983; Hübner 1984; Dunn 1992; Watson 2007.

10. Among other works, see e.g., Gathercole 2002; Thielman 1987, 1994; Talbert 2001; Cairus 2004; Seifrid 1992: 78–135; Quarles 1996; Hagner 1993; Eskola 1998: 28–60; idem 2002; Carson, O'Brien, and Seifrid 2001; esp. Avemarie 1996 (particularly 36–43); see also discussion in Bird 2007. Sanders 2009 has forcefully reiterated and explained what he intended as the primary *point* of his argument; for the weighty intellectual history of his approach, see Sanders 2008: 18–25.

Synthesizing Various Factors

Part of the debate depends on the meaning of "legalism" and "works righteousness." Thus, Sanders would point out that the NT sources themselves often speak of reward and even eternal salvation on the basis of works, yet in the larger context of God's covenant grace. With some critics, one helpful approach to the varied evidence of Jewish sources is to recognize that diverse approaches existed, a variety that many teachers never sought to harmonize and Judaism as a whole certainly could not harmonize. It is indeed hard to imagine otherwise. For example, despite the heavy teaching on grace in the New Testament, many Christians today are what other Christians would consider "legalistic."[11] Ancient Judaism surely included its share of this sort of "legalism," too, whatever the approach of those who most emphasized grace. (We did, after all, open this section by affirming the diversity of ancient Judaism in many other respects.)

Aside from this question, we should also allow for some other factors when hearing Paul. First, Paul is ready to use *reductio ad absurdum* where necessary (cf. e.g., Rom 2:17–24); ancient polemic could focus on a weakness in an opposing position that its supporters might not regard as fundamental to or characteristic of the position. Moreover, the center of Paul's argument is not simply any gracious act, but God's grace specifically in Christ, which was for Paul (and for other Christians) the climax of salvific history. This *specific* understanding of grace informs the distinction of his position from that of contemporaries who rejected his understanding of Christ. Finally, Paul is often addressing not Judaism as a whole, but (especially in Galatians) the demands of some fellow Jewish Christians who sought to accommodate the strictest Jewish expectations for full converts to Judaism. It was the status of Gentile converts that generated the conflict most starkly (hence the increased prominence of righteousness by faith in letters addressing Gentile believers' relation to Judaism).[12]

Thus, most Jews welcomed Gentile interest in Judaism and even affirmed the future "salvation" of monotheistic, sexually pure Gentiles, yet believed that sharing in Israel's covenant required circumcision and acceptance of the law, including those parts specific to Israel. Jews could

11. Historically, cf. e.g., Vidler 1974: 279.

12. Many have noted this greater prominence in Romans and Galatians (cf. also Ephesians), especially since Stendahl 1976 (esp. 2–4).

keep the law as a natural part of their culture regardless of the question of salvation. By contrast, for Gentiles to keep it as a condition for belonging to the covenant, and still more (on some particularly strict views) for salvation,[13] was to demand new "works" as a condition for inclusion rather than simply a sign of inner transformation. (One might compare Western missionaries one or two centuries ago obligating new believers in some parts of the world to adopt Western names and dress to confirm their conversion to Christianity.) Although ethnically distinctive markers in the law are not the only ones Paul addresses (his language is too broad for that), these are the features that provoked the most complaint in Rome and that seem a central problem in the practical relation of Roman believers addressed in Romans 14.

For Paul, to insist on maintaining literally all the distinctives mandated specifically for ancient Israel was to ignore the climax of salvation history, what God had accomplished in Christ. He treated outward circumcision as secondary to the spiritual covenant commitment it signified, and insisted that the new covenant in the heart obviated the details of the earlier covenant that merely prepared the way for it. From Paul's perspective, this was simply following his own biblical Jewish faith to its logical conclusion, in light of the coming of Christ and the Spirit. Many of his contemporaries understandably disagreed, and their debates (albeit usually from the Pauline side) surface repeatedly in the NT texts.

PAUL, JUDAISM, AND RHETORIC

Our problems reconciling what we know of ancient Judaism with Paul's arguments stem not only from the diversity of ancient Judaism but from our unfamiliarity with ancient rhetoric. Polemic regularly caricatured opponents, sometimes using hyperbole to reduce their position to the absurd (see e.g., Matt 23:24). An ancient audience could recognize and appreciate such strategies (except when recycling the language polemically themselves).

Most scholars today recognize that Paul sometimes employs ad hoc arguments (e.g., in 1 Cor 11:3–16).[14] Some such arguments appear in Romans, where, for example, his caricature of a distinctly unreliable

13. In Galatia, Paul's opponents possibly meant merely the former; if so, Paul prefers a rigorous consistency that identifies membership in the covenant with salvation.

14. See discussion in Keener 1992: 19–69; additional background in idem 2000a.

Jewish teacher (2:17–24) and his recycling of several more general texts to regard all Jews as sinful (the Psalm texts in 3:10–20) would not actually condemn every individual Jewish person. To notice this apparent anomaly is not to suggest that Paul would have relinquished his view that all people were sinners (a view that most Jews shared anyway), but to suggest that if had he written for a modern audience he sometimes would have used a different style of argumentation. His rhetoric, no less than his use of Greek language, is constructed to appeal specifically within a particular cultural setting. Such polemical rhetoric was expected and necessary for successful debate in Paul's day. Indeed, Paul fashions his polemic in such a way that even his detractors would have been forced to condemn the figure he caricatures. Today we can learn from Paul's message while aesthetically appreciating his plethora of figures of speech and rhetorical devices that displayed his brilliance while holding his original audience's attention.

Some of Paul's arguments reflect earlier Christian tradition, and some may have generated such tradition. For example, the polemic regarding true children of Abraham (4:11–17; cf. 9:6–13) reflects a debate already found in the early Palestinian gospel tradition (Matt 3:9/Luke 3:8; cf. John 8:39–41). Likewise, Paul's treatment of faith and works (here or more generally) seems to have been caricatured (either to exploit it or to denigrate it; cf. 3:8), inviting a rejoinder to that caricature in Jas 2:18–24.[15]

THE SETTING OF THE CHURCH IN ROME

Even letter-essays sometimes addressed the receiver's situation or interests (e.g., the need for consolation), and other sorts of letters did so even more regularly. Ancient orators and writers tried to be sensitive to the settings they were addressing, and (contrary to what some scholars argue in the case of Romans) Paul is no exception. Paul writes this letter from Corinth (cf. Rom 16:1; Acts 20:2–3), a colony closely tied with Rome (e.g., merchants regularly traveled between them). Given the list of people Paul knew in Rome (see Rom 16:3–15), he was undoubtedly well-informed about issues there. This does not mean that Paul lacks interest in larger principles (he does in fact work from a larger argument that resembles

15. For the point-by-point, sequential comparison, see Dunn 1988: 1:197.

some of his preaching elsewhere); rather, he brings those principles to bear pastorally on a local situation.

Jews in Rome[16]

Estimates of Rome's Jewish population tend to run between about twenty thousand and fifty thousand; such estimates are at best educated guesses, but they probably suggest the right order of magnitude.[17] Estimates of Rome's population also vary, from perhaps a quarter of a million (extrapolated from water supplies) to over a million for its metropolitan area (extrapolated, in my opinion more reliably, from concrete census figures from ancient historians).[18] It is at any rate clear that the Jewish community was a small minority, though significant among the Greek-speaking minority immigrant populations from the eastern Roman Empire.

Jewish people lived together in several suburbs of the city, generally in mostly ethnically segregated neighborhoods. The majority remained in their original area, Transtiberinum (what is today Trastevere), across the Tiber from the city's center. Archaeology indicates that most Jews there were poor; many probably worked at the Tiber's docks.[19] Nevertheless, there were well-to-do members. We know the names of three to five Roman synagogues from this period, which appear to have been connected only loosely, since Rome did not allow any unifying leadership as, e.g., in Alexandria. Archaeological evidence suggests that many had settled from various parts of the Diaspora and were thus fairly diverse. This loose structure may have helped facilitate the free spread of the message about Jesus in some of the synagogues.

16. See Leon 1960; Lampe 2003a; essays in Donfried and Richardson 1998.

17. See Suetonius *Tib.* 36; Josephus *Ant.* 18.84; idem *J.W.* 2.80.

18. See Clarke 1994: 464–66; Garnsey and Saller 1987: 83; for estimates approaching a million, see Stambaugh 1988: 89; Packer 1967: 87; below a quarter million, Rohrbaugh 1991: 133. For earlier periods, with over one hundred thousand adult citizens (thus not counting children, slaves, and non-citizen residents), see e.g., Dionysius of Halicarnassus *Ant. rom.* 5.20.1; 5.75.3; 6.96.4; 9.15.2; 9.36.3; cf. Plutarch *Caesar* 55.3; Suetonius *Jul.* 41. Some estimates are much higher (e.g., Carcopino 1940: 20–21). Ancients could speak either of the area inside the city walls (e.g., Pliny the Elder *Nat.* 3.5.66) or of larger Rome (idem 3.5.67).

19. Jeffers 1998: 131. In Rome as a whole, rich and poor often lived side by side, the latter especially in crowded tenements, with the poorest tending to live higher up in the sometimes flimsy and flammable structures.

Over half of Rome's Jews have Latin names.[20] A large number prob-ably descended from Jewish slaves originally brought to Rome by Pompey over a century earlier, then bought and freed by Jews already living in Rome (Philo *Embassy* 155). Although many remained predominantly Greek speaking even by this period (over three quarters of their inscrip-tions are in Greek, and not quite a quarter are in Latin),[21] many were Roman citizens (Philo *Embassy* 155). When Roman citizens freed their slaves under particular conditions, those freed became Roman citizens; Paul himself may have descended from Jewish slaves freed in Rome (cf. Acts 6:9; 16:37; 22:28). Certain features made this community ripe for the spread of the message about Jesus: they were apparently open to the dominant culture, providing tolerance for new ideas, while their distinc-tive ethnic status also connected them with other Judeans who followed Jesus.

Nevertheless, Jews often faced prejudice from the larger Roman soci-ety.[22] Rome was tolerant of many cultures in its empire, but many Romans guarded more jealously their own city's traditions, and particularly re-sented Jewish success at winning converts and sympathizers (especially among Roman matrons). Roman sources explicitly condemn Jews for circumcision (cf. Rom 2:25–29; 4:9–12), which they viewed as a form of mutilation; the Sabbath (cf. Rom 14:5-6), which they viewed as an excuse for laziness (in contrast to Roman market days); and their food customs (cf. Rom 14:2–23). Under extreme circumstances, the Jewish community could even face banishment from Rome (see discussion below).

Jewish and Gentile Elements in the Church

The church's origins in Rome probably stemmed from Jewish believers there (cf. Acts 2:10),[23] but clearly it spread beyond them. Paul's audi-

20. Mostly regular Gentile names, including many that recall names of deities (but without polytheistic intent; they likewise used some Roman decorations, but preferred distinctive Jewish symbols like the menorah to major Roman ones). Only about 15 per-cent have traditional Semitic names.

21. Leon 1960: 76.

22. See e.g., Juvenal *Sat.* 14.100–104; see especially Gager 1983; Sevenster 1975.

23. So also Ambrosiaster in the fourth century, who believed that the founders ex-pected law observance (Lane 1998: 203). Paul assumes a high degree of biblical literacy and familiarity with Jewish tradition (though cf. also Galatians), and the many travelers to the capital carried new ideas there quickly.

ence was "among the Gentiles" (Rom 1:5); they were least partly Gentile (11:13) and probably mostly Gentile (1:13; cf. 16:4). Many contend that Jewish believers and God-fearing Gentiles[24] remained in the synagogues in Rome for some time, explaining why Paul can presuppose so much knowledge of Scripture and Jewish perspective in the letter (cf. 7:1). At some point in the 40s CE the Jewish community in Rome was apparently divided over questions of the identity of the Messiah, probably Jesus. As a result, the emperor Claudius followed the precedent of the earlier emperor Tiberius and banished the Jews from Rome (cf. the garbled account in Suetonius *Claud.* 25.4). Given the context in our sources, this may have happened in about the year 49 CE.

Scholars debate whether the entire Jewish community actually left; it would be difficult to reclaim property, hence difficult to imagine generations of Jewish occupation coming to a complete end, then resuming their lives in Rome after Claudius's edict was repealed (on his death in 54 CE). Certainly the many Jews who were Roman citizens would not have been expelled. Nevertheless, Luke, like Suetonius, speaks of Jews being expelled (Acts 18:2, though prudently omitting the cause). Whether all were expelled (and whether all who were officially expelled actually left), at least those visible in the original conflict must have left. Luke indicates that Priscilla and Aquila, Jews in Rome who were apparently already believers (and possibly church leaders) when Paul met them, had left. It is likely that a substantial number of Jewish Christians, and perhaps all their leaders, left Rome at this point. This means that Gentile Christians had probably constituted the bulk of the Roman church and its leadership for at least five years, and may represent a number of the house churches greeted in Romans 16. (Those with Jewish leaders, as in 16:5, 7, may have organized after many Jews returned.)

Given the different cultural orientation of congregations in the same city, probably at least as loosely connected as the different synagogues, it is not surprising that misunderstandings would arise between groups with a predominantly Jewish ethos. Some Gentiles (especially former

24. Rome's synagogues had many Godfearers to begin with; proselytism and attraction to Judaism constituted major causes of resentment among traditional Romans against Roman Judaism (see Parkes 1979: 25–26; Gager 1983: 55–56). For proselytes in Rome, see e.g., Leon 1960: 250–56. Nanos (1996) argues that the believers in Rome, who are Gentiles, remain in the synagogues, so that Paul encourages them to honor Jewish concerns.

adherents of the synagogue) may have held the "Jewish" position, and some especially culturally sensitive Jews (probably including Aquila and Priscilla) may not have insisted on Gentiles observing the whole law, but at least two basic "sides" seem to have existed nonetheless.

Jews and Gentiles in Paul's Letter

Committed to building up the believers in Rome (Rom 1:11), Paul naturally targets a key issue among them. His letter addresses the relationship between Jewish and Gentile believers (1:16; 2:9-10; 3:9; 9:24; 10:12).[25] In Romans 1–3, he establishes everyone's equal need before God: not only Gentiles (1:18–32) but also Jews (2:1—3:20) are damned. He shows how the law itself need not make Jews better than Gentiles (e.g., 2:14). He shows how the law itself establishes righteousness by faith (3:21, 27, 31), focusing on the example of Abraham (ch. 4). Against Jewish dependence on their corporate chosenness in Abraham, Paul shows that it is those who are of faith who are Abraham's *spiritual* heirs (4:11–16), and reminds those inclined to depend on genetic ancestry that *all* are descended from Adam (5:12–21). The way of faith makes people more righteous, not less (6:1—8:13). Possessing the law does not make Jewish people righteous (ch. 7), and all believers share in a new experience of redemption akin to the promised new exodus (ch. 8). Jewish people believed that they were chosen in Abraham, but Paul shows that God's sovereignty means that chosenness for salvation need not rest on ethnicity (ch. 9, especially vv. 6–13).

Having established that Gentiles and those who do not observe ancient Israel's law need not view themselves as inferior, he quickly challenges their inclination to view themselves as superior. God has not abandoned his plan for the Jewish people, and uses Gentile converts as part of that plan; they must not look down on Jewish people who do not follow Jesus (ch. 11). Believers must serve one another (12:1–13) and love

---

25. Although views of Romans' purpose diverge widely (see Donfried 1991), the apparent majority of contemporary scholars (e.g., Wiefel, Sanders, Stendahl, Dunn, Lung-Kwong) rightly recognize that Jewish-Gentile tensions are a factor in Romans. Even if the Roman church was *completely* Gentile by this period, its relationship to Judaism (as an intrinsic part of its heritage) remains key (cf. discussion in Das 2007). Some think that Jewish antipathy toward Gentile governments in Judea may also affect the situation (cf. Rom 13:1–7); most northern Mediterranean Jews, however, stayed clear of hints of resistance.

one another (the heart of the law, 13:8–10). Those not attached to kosher laws must stop looking down on believers who keep them (14:1—15:7). Framing his concern with division over food and holy days in 14:1–23, he calls believers to welcome one another (14:1–2; 15:7), then biblically grounds his exhortation to Jews and Gentiles uniting for God (15:8–12). Paul offers both Jesus (15:7–12) and himself (15:16–29) as examples of Jews who ministered to Gentiles, and speaks of Gentile believers' extraordinary debt to Jewish believers (15:26–27). His likely final closing exhortation warns against those who cause division (16:17).

The Roman situation invited Paul to articulate the sort of message he often preached that was relevant for Jew and Gentile alike (1:16; 10:12), and hence invited unity in Christ's church.[26] (Paul's own setting suggests that such implications were on his mind for additional reasons; see 15:25–27, 31.) In practical terms (highlighted in ch. 14), such unity would require a common understanding of the law that provided obedience to its spirit without constraining Gentiles to adopt its Israelite-specific details (cf. 2:14, 29; 3:27, 31; 8:2–4; 13:8–10).

Indeed, Paul clinches this point toward the conclusion of his argument in the letter body. After using Scripture to argue his case throughout the body of the letter, he concludes that Scripture was meant to sustain hope through "endurance" (NRSV "steadfastness") and "encouragement" (15:4). Based on what he has sought to provide them from Scripture, Paul prays that God will give them the same mind toward one another (15:5). That is, Paul's exhortations from Scripture throughout this letter have been to bring them to unity.

An inductive reading of the situation that Romans seems to address thus fits well with what we independently know of the situation. Modern scholars are not the first to notice this situation; Origen, for example, recalls that Priscilla and Aquila left due to the decree and presumably returned in its aftermath,[27] and explicitly recognizes that in this letter Paul arbitrates between Jewish and Gentile believers.[28] Later, when Paul visits

26. Because the Jewish-Gentile barrier was one established in Scripture itself, Paul's emphasis on ethnic unity would have even greater implications for any other ethnic divisions (e.g., Keener 2003c: esp. 208–10); it has also been applied against nationalism (e.g., Schlatter 1995: 31, in the context of rising German nationalism) and ethnocentric imperialism (Jewett cites South African Bishop John William Colenso in 1863).

27. Origen *Comm. Rom.* on 16:3 (Bray 1998: 370).

28. See Reasoner 2005: xxv, and sources cited there. Other early readers recognized

Rome, believers do welcome him, probably without being divided in factions (we cannot be sure whether the two delegations in Acts 28:15 reflect different house churches or perhaps simply different work schedules). So far as one might gather from our limited reports of Nero's persecution (from a decade after Jewish believers returned and perhaps six years after Paul composed this letter), Christians may have been at that time united as a movement.[29] The church must have been massive by that point; Nero seems to have killed hundreds (or possibly thousands) of suspected Christians (Tacitus *Ann.* 15.44), yet the church continued to flourish after his death a few years later.

Because Roman historians concentrated on Rome, their information provides us more of an external framework for understanding this church's situation than we have for most of Paul's letters. Depending on one's chronology of later events in Paul's life, Paul writes between 55 and 58 CE (I incline toward the latter end of that spectrum)—hence one to four years after some of the Jewish believers expelled from Rome have begun to return and six to nine years before Nero began slaughtering Christians.

Other possible reasons for Paul writing Romans, not inherently incompatible with this one, include building a relationship with this Christian community that will provide the base for his planned mission to Roman Spain (15:24, 28; emphasized, e.g., by Jewett). Paul's failure to visit them already is due to the very urgency of his mission to the unreached (15:20–22), which will compel him to move beyond them to the west (15:23–24; cf. 1:13–14). Nevertheless, his Spanish mission and his collection from Diaspora churches both relate to his ministry of building a church that brings together Jew and Gentile, examples relevant to the Roman church.

Paul certainly also summarizes his gospel, as many scholars point out; nevertheless, as we have noted above, he is not simply giving a random audience a random overview of it. It has practical implications for

---

that Paul sought to reconcile discord in the church (Theodoret of Cyr *Interp. Rom.* on 15:33; Pelagius *Comm. Rom.* on 15:33; Bray 1998: 368) and that tensions over the law inform the differences between the groups in Rom 14 (Ambrosiaster *Commentary on Paul's Epistles* on Rom 14:1; Theodoret of Cyr *Interp. Rom.* on 14:1; though contrast Pseudo-Constantius *Holy Letter of St. Paul to the Romans* on 14:1; Bray 1998: 337–38).

29. Tacitus *Ann.* 15.44; cf. also the lack of concern over local division in 2 Tim, 1 Pet, or Heb 13:23–24; and the interest of *1 Clem.* (e.g., 46.5–9) in Corinthian believers' unity. Persecution, of course, could have unified the church in any case.

their situation, and the fact that half of the explicit biblical citations found in all his writings appear in this one letter suggests that this presentation of the gospel is directed toward a situation concerned with the status of Gentile believers vis-à-vis the law (likely a major point of division in a conflict between Jewish and Gentile factions).

Romans and Pauline Theology

Whereas Paul's rhetoric in addressing the law is combative and hyperbolic in Galatians, it seems more nuanced in Romans, where he writes to persuade rather than to rebuke. (Both kinds of letter and rhetoric are known in antiquity, and Paul shows skill in writing in both styles where necessary.) He addresses a setting less polemical than in Galatians (although he is still ready to address opponents on the issue polemically in Philippians [3:2, 18–19], which in my view was written after Romans). Paul may have critics in Rome (perhaps those mentioned in 3:8), but it seems less likely that he has actual opponents (unlike he did in Galatia), despite those he denounces in 16:17–18. Here he deploys some arguments familiar to us from the earlier letter, while he avoids leaving misimpressions on the many believers in Rome who (in contrast to those in Galatia) lack fuller acquaintance with his teaching. Still, even in Romans Paul can presuppose familiarity with common early Christian teaching, explanations if necessary by colleagues who know him (such as Priscilla and Aquila), and more detailed explanations from the letter bearer, Phoebe.

While the situation calls for a particular articulation of Paul's message that is characteristic of Romans, as opposed to, say, First or Second Corinthians, its theme does reflect a broadly characteristic Pauline emphasis. The letter's central theme is the gospel that is the same for Jew and Gentile alike, a gospel emphasizing dependence on God's initiative rather than weak human power (1:16–17). In Romans, Paul argues that Jews cannot boast that their law keeping or election makes them superior to Gentile believers; God produces true righteousness not by ethnic identity or human observance of regulations, but by the transformed life of a new humanity empowered directly by him.

Scholars have sometimes been divided between those who think that Paul addresses a universal human problem and those who think he addresses a specific local one, but this dichotomy is unnecessary. Although Paul focuses much attention specifically on the law because of the Jewish-

Gentile issue in Rome, the rest of his theology makes clear that the fundamental principle from which he reasons extends far beyond the law. He is clear that the problem is not with the content of the law, but with sin (2:14–16) and the flesh—weak humanity's inability to reflect God's righteousness (Rom 7:7–8, 13–14; 8:2–4; Gal 2:21; 3:3; 5:16–21). The new life of Christ and the Spirit should evidence a deeper and more complete righteousness, because God empowers it. Pauline theology involves dependence on God not only for forensic justification, but for new life (e.g., 8:2–17), gifting for ministry to one another (12:3–8), love (13:8–10), and everything else.

Useful Commentaries

A number of useful commentaries exist for English readers, each helpful in its own way. I offer here a mere sample of some of these commentaries below. (I have included here a few works that are not commentaries in the traditional sense, yet cover most of the text of Romans.) I have omitted some older works (though some, like Barrett 1956, Cranfield 1975, and Käsemann 1980, are particularly noteworthy) in order to emphasize more recent ones; I also omit useful and important reference works on Romans (e.g., Donfried 1991; Donfried and Richardson 1998; Haacker 2003; Das 2007). Among commentaries, the present commentary falls within the popular to midrange categories (more so the former, if one skips the notes).

Popular commentaries (or works covering many passages) include Grieb 2002; Hunter 1955; Robinson 1979; and Wright 2004. Midrange works include Byrne 1996; Johnson 2001; Stowers 1994; Stuhlmacher 1994; Talbert 2002; and Tobin 2004. Heavily academic works (all impressive) include Dunn 1988; Fitzmyer 1993; Jewett 2007; Moo 1996; and Schreiner 1998. I also cite some others later in the commentary itself. For a survey of early readings of Romans, see, e.g., Reasoner 2005; Gaca and Welborn 2005; and at greater length and reproducing many relevant texts (from which I have drawn most patristic opinions mentioned in this commentary), Bray 1998; for readings through history more broadly, Greenman and Larsen 2005; also ad loc. in Fitzmyer 1993.

ROMANS 1

INTRODUCTION (1:1–17)

The letter's title matches the titles of other Pauline letters, naming the recipients (specified here in 1:7). The need for a title stems from the time that Christians later collected Paul's letters; otherwise the title might have been borrowed directly from Paul's probable statement of purpose in 1:16–17.[1]

Paul's Greeting (1:1–7)

Just as today's letters often open with "Dear" (and e-mails with "Hi"), ancient letters followed particular conventions. The writer could begin by identifying him- or her-self, then the addressee, and finally giving the conventional greeting. Although such introductions were typically simple,[2] writers could expand any of these elements as needed.[3] Because Paul here is writing to a congregation he has not visited, he may expand the first element (his identity) at greater length than usual. But introductions (whether of speeches, laws, books, or other works) typically introduced a work's primary themes,[4] and Paul hints at some of these even in

---

1. For purpose statements as titles, see Porphyry *Ar. Cat.* 57.15–19. Because 1:16–17 is not explicit that it so functions, however, ancient commentators (in contrast to modern ones) do not seem to have identified it as such.

2. Weima 2000: 328; Aune 1987: 163. This is true even when orators write the letters (e.g., Seneca *Controv.* 2.pref. intro).

3. See Stowers 1986: 20–21, 66. Paul's expansions reflect rhetorical interest (Anderson 1999: 113) and are unusual (Anderson 1999: 207 n. 45); for connections to the letter body, cf. Wuellner 1976: 335.

4. See e.g., *Rhet. Alex.* 29, 1436a, lines 33–39; Dionysius of Halicarnassus *Lys.* 24; Seneca *Controv.* 1.pref.21; Quintilian *Inst.* 4.1.35. Outside speeches, see e.g., Polybius 3.1.3—3.5.9; 11.1.4–5; Dionysius of Halicarnassus *Thuc.* 19; Virgil *Aen.* 1.1–6; Aulus Gellius *Noct. att.* pref. 25.

this letter's opening. (He becomes more specific, however, in 1:8–17, esp. 1:16–17.)

Paul[5] begins by identifying himself as a slave of Christ, a called apostle, and one set apart for God's good news. Although apostleship may be his distinctive gift (1:5; 11:13), he will return to many of these descriptions with regard to believers more generally: their slavery to God versus slavery to sin (6:6, 16–22; 7:6, 25; 8:15; 12:11; 14:18; 16:18), their God-initiated "calling" (1:6–7; 8:28, 30; 9:7, 12, 24–26), and their being "set apart" for God (1:7; 6:19, 22; 8:27; 11:16; 12:1, 13; 15:16, 25–26, 31; 16:2, 15). The "good news" ("gospel") is one of his major themes in the letter and lies at the heart of his own mission (1:9, 15–16; 2:16; 10:15–16; 11:28; 15:16, 19–20; 16:25; see comment on 1:16).

Although free persons normally did not consider "slavery" an honorable status, slaves were not all of one kind. Some slaves of Caesar wielded more power than free aristocrats, and some aristocratic women even married into slavery (in Caesar's household) to improve their status. Slavery to the supreme Lord Jesus was no dishonor; it resembled the OT situation of the prophets and some other godly leaders of Israel as "servants of God."[6] The nature of Paul's slavery to Christ is connected with his being "set apart" (in God's plan, even from the womb; cf. Gal 1:15) for the good news. God had revealed this purpose for Paul at his calling, when he was converted (cf. Gal 1:16; Acts 26:16).

Paul cannot introduce himself and his mission without talking about the God he serves. Sophisticated Greek writers sometimes circled back to their point, as Paul does here:[7] he returns to his apostleship as a mission to the Gentiles in 1:5, but first he explicates the content of the good news he mentioned in 1:1. The good news Paul proclaims is just what the prophets announced (1:2; cf. 3:21; 16:26), hence Paul's heavy use of Scripture in this letter focused on his gospel. (Roughly half of Paul's extant quotations

5. Paul's Roman name itself was most often a Roman cognomen usually belonging to Roman citizens and typically associated with high status (cf. Judge 1982: 36 n. 20). Roman Jews usually avoided using their full (three-part) Roman names, and most letters omit such full names anyway, but Romans would likely infer Paul's citizen status (cf. Rapske 1994: 85–86; Lüdemann 1989: 241). Paul's own interest, however, is in communicating his divinely ordained mission.

6. See discussion and sources on ancient slavery in e.g., Keener 2003b: 448–49, 748; see also Martin 1990 (positively, see esp. 47–49, 55–56); Buckland 1908; Barrow 1968. For "slaves of God" as a positive image in Judaism, see Hezser 2003: 418–20.

7. See Aune 2003: 347; but cf. BDF §464.

of Scripture appear in this letter.) In the Prophets proper, the "good news" is especially the promise that God would establish peace and blessing for his people (Isa 40:9; 52:7; 60:6; 61:1), and Paul proclaims that this ancient promise is now being fulfilled in Jesus (see comment on 1:16), a theme to which he will often return (see "promise" in 4:13, 14, 16, 20, 21; 9:4, 8, 9; 15:8).

What is the content of the good news foretold by the prophets? The prophets associated their good news of Israel's restoration with the coming of the promised Davidic king and the hope of resurrection. In 1:3–4 Paul declares that his good news concerns God's "Son."[8] As a descendant of David (1:3; cf. 15:12), Jesus could be rightful heir to Israel's throne; but once a king was enthroned, he was adopted by God (2 Sam 7:14–16; Pss 2:6–7; 89:26–33). Jesus was not only descended from David (as some other people were), but attested as God's Son by the Spirit, who raised him from the dead and hence exalted him as Lord.[9] Of course, Jesus is not God's "Son" only in the ordinary royal sense (cf. Rom 8:3, 29; Isa 9:6–7), but the good news that God has established[10] a king, and hence his kingdom, sets Paul's preaching of Jesus squarely in the context of the OT promises.[11]

Many Judeans regularly praised God for his power that would one day be expressed in raising the dead;[12] Paul likewise treats resurrection

8. Reusing earlier poetry was common (Menander Rhetor 2.4.393, lines 9–12), and many argue forcefully that Paul draws here on a pre-Pauline tradition (Beasley-Murray 1980: 147–54; Dunn 1988: 1:5; Jewett 2007: 24–25, 97–108); their evidence allows this usage but need not require it (see Poythress 1976; Moo 1996: 45–46; Haacker 2003: 108–9; Anderson 1999: 207 n. 45). Paul might simply shift to grand epideictic style, appropriate to discussing the sublime or deities, when elaborating Christology. At the least it cannot be a "hymn," since it lacks meter.

9. The contrast between "flesh" and "Spirit" here lays emphasis on the divine empowerment involved in the latter (see 8:4, 5, 6, 9, 13). It does not denigrate the fleshly relationship, but relativizes its importance (cf. 4:1; 9:3, 5), perhaps why Paul rarely emphasizes this aspect of messiahship relevant to his contemporaries (but cf. also Mark 12:35–37).

10. On *horizō* as "appointed" or "established" with reference to Jesus, see also Acts 10:42; 17:31.

11. Although not relevant exclusively to Rome, this central message of Jesus as Israel's messianic ruler would reaffirm Roman believers who had apparently already suffered for that claim (Suetonius *Claud.* 25.4; see our introduction). It also contrasted with the "merely procedural" deifications of Roman emperors (Elliott 2008: 71–72).

12. In the second of the "Eighteen Benedictions" (cf. *m. Roš Haš.* 4:5); similarly in later Islam (Qur'an 42.9; 46.33; 57.2). Contrast pagan deities (e.g., Ovid *Metam.* 2.617–18).

as the ultimate display of God's power (Rom 1:4; 1 Cor 6:14; 15:43; Eph 1:19–20; Phil 3:10, 21). Jesus's followers, however, recognize this resurrection as not merely a theoretical hope for the future, but a future reality already initiated in history: Paul speaks literally here of Jesus's resurrection "from among the dead ones," implying that Jesus's resurrection is the first installment of the future promise of resurrection for the righteous (cf. Acts 4:2). Paul elsewhere associates God's Holy Spirit[13] with power (Rom 15:13, 19; 1 Cor 2:4; Eph 3:16; 1 Thess 1:5; cf. also Mic 3:8; Zech 4:6; Luke 1:35; 4:14; Acts 1:8; 10:38), and affirms that the same Spirit who raised Jesus will also raise all believers (Rom 8:11).[14] Paul stresses Jesus's resurrection as a prominent element of the good news (4:24–25; 6:4–5, 9; 7:4; 8:11, 34; 10:9).

Through Jesus Paul has received "grace" for his apostolic mission (1:5). Each believer received God's generous, unmerited gifting or "grace," empowering them for their own special role or purpose in serving his people (Rom 12:6; cf. 1 Cor 1:7; 12:4, 9, 28–31; Eph 4:7); Paul's grace is expressed in this letter by serving them (12:3; 15:15). Paul's mission is to bring Gentiles to the obedience of faith, hence his desire to share his message with Christ's followers in Rome, who are among the Gentiles (1:5; cf. 1:13–15).[15] What does Paul mean by "obedience of faith"? The Greek phrase could be understood in several ways, but Paul is concerned that believers obey God rather than sin (6:12, 16–17; cf. 5:19), and elsewhere speaks of their obedience (16:19) and his mission to bring Gentiles to obedience (15:18). Paul also emphasizes "faith" often in Romans (some forty times, plus twenty-one uses of the cognate verb). He is clear from the beginning that genuine faith in Christ (itself obedience to the gospel; cf. 6:17) should, if carried out, produce a righteous lifestyle (see ch. 6).[16]

---

13. "Spirit of holiness" may associate the Spirit with being set apart for God (1 Thess 4:7–8; cf. Dunn 1970: 105–6; Smith 2006: 98; Keener 1997: 8–10) but is also simply a good Semitic way of speaking of the "Holy Spirit" (for both concepts together, cf. e.g., 1QS 3.7; 4.21).

14. For the Spirit and resurrection, see also *m. Sotah* 9:15.

15. Some take "among the Gentiles" as indicating that they were predominantly Gentile. Literally, it might simply locate them in the Diaspora; one may infer their largely Gentile status, however, in 1:13–15.

16. Cf. also discussion in Schlatter 1995: 11; Jewett 2007: 110. For the nations' promised obedience, cf. Gen 49:10; Isa 45:14; 49:23; 60:14. Paul's vision of Gentiles' incorporation as Abraham's children (see ch. 4) contrasts with the empire's subjugation of nations (see Lopez 2008).

Paul probably returns to this crucial point in 16:26. Disobedience brings reproach on Christ (cf. 2:24); God saves a people for his "name," that is, for his glory or honor.[17] (Roman society had a keen sense of honor and shame, and would appreciate the importance of God's honor.)

"Saints" (in some translations of 1:7) means "those who have been set apart" (cf. 1:1). Scripture portrayed Israel as "beloved" (cf. 11:28), "called" (cf. 11:29), and as "set apart" for God (cf. 11:16).[18] Paul readily applies all these titles to a majority Gentile congregation (cf. 1:13), since all who serve Israel's rightful king (1:3–4) are grafted into Israel's heritage (cf. 11:16–17). They, too, are special objects of God's love (5:5, 8; 8:35, 39; and probably 15:30).[19] It was customary to build rapport with one's audience toward the beginning of one's work, when possible,[20] and clearly Paul shares this sensitivity.

Significantly, in 1:7 Paul adapts the conventional greeting of his day (as elsewhere in his and some other early Christian letters). Greek greetings were normally simply *chairein* ("greetings");[21] Paul and some other early Christian writers adapt this to *charis* ("grace"; divine "generosity") and include the typical Judean (and Eastern) greeting "peace" (reflecting Hebrew *shalom*, which is analogous to the contemporary English greeting "God bless you").[22] Paul's major adaptation, however, is more significant. Letters typically included prayers or wishes invoking deities on behalf of the recipients' health or welfare. Paul here blesses the believers by invoking not only God the Father, but also the Lord Jesus Christ. Although post-Nicene readers might suppose that Paul envisions

17. Schreiner (1998: 23, 35–36) rightly emphasizes the centrality of God's glory and honor in this letter. See e.g., Rom 1:21, 23; 2:24; 3:23; 4:20; 9:17, 23; 11:36; 14:6; 15:6–9.

18. Although the churches in Rome may not have been more unified at this time than Rome's synagogues were, we should not read much into Paul's lack of mention of "church" here (in contrast to Jewett 2007: 61; cf. Rom 16:5), any more than we should, say, in Phil 1:1.

19. Also of Paul's (12:19; cf. 16:5, 8, 9, 12).

20. E.g., *Rhet. Alex.* 29, 1436b.17–40; Cicero *Inv.* 1.15.20; idem *De or.* 1.31.143; idem *Fam.* 13.66.1; Statius *Silvae* 2.preface; Quintilian *Inst.* 4.1.5.

21. E.g., Demosthenes *Epitaph.* 1.1; Chariton *Chaer.* 4.5.8; 8.4.5; Josephus *Life* 365–66; Acts 15:23; Jas 1:1; Deissmann 1978: 150–204 passim; Kim 1972: 10–20, esp. 11.

22. Jewish letters in Greek sometimes combined *chairein* with "peace" (2 Macc 1:1); a Hebrew letter could combine "mercy" and "peace" in a greeting (2 *Bar.* 78:2–3). Paul is not the only early Christian writer to combine "grace" and "peace" (1 Pet 1:2; 2 Pet 1:2; 2 John 3; Rev 1:4; 1 *Clem.* title; cf. Ign. *Smyrn.* 12.2).

Jesus's deity only where he uses the explicit title "God" (cf. perhaps 9:5), he actually assumes Jesus's deity fairly often. In fact, for Paul, "Lord" can be a divine title no less than "God" is (cf. 1 Cor 8:5–6); Paul employs this title for Jesus, and sometimes the Father, roughly thirty-seven times in Romans.

Thanksgiving (1:8–15)

In what constitutes a single long sentence in Greek, Paul emphasizes his appreciation for the Roman believers. He explains that he would have eagerly visited them to serve them with his apostolic ministry, as he has been gifted to serve all the Gentiles, but that he has been detained so far (1:8–15). Toward the end of his letter he will indicate that he has been detained by spiritually needier destinations (15:19–22).

Paul starts by thanking God for them (1:8). Thanksgivings were common (though by no means pervasive) in ancient letters, and Paul nearly always thanks God for the churches to whom he writes (though this feature is conspicuously omitted in his opening rebuke to the Galatians).[23] Paul not only thanks God for them, but regularly prays for them (1:9);[24] calling a deity to "witness" underlined the veracity of one's claim, since deities were expected to avenge false claims about them.[25] Paul prays especially that he might visit them (1:10) so he can serve them the way God has gifted him to do (1:11).[26] "In God's will" (1:10) does not absolutely

---

23. If humanity in general can be charged with failing to thank God (1:21), the same charge can hardly be laid against Paul (6:17; 7:25; 16:4; and passim in his letters)! On thanksgivings, see Schubert 1939; esp. O'Brien 1977; cf. e.g., Fronto *Ad M. Caes.* 5.41 (56).

24. Letter writers often expressed prayers (or wishes) for their recipients; e.g., P. Giess. 17.3–4; P. Lond. 42.2–4; P. Oxy. 1296.4–5; Fronto *Ad M. Caes.* 1.2.2; 5.25 (40). "Unceasingly" may involve greater frequency than daily prayer times, but might be hyperbolic (a common figure, e.g., *Rhet. Her.* 4.33.44); "unceasing mention" seems to refer to times of feasts and sacrifices in 1 Macc 12:11.

25. For Jewish people calling God to witness, see e.g., Josephus *Ant.* 4.40, 46; *T. Reu.* 1:6; 6:9; among Gentiles, e.g., Homer *Od.* 1.273; 14.158; Xenophon *Cyr.* 4.6.10.

26. Letters often expressed a genuine desire to visit (Anderson 1999: 207); even more frequently, they expressed deep affection (Cicero *Fam.* 7.14.2; Pliny *Ep.* 3.3.1; Fronto *Ad M. Caes.* 1.3.1–5; 2.2.2; 3.9.1; 4.2.1) and longing (P. Oxy. 528.6–9; Cicero *Fam.* 1.9.1; 16.1.1; *Att.* 2.18; 12.3; Dio Chrysostom *Ep.* 3; Pliny the Younger *Ep.* 3.17.1–3; 6.4.2–5; 6.7.1–3; 7.5.1–2; Fronto *Ad M. Caes.* 2.4; 2.10.3; 2.14; 3.9.2; 3.19; 4.5.3; 4.9). One might also explain reasons for one's delay (*CPJ* 2:219, §431).

promise his coming, but acknowledges that, while he plans to come, only God knows whether future circumstances will fully permit it. This was a common enough caveat (cf. 1 Cor 4:19; 16:7),[27] and Paul undoubtedly thinks also of dangers he may face (Rom 15:31–32).

Paul did not found the Roman church, so he writes more as a brother than as a father (contrast 1 Cor 4:15–16). Thus, he speaks unobtrusively of "some" Spirit-inspired gift (1:11) and even insists that he and they will be mutually "encouraged" by the other's faith (1:12).[28] Nevertheless, Paul knows that some are more gifted for "exhortation" or "encouragement" than others (12:8), and offers some such exhortations in this letter (12:1; 15:30; 16:17; all using a cognate of the verb for "encourage"). Certainly he has already set about to encourage their "faith," a key theme in Romans (see comment on 1:17). His delay so far may have involved the temporary prohibition of Jews settling there (cf. Acts 18:2), but, as his audience will learn later, particularly involves the compelling priority of his mission to unevangelized regions (15:19–23).

Still, Paul's desire to visit them and encourage their faith (1:11–12) flows, as apparently everything else in his life does, from his life's mission and purpose to reach the nations (1:5, 13–15). Paul treats this mission as a divine obligation (Rom 1:14; cf. 1 Cor 9:16–17)[29] to reach the entire range of "Gentiles" (1:13). These included both Greeks and "barbarians" (non-Greeks), both those whom Greeks considered wise and those they considered foolish.[30] (Greeks usually divided humanity into Greek and "barbarian"; mentioning both together meant "everyone."[31] Romans and Jews sometimes adopted these conventional labels.)[32] The dominant

27. A common caveat (e.g., Xenophon *Hell.* 2.4.17; *Anab.* 7.3.43; Epictetus *Disc.* 1.1.17; Josephus *Ant.* 2.333; 7.373; 20.267).

28. Reciprocity was a conventional expectation (Pliny *Ep.* 6.6.3; Statius *Silvae* 4.9; Herman 2003; Highet 2003; Harrison 2003: 1, 15, 40–43, 50–53), but Paul expresses it in terms expected for peers. For Paul, "spiritual" alludes to the Spirit (Fee 1994b: 28–31).

29. Ancient culture heavily emphasized obligation (cf. Rom 13:8; 15:1, 27), but the expression was not limited to money and was often used figuratively (Musonius Rufus 17, p. 110.2–3; Dio Chrysostom *Or.* 44.4; Pliny *Ep.* 7.19.10), including for a debt to a people (Cicero *Quint. fratr.* 1.1.9.28; Valerius Maximus 5.6. ext. 2).

30. On Greek disdain for barbarians' lack of Greek education, see e.g., Diodorus Siculus 1.2.6; Iamblichus *V.P.* 8.44.

31. E.g., Plato *Alcib.* 2.141C; Dio Chrysostom *Or.* 1.14; 9.12; Diodorus Siculus 1.4.5–6; Dionysius of Halicarnassus *Ant. rom.* 3.11.10.

32. E.g., Cicero *Inv.* 1.24.35; Seneca *Dial.* 5.2.1; Josephus *J.W.* 5.17; idem *Ant.* 1.107.

culture of the urban eastern Empire was Greek, and that culture also influenced the Greek-speaking eastern immigrant community in Rome (including most of its Jewish population) where the church had first taken root.

Good News of Salvation (1:16–17)

We must offer special, hence more detailed than usual, attention to 1:16–17. Ancient writers often (though not always) stated their themes and purpose in a proposition before their main argument,[33] and most commentators of recent centuries believe that Paul does so here. Commentators differ over the central theme involved, though some proposals dominate only particular parts of the letter. Nevertheless, God's righteousness (most explicitly through ch. 10), faith (most explicitly in chs. 1, 3–4, 10, and 14), and the Jewish-Gentile issue (most explicitly in chs. 9–11) seem to pervade it. Others offer the more general theme of the "gospel," which integrates a number of these factors (and for which, in Romans, God's righteousness is a key element).[34] That all these themes reflect the language of prophetic promises to Israel (Ps 98:2–3; Isa 51:4–5; 52:10)[35] reinforces Paul's claim that Scripture is the source of his gospel (1:1–2).

The gospel is the object of faith, and its subject is God's Son (1:9), Jesus Christ (15:19, 20; 16:25). Scholars propose various reasons why Paul claims to be "unashamed" of the gospel. Certainly, interest in honor and shame dominated ancient Mediterranean urban culture, including Rome, and Paul's message involved folly and weakness to a status-conscious cul-

---

Some texts add Romans as a third category (Juvenal *Sat.* 10.138; Quintilian *Inst.* 5.10.24; as Greeks in Dionysius of Halicarnassus *Ant. rom.* 7.70.5); most included Jews in the barbarian category (Strabo 16.2.38; Josephus *J.W.* 1.3; 4.45; but cf. Josephus *Ant.* 18.47).

33. E.g., Dionysius of Halicarnassus *Lys.* 17; Cicero *Or. Brut.* 40.137; idem *Quinct.* 10.36; Quintilian *Inst.* 4.4.1–8; Pliny the Elder *Nat.* 8.1.1; 18.1.1; Dio Chrysostom *Or.* 1.11; 38.5–6. Technically a "thesis" involved a hypothetical topic and a "hypothesis" a concrete one (Theon *Progymn.* 1.60 [cf. 2.91–104; 11.2–6, 240–43]; Hermogenes *Progymn.* 11, On Thesis 24–26; Anderson 2000: 63–65). Paul's might resemble a philosophic thesis, though Stoics omitted these (Anderson 1999: 61, 241–42). Paul's form may differ from conventional rhetorical expectations (cf. Elliott 1990: 62–63, 82–83, doubting that it is a thesis).

34. Moo 1996: 29, 32, 65; Jewett 2007: 135.

35. See especially Hays 1989: 36–38; idem 2005: 45, 94, 137, citing these texts, and noting the texts to which Paul appeals in Rom 9:27–33; 11:26–27; 15:7–13, 21.

ture (1 Cor 1:18–23).[36] The world's hostility could provide temptation to be ashamed (cf. 2 Tim 1:8, 12, 16; 1 Pet 4:16), but God's servants could trust that they would not be shamed eschatologically (Rom 5:5; 9:33; 10:11).[37] "Unashamed" may also constitute litotes; Paul is positively eager to preach this message (cf. Phil 1:20; Heb 2:11; 11:16).[38]

God's "power" for salvation might recall his "power" to create (1:20), act in history (9:17, 22), or provide miraculous attestation (15:19). But it especially recalls his power to raise the dead (1:4, including a central point of the gospel message; cf. Eph 1:19–20), hence to transform by providing new life (cf. Rom 15:13; 1 Cor 1:18). He may also think of the Spirit's activity in the gospel to convince people of the truth of the message (1 Cor 2:4–5; 1 Thess 1:5).

In the context (Rom 1:5, 13–15), Paul certainly wants to emphasize that the gospel is for all peoples, Jew and Gentile alike.[39] Yet there is also a sense in which the good news, rooted in promises to Israel, is "to the Jew first"; it will take Paul all of chapters 9–11 to resolve the tension between these emphases. Paul's evangelistic prioritization of ethnic Israel fits Jesus's teaching (Mark 7:27) and the portrayal of Paul's own ministry in Acts (e.g., 13:5; 28:17), yet he will argue that God saves both Jew and Gentile by the same means.

Paul's audience in Rome may influence him in speaking of the gospel going next to the "Greeks":[40] they are mostly Gentiles (1:13), which includes Greeks and barbarians (1:14), and of these two groups they are largely the former (1:16). The Roman congregations were mostly Greek speaking at this time (as the earliest Christian inscriptions and leadership lists show). Romans also often considered themselves "Greek" rather than "barbarian," which was not a flattering designation. But Paul often employs the contrast between "Jew" and "Greek" (2:9–10; 3:9; 10:12), and

36. Cf. similarly Apollinaris of Laodicea (Bray 1998: 29); John Chrysostom. *Hom. Rom.* 2.

37. Paul drew on Isa 28:16 LXX in two of these texts, and knew Isaiah's broader expectation (Isa 45:17; 54:4; 65:13; 66:5; see more fully Hays 1989: 38–39). He may have also known Jesus's saying in Mark 8:38 (cf. John 12:26).

38. E.g., Porter 1997: 579; cf. again John Chrysostom *Hom. Rom.* 2; on litotes, Rowe 1997: 128.

39. So also Origen *Comm. Rom.* on 1:16 (in Bray 1998: 30).

40. Paul may speak of the gospel going next to Greeks possibly because Greeks (broadly defined, since Alexander) were the next ones to receive it; "Greeks" constituted the primary mission field of Paul's day, at least in his cultural sphere.

not only in this letter (see 1 Cor 1:22, 24; 10:32; 12:13; Gal 3:28; Col 3:11; cf. Acts 14:1; 18:4; 19:10, 17; 20:21), as equivalent to "Jew" and "Gentile" (Rom 3:29; 9:24; 1 Cor 1:23). "Greek" provided a natural metonymy for the larger category of "Gentile." Josephus often uses "Greeks" for all non-Jewish urban residents,[41] and Jews had longstanding severe conflicts with Greeks, the dominant urban culture in the eastern Mediterranean.[42]

As the introductory "for" (*gar*) indicates, Paul now explains *why* the good news brings salvation to Gentiles as well as Jews: God's way of implementing his righteousness is through faith (1:17). Scholars read this explanation, however, in different ways, regarding both "God's righteousness" (*dikaiosunē*) and "faith" (*pistis*). Both are clearly key concepts: if we include their cognates, Paul employs each term over fifty times in Romans. Here I must digress to address *dikaiosunē* more fully.

Excursus: *Dikaiosunē* in Romans

In common Greek, *dikaiosunē* normally meant "justice."[43] In what sense would God's "justice"[44] or "righteousness" (Rom 1:17; 3:5, 21–22; 10:3) put people right with him (cf. 3:26)? Scripture often connects God's righteousness with his faithfulness and/or covenant love (e.g., Pss 36:5–6, 10; 40:10; 88:11–12; 98:2–3; 103:17; 111:3–4; 119:40–41; 141:1; 143:1, 11–12; 145:7). In the Psalms, God's righteousness causes him to act justly (e.g., Pss 31:1; 35:24) or mercifully (Pss 5:8; 71:2, 15–16, 19, 24; 88:12) in favor of his servant. When forgiven, the psalmist will praise God's righteousness (Ps 51:14).[45]

---

41. Rajak 1995: 1, 11–13; cf. Josephus *Ant.* 19.278. This is often true of Luke as well (e.g., Acts 14:1; 16:3).

42. For ethnic conflicts between Jews and Greeks, see Stanley 1996.

43. Certainly appropriate in a thesis statement such as Rom 1:17; "justice" came to be viewed as a standard category of reasoning for developing a thesis (Hermogenes *Progymn.* 11, On Thesis 26).

44. "Justice" may depict an aspect of God's nature as do God's wrath (1:18) and God's power (1:20). Elliott (2008: 76–77) finds in God's justice a critique of human injustice, focusing on the empire.

45. God answering in righteousness (Ps 143:1) need not include judging, since no mortal could meet God's standard (Ps 143:2).

In the Greek version of the OT, the cognate verb *dikaioō* did not imply a legal fiction, but recognizing one as righteous,[46] including in forensic contexts (cf. Gen 44:16; Isa 43:9, 26; Ezek 44:24): judges must not "acquit the guilty" (Exod 23:7), but must "justify," i.e., pronounce righteous, the innocent (Deut 25:1).[47] God himself would punish the guilty but "justify" and vindicate the righteous (1 Kgs 8:32; 2 Chr 6:23); he himself was "justified," or "shown to be right," when he pronounced just judgment, even against the psalmist (Ps 51:4, in Rom 3:4). Thus for God to "justify," "acquit," or "vindicate" someone who was a morally guilty person, as in Rom 4:5, might shock hearers.

Nevertheless, those immersed in Scripture could also understand God rendering judgment in favor of someone based on his mercy. For example, God pronounced judgment justly against Israel (Dan 9:7, 14); but they could entreat him to forgive them according to his "righteousness" (Dan 9:16). God might punish the guilty, yet ultimately plead their case, "justifying" them to see his "righteousness" (Mic 7:9). Israel hoped for God's promise of vindication someday (Isa 45:25; 50:8; 58:8), including through the righteous servant who would bear their sins (Is 53:11; cf. Rom 4:25).[48] God being "righteous" meant that he would honor the promise to Abraham, whom he found "faithful" (Neh 9:8).[49]

For Paul, God's righteousness is incompatible with dependence on mere human righteousness (Rom 9:30—10:6; Phil 3:9). Divine righteousness is not a goal to be reached by human effort, but a relational premise that should dictate the new life of faithfulness to Christ. Often Romans uses the verb cognate (*dikaioō*) for God putting believers right with himself, reinforcing the possibility that this is how Paul uses the noun here.[50] This verb can signify just vindication; in a forensic context it may entail "justification" (as many

46. Gen 38:26; cf. Job 33:32; Sir 1:22; 23:11; 26:29; 31[34]:5; of God in Sir 18:2; used in a comparative sense in Jer 3:11; Ezek 16:51–52. Cf. 1QS 3.3; *Gen. Rab.* 65:6.

47. To "justify" was also to "render justice" on someone's behalf (2 Sam 15:4); one should "justify," "vindicate," "defend the rights of" the widow (Isa 1:17) and the poor (Ps 82:3).

48. In the Greek version of Isa 53:11, it is the servant who is justified.

49. Some other Jews also depended on God's "righteousness" to vindicate or save them (1QS 11.5, 9–14; cf. 1QH 4.29–37; 11.10–11; 1QM 11.3–4; *Gen. Rab.* 33:1; for a fuller range of biblical (and some early Jewish) background, see e.g., Stuhlmacher 2001: 13–24).

50. Cf. also Phil 3:9; Ambrosiaster *Commentary on Paul's Epistles* (CSEL 81:37); John Chrysostom *Hom. Rom.* 2; Basil *Humility* 20 (Bray 1998: 31–32).

translations render some of its occurrences in Romans) or acquittal. Those who argue for legal acquittal rightly emphasize God's generosity, or "grace," as opposed to human achievement.

Nevertheless, Paul does not think only of "acquittal," which is only one element of the term's normal sense. Acquittal does not dominate the entire letter, which goes on to address conduct (Rom 6; 12:1—15:7);[51] moreover, when God pronounces something done, one expects this to happen, not merely produce a legal fiction (Gen 1:3; 2 Cor 4:6).[52] In Romans, *righteousness* is a *transforming* gift. It is a divine gift rather than human achievement (Rom 5:17, 21), but God's gift also enables obedience (cf. 1:5; 2:8; 5:19; 15:18), i.e., right living (6:16–18; 8:2–4; 13:14). In theological terms, justification is inseparable from regeneration.

Although disputed, "from faith to faith" may simply mean that God's righteousness revealed in the gospel is a matter of faith from start to finish.[53] Romans often uses *pistis* ("faith") and its verb cognate *pisteuō* ("believe"). Apart from disputed instances (e.g., 3:22), faith is normally in God or Christ (most obvious in cases where the verb is being used). Whatever else "faith" means for Paul, it is not a human work, whether physical or (as sometimes in Protestantism) mental in nature (Rom 3:27–28; 4:5; 9:32; Gal 2:16; 3:2, 5). It involves dependence on God's righteousness. This means not a Kierkegaardian "leap into the dark" (reacting to the Kantian consignment of faith to the category of subjectivity), but embracing truth in the gospel (in contrast to the false ideologies of the world; cf. Rom 1:18–23, 28). We should note, however, that just as "righteousness" involves transformation, so the term *pistis* includes the sense of "faithfulness"—loyalty and allegiance—and not simply an intellectual

51. Schlatter 1995: 26–27.

52. This "transformative" righteousness view (vs. mere acquittal) is the one dominant in most of church history (Fitzmyer 1993: 118–19).

53. Cf. the construction in 2 Cor 2:16 (a rhetorical flourish, as in Menander Rhetor 2.3, 378.29–30; Ps 84:7; Jer 9:3). Alternatively, God's righteousness may be revealed on the basis of faith in the gospel, generating more faith (cf. Rom 10:17; the construction in Gal 6:8). "From faith" might counter the assertion that it was "from works" (cf. 3:20; 4:2; 9:11, 32; 11:6); it also reflects Hab 2:4 LXX. Many understand it as from God's faithfulness (3:3) to human faithfulness, yet one would expect Paul's context to clarify such different uses more adequately.

acknowledgment. Genuine dependence on Christ invites genuine loyalty to him, not simply reciting a statement about him as if nothing is truly at stake.[54]

As in the rest of Romans, Paul now turns to Scripture to demonstrate a controversial point, using a familiar early Jewish and Christian citation formula.[55] Paul here cites Hab 2:4, which concerns God preserving the righteous in the time of impending judgment. Some interpreters take "righteous one" here as Jesus (cf. Acts 3:14; 7:52), but none of the other sixteen uses of *dikaios* ("righteous") in Pauline literature in context refer to Jesus (including in the quotation of this same passage in Gal 3:11).

Scholars also debate whose faith(fulness) is in view in this Habakkuk quotation. Although the dominant Greek version of Hab 2:4 says, "my [God's] faith [*pistis*]," Paul undoubtedly knows that the Hebrew speaks of the faith of the righteous person; Paul simply omits the debatable pronoun. Scholars have taken him in one or both ways here; Paul does speak later of God's faithfulness (*pistis*, 3:3). Yet it would have been easy for him to have followed the Greek rendering familiar to his audience, which he chooses not to do,[56] and in Romans he far more often speaks of believers' *pistis* (e.g., 1:8, 12), even when echoing the text here (4:5). Elsewhere (Gal 3:6, 11) Paul midrashically links the two biblical texts that mention both righteousness and faith, and the other text clearly refers to a believer's (Abraham's) faith (Gen 15:6). Thus Paul probably refers to the believer's faith here.

Like some other Pharisaic interpreters,[57] Paul presumably applies "live" to eternal life, the resurrection life of the coming age (2:7; 5:21; 6:22–23; 8:13; 10:5; 14:9), even though in a sense believers have already entered it (6:10–13; 8:2, 6). Thus Paul presumably here cites Habakkuk to affirm that God preserves from his wrath those who trust in him.

---

54. Scholars debate whether "faith" here attaches to "live" or to "righteous"; normally in Romans Paul connects faith with righteousness (3:22, 26, 28, 30; 4:3, 5, 9, 11, 13; 5:1; 9:30; 10:4, 6, 10), though in any case all *three* terms are closely connected here.

55. Cf. e.g., 2 Chron 23:18; 1QS 5.15, 17; CD 5.1; 7.10; 11.18, 20. On Paul and ancient citation techniques, including adaptation of wording to fit the context, see especially Stanley 1992 passim.

56. Some think that Paul alludes to both the Greek and Hebrew versions, but his audience likely was unacquainted with the Hebrew version.

57. *T. Hul.* 10:16; *Sipra A.M.* par. 8.193.1.10; *Sipre Deut.* 336.1.1; *'Abot R. Nat.* 40 A; *y. Hag.* 2:1, §9; cf. Ezek 33:14–16, 19; *4 Ezra* 7:21; *m. 'Abot* 6:7; but contrast *L.A.B.* 11:9.

MADE RIGHT BY TRUSTING CHRIST (1:18—5:11)

Modern outlines cannot do justice to Paul's careful thinking in Romans, which often transitions seamlessly from one point in his argument to the next. It is not possible to sever 1:18–23 from 1:16–17, but we have followed the traditional division here. In 1:18—5:11, Paul argues at length that Jew and Gentile alike are made righteous only through depending on Christ.

Inexcusable Idolatry (1:18–23)

Instead of believing truth in the gospel, some corrupt even the truth they have in nature. While God's saving righteousness is "revealed" in the gospel for those who trust it (1:16–17), God's wrath is "revealed" against those who suppress the truth by unrighteousness (1:18–23).[58] The truth they unrighteously suppress is the truth about God (1:25; cf. 2:8), which they suppress, ultimately, by idolatry (1:19–23).[59]

This denunciation offers a key transition in Paul's larger argument that shows that both Gentiles and Jews need the gospel. Jewish people regarded idolatry (1:23) and sexual vice (1:24–25), especially homosexual behavior (1:26–27), as characteristically Gentile sins. But after Paul denounces such sins to his audience's applause, he quickly turns to more universal sins (1:29–31), finally consigning his own people, knowledgeable of the law, to judgment as well (2:17–29; 3:9, 19–20). (Cf. the same tactic in Amos 1:3—2:8.) Although condemning Gentiles in 1:18–32, Paul employs for this condemnation biblical language regarding Israel, probably evoking such texts in the memories of his more biblically informed hearers and preparing for his wider argument in the next chapter.[60]

Although God's wrath (1:18) has a future aspect (e.g., 2:5, 8; 9:22), it is revealed in the present here especially through God "handing over" sinners to the consequences of their own sinfulness (1:24, 26, 28; cf.

58. Salvation and wrath seem to be two sides of God's righteousness (1:16–18); the latter responds to human *un*righteousness (1:18). The gospel reveals the former (1:16) and presupposes the situation (depicted in 1:18–32) of the latter.

59. Recognized also by Ambrosiaster and Apollinaris of Laodicea (Bray 1998: 35).

60. E.g., the language of Ps 94:11 in Rom 1:21; exchanging God's glory for idols (1:23) in Ps 106:20 (cf. Jer 2:11; possibly language from Deut 4:16–18); perhaps also moral hardening (cf. Rom 1:28; 11:7, 25) and the handing over to their sins (Rom 1:24; Ps 81:12).

Acts 7:42).[61] As God's righteousness appears in the truth of the gospel (1:16–17), their unrighteousness (1:18) appears in suppressing the truth of God's character (1:19–23). Saving faith (1:16–17) is thus not a guess or wishful thinking, but embracing the genuine truth in contrast to lies that seem progressively more plausible to depraved humanity.

Whereas some philosophers believed that true knowledge would lead to right living, Paul believes that knowledge merely increases moral responsibility ("without excuse," 1:20; cf. 2:1, 15). God revealed enough for Gentiles to be damned, though people who know the Scriptures are more damned than those who have only nature and conscience (2:14–18). God revealed the truth about God within people (1:19), an internal knowledge based on being made in God's image (Gen 1:26–27). More generally, God revealed his power and divinity, as well as benevolence in providing creation, so those who fail to recognize his power and character, worshiping mere idols or human conceptions, are without excuse (1:20).

Even Gentile intellectuals could have followed Paul's argument here. Apart from the more skeptical Epicureans, most Greek and Roman intellectuals recognized divine design in nature;[62] many reckoned as absurd the alternatives, namely, that the universe resulted from chance or human activity.[63] Various philosophers affirmed that the supreme deity was present in and known by his works.[64] Many of these writers also affirmed, like Paul, that one could infer much about God's character from creation. For example, some believed that God's character transcended merely human religion,[65] or that deities were benevolent and cared for people.[66] Paul would not have endorsed all their inferences;[67] many of these philosophers still accepted their culture's belief in many deities. But many Stoic

---

61. The judgment of consequences of false belief appears elsewhere (cf. Isa 29:9–14; *Jub.* 21:22; Josephus *J.W.* 5.343; Epictetus *Disc.* 1.12.21–22; 3.11.1–3; Porphyry *Marc.* 22.348–360).

62. So Dio Chrysostom *Or.* 12.29, 34, 36–37; for examples, cf. Plutarch *Isis* 76, *Mor.* 382A; in Jewish sources, *Let. Aris.* 132.

63. A Pythagorean in Diodorus Siculus 12.20.2.

64. Epictetus *Disc.* 1.6.23–24; Josephus *Ag. Ap.* 2.190, 192; cf. 2.167.

65. Ps.-Heraclitus *Ep.* 4, 9.

66. Socrates in Xenophon *Mem.* 4.3.12–13; for their benevolence, cf. also Seneca *Ep. Lucil.* 95.50.

67. Some decided that the divine nature must be spherical, since this was the perfect shape (Cicero *Nat. d.* 2.17.45–46)!

thinkers by Paul's day ultimately believed in one divine designer behind everything (including the other gods).[68]

Thus, after arguing for the necessity of a cause,[69] the late first-century Stoic philosopher Epictetus argues from the structure of objects that they reflect a designer and not mere chance:[70] "Assuredly from the very structure of all made objects we are accustomed to prove that the work is certainly the product of some artificer, and has not been constructed at random."[71] Anyone who observes the facts of nature, yet denies the existence of a creator, he opines, is stupid.[72] Epictetus believed that human beings, and especially their intellect, most complex of all, particularly revealed the designer.[73] Many others (including Cicero and Seneca) concurred: humans,[74] and especially their intellect,[75] were inexplicable apart from design. Jewish thinkers in the Greek world had adapted such ideas for a purer monotheism centuries before Paul,[76] making his missionary job much easier.[77] Jewish intellectuals like Paul, however, believed that such reasonings simply confirmed what was obvious in Genesis.

68. Cf. Diogenes Laertius 7.1.134; cf. earlier Heraclitus in Diogenes Laertius 9.1.1. Some earlier Stoics tended toward pantheism, but Stoicism generally distinguished between matter and the logical principle (the *logos*) which organized matter (I explore some of these ideas further in Keener 2003b: 341–47).

69. Epictetus *Disc.* 1.6.3–6.

70. Epictetus *Disc.* 1.6.7.

71. Epictetus *Disc.* 1.6.7 (LCL translation, 1:41).

72. Epictetus *Disc.* 1.16.8.

73. Epictetus *Disc.* 1.6.10; cf. Rom 1:19.

74. Cicero *Nat. d.* 2.54.133—58.146; Seneca *Ben.* 6.23.6–7; cf. Cicero *Fin.* 5.12.35–36; *Let. Aris.* 156–57.

75. E.g., Cicero *Nat. d.* 2.59.147—61.153; Porphyry *Marc.* 26.410–11. They viewed knowledge of a deity as innate in people (Seneca *Ep. Lucil.* 117.6; Dio Chrysostom *Or.* 12.27–28; Iamblichus *Myst.* 1.3). Some also adduced in favor of deities' existence the universal pervasiveness of belief in them (Cicero *Tusc.* 1.13.30; cf. Maximus of Tyre *Or.* 11.5).

76. For example, the Jewish philosopher Philo borrows various philosophers' arguments for God's existence (Wolfson 1968: vol. 2, 73–93), including Plato's argument from creation (p. 74) and material from Stoic sources (pp. 75–83).

77. He may especially draw on the Wisdom of Solomon, a widely circulated Jewish work in Greek (cf. Wis 13:1–9, including "without excuse" in 13:8); there the consequences of idolatry culminate in a vice list (Wis 14:12–31). Cf. also Jewish stories about Abram reasoning back to a first cause and resisting idolatry. For subsequent Christian approaches to "natural theology" here, see concisely Bray 1998: 34, 37–38; Reasoner 2005: 11–17.

Thus, humanity "knew" God, but because they refused to "glorify" him (1:21),[78] they ended up exchanging his "glory" and image for that of mortal, earthly creations (1:23). They were God's image (Gen 1:26–27), but by corrupting God's image in worshiping things other than God they gave up and lost his glory (cf. Rom 3:23).[79] God punished their failure to act according to the truth by delivering them to their moral insanity (1:21–22).[80] Jewish people considered idolatry the climax of human evil.[81] Even Greeks, whose deities looked human, disdained the Egyptian animal images also mentioned here.[82]

Sexual Sin (1:24–27)

Paul has narrated that humanity exchanged the truth about God for idolatry (1:19–23), which he here calls a "lie," the opposite of truth (1:25). A direct consequence of this behavior was that God handed them over to defile their own bodies sexually (1:24), including in same-sex intercourse, which was "against nature" (1:26–27), i.e., (for a Jew) against the way God created things to be. In the primeval era of the "creation" (Rom 1:20), God revealed his character and made humanity in his image (Gen 1:26–27); yet they distorted God's image by worshiping other images (Rom 1:23).[83] Exchanging God's truth for lie involved idolatry (1:23, 25), but also a perversion of right sexuality in God's image to distorted sexuality (1:24, 26).

78. For humanity abandoning gratitude toward God, see also Josephus *Ant.* 1.72. Ingratitude was among the most despised vices in Mediterranean antiquity (e.g., Xenophon *Cyr.* 1.2.6; *Mem.* 2.2.2–3; Cicero *Att.* 8.4; Heraclitus *Hom. Prob.* 4.4; Seneca *Ben.* 1.10.4; *Ep.* 81.1; '*Abot R. Nat.* 46, §128 B).

79. Useful for Paul's audience, Greeks and Romans also believed that humanity had declined from a primeval golden age (Hesiod *Op.* 110–201; Ovid *Metam.* 1.89–312), but Paul's biblical allusions and polemic against idolatry infuse his narrative with the Jewish subtext of Genesis (without claiming detailed allusions to Adam's fall here, as some do). The glory and image are restored in Christ (Rom 8:29–30).

80. The term *mataios* ("vain," "futile") in 1:21 was sometimes associated with idols (e.g., Acts 14:15; 1 Kgs 16:26 LXX; Jer 8:19; 10:3, 15; Ezek 8:10; Wis 13:1; *Sib. Or.* 3.29, 547–48, 555), though the language here echoes Ps 94:11.

81. E.g., Wis 14:27; *t. Bek.* 3:12; *Mek. Pisha* 5.40–41; *Sipre Deut.* 43.4.1; 54.3.2. Later rabbis said it was the final stage to which the evil impulse would lead one.

82. E.g., Lucian *Imag.* 11; Philostratus *Vit. Apoll.* 6.18–19; *Let. Aris.* 138; Josephus *Ag. Ap.* 2.81, 128, 224.

83. "Beginning" included the entire primeval period, including the first people (e.g., Mark 10:6; *L.A.B.* 1:1).

Once they had perverted God's image directly, they distorted it also in themselves. God's image in humanity included the complementarity of male and female (Gen 1:27),[84] and the distortion of his image led to same-sex intercourse against "nature," which for Paul meant against the way God had created humans to function. (That Paul has Genesis in mind is made likelier by the distinctive terms he employs for "male" and "female" in Rom 1:26–27, terms that appear together prominently in Genesis, though not exclusively; cf. Gen 1:27; 5:2; Mark 10:6.) Possibly the penalty "in themselves" (1:27) involved not only the physical consequences of their behavior but the further effacing of God's character and image in them (cf. 1:19, 24; contrast 8:23). Greek myths portrayed their deities committing all kinds of immorality, including sexual immorality,[85] behavior that Jewish apologists connected with Greek male lifestyles and often ridiculed.[86]

Fusing the Horizons: Homosexual Activity

Scholars diverge fairly widely in their views about how to interpret Paul in 1:26–27, although a majority recognizes that Paul condemns homosexual behavior generally. Interpreters differ still more widely over how (and whether) to apply Paul today. In view of this disparity, we need to understand the historical context of Paul's argument.

Homosexual Activity in Antiquity

Homosexual activity was common in the ancient Mediterranean world.[87] It was usually bisexual rather than exclusively homosexual.[88] Most of those who courted or molested boys planned to eventually marry women and have chil-

84. This complementarity was especially sexual, designed for procreation (Gen 1:28).

85. E.g., Pliny *Nat.* 2.5.17; Lucian *Prom.* 17; *Deor. conc.* 7; *Philops.* 2.

86. Josephus *Ag. Ap.* 2.232–49, 275; cf. later Athenagoras 20–22; Theophilus 1.9; Tatian 33–34.

87. For discussions, see e.g., Dover 1978; Greenberg 1988. On Paul's view, see contrary arguments in e.g., Scroggs 1983; Gagnon 2001.

88. The latter practice did exist, although it was sometimes stereotypically associated with misogyny.

dren of their own. Although various Greek sources report its occurrence among Gauls, Persians (especially with eunuchs), and others, the dominant cultural influence for it was Greek. This practice pervaded Greek society and was even attributed to deities.[89]

Homosexual practices are attested in Rome from an early period, but Greek influence multiplied these practices in Roman society, especially among the leisured aristocracy. Romans had often denounced these practices as due to Greek influence, and some Roman thinkers continued to reject the practice (see further discussion below), but it was now widely entrenched within aristocratic Roman society. Paul is thus not simply playing to Roman Gentiles who opposed the practice because of their cultural backgrounds. Indeed, Paul writes in Greek to a majority audience of Greek speakers in Rome, probably most of them immigrants from, or recent descendants of those who had immigrated from, the east. Their shared antipathy to homosexual practice is rooted not primarily in traditional Roman values (although it undoubtedly appealed to them) but in Jewish beliefs also adopted by Gentile adherents to Judaism and the early Christian movement.

As in most cultures, particular features of a society are linked with other characteristics of that society. In the Greek (and to lesser extent, Roman) world fathers could insist, often for economic reasons, that unwanted babies be abandoned on trash heaps.[90] Although the matter is debated, there is still reason to believe that Greeks abandoned female babies more often than male babies, given the disparity in genders and consequent disparity in age at marriage. On average, Greek men seem to have married around age thirty, marrying young women twelve years their junior. This meant that young men in that society looked for other sexual outlets before marriage: slaves, prostitutes, and (more affordably) each other. The particular sexual practices dominant varied from one Greek city-state to another, but in this period the old traditions of Athens were most influential.

89. Zeus, for example, seduced and raped not only women, but the boy Ganymede, whom he eventually took up to heaven (e.g., Homer *Il.* 20.232–35; Ovid *Metam.* 10.155–61); as the satirist Lucian wryly points out, his wife Hera apparently tolerated this boy on Olympus more than her earthly women rivals (Lucian *Dial. d.* 213–14 [8/5, *Zeus and Hera*]). Other deities also loved boys sexually (e.g., Apollodorus *Library* 1.3.3; Ovid *Metam.* 10.162–219); Josephus ridiculed such portrayals (*Ag. Ap.* 2.275).

90. The babies so abandoned could be eaten by vultures or dogs, but were often adopted and raised as slaves. Jews and Egyptians, however, rejected this practice of child abandonment.

Pederasty and Other Exploitation

The vast majority of homosexual affection in the ancient Mediterranean world was directed toward boys (pederasty) or young men.[91] Greeks openly admired young men's beauty,[92] but it was held to decline with puberty and the attendant growth of facial hair and other specifically masculine characteristics. Some slaveholders, mocked by many of their contemporaries, tried to prevent masculinization by having hairs plucked or, worse, turning boys into eunuchs.[93] Some remained objects of homosexual affection through their teens, and some, like Alcibiades, drew comments about their handsomeness much later. We do read of homosexual relations between fully mature men, but by far the predominant form of homosexual interest remained that of men toward prepubescent and adolescent males. The unequal status of the partners was compared to that of men with women (whose status had been notoriously low in classical Athens), with the dominant partner on top when intercourse occurred.

This interest often took the form of courting with gifts and interest, which many Greeks found entertaining. Although today any such behavior would be considered exploitive, Greeks counted only excesses, such as more blatant seduction or rape, as taking unfair advantage of a boy and inviting severe punishments. Even such crimes generated outrage only when committed against boys who were free; even aristocratic Romans by this period employed slave boys at banquets who, like female slaves and prostitutes, could be exploited sexually. It was preferred that they remain "effeminate," a behavior counted undignified and mocked when practiced by free men. (Those whose masculinity was physically impaired, such as eunuchs, generally faced the same derision.) Men could also find sexual outlets with male prostitutes; whereas pimps could exploit slaves for this role without public protest, the voluntary involvement of free young men invited disrespect toward the latter.[94] Teachers, conquerors, and emperors were all reputed to sexually exploit boys (as well as, when available, young women).

91. On this point, Scroggs 1983: 29–43, is certainly correct.

92. Socrates was known for having spent much time with handsome young men enjoying their beauty without intercourse (although satirists like Lucian suggested that everyone really knew better; Lucian *Ver. hist.* 2.19; *Vit. auct.* 15).

93. Cf. e.g., Seneca *Ep.* 47.7; Dio Chrysostom *Or.* 77/78.36; Suetonius *Dom.* 7.1; Bradley 1987: 115; cf. Ps.-Lucian *Am.* 10.

94. See Höcker 2008: 59–60; Hartmann 2005: 469–70; cf. Aeschines *Tim.* 21, 51–53, 74, 137; Polybius 8.9.12; Dionysius *Epid.* 7.291; Lucian *Alex.* 5–6.

Views Regarding Homosexual Behavior in Antiquity

Some Gentiles criticized homosexual behavior, for various reasons. Some criticized it out of personal preference; some Romans considered it unmanly or un-Roman.[95] Many Roman philosophers associated the pursuit of boys with excesses like gluttony and drunkenness. Some also criticized it as being against nature (a point we will address more thoroughly, given its relevance in 1:26–27).

More often, people regarded it as a personal preference or a common practice. Some even defended it as being preferable to heterosexual affection, which was said to be driven by animal passion rather than philosophic appreciation. Anal intercourse was common enough that men also used it at times with women (perhaps prostitutes), as attested on some of the many ancient vase paintings that would today be classified as pornographic.

Jewish people, however, unanimously rejected homosexual behavior. Some Diaspora Jews in contact with Greek culture considered it against nature.[96] Contrary to what some have argued, Jewish people included homosexual behavior among Sodom's sins. Most characteristically, Jewish people associated homosexual activity especially (and probably largely accurately) with Gentiles. Although Jewish sources report Jewish adulterers, johns, and murderers, Jewish homosexual practice was nearly unknown.[97] The obvious contrast with ancient Greek culture suggests the prominent role played by socialization in sexual formation.

Interpreting Paul

Could Paul have envisioned the issue of gay marriage? This is not likely. Some time after Paul wrote Romans, it is reported that the young emperor Nero "married" both a boy (whom he had castrated) and another man (Suetonius *Nero* 28.1; 29; Tacitus *Ann.* 15.37). Even the reporters, however, offer these

---

95. Still, it could be better than being accused of adultery with a free matron (Valerius Maximus 8.1. acquittals 12).

96. Philo *Abraham* 135–37; *Spec. Laws* 3.37–39; Josephus *Ag. Ap.* 2.273–75; Ps.-Phoc. 190–92; *T. Naph.* 3:4–5; cf. the later recension of 2 *En.* 10:4. More generally, Lev 18:22; 20:13; Josephus *Ag. Ap.* 2.199, 215; idem *Ant.* 3.275; Ps.-Phoc. 3; *Sib. Or.* 3.764; 4.34; 5.166, 387, 430.

97. On homosexual behavior as a Gentile sin, see e.g., *Let. Aris.* 152; *Sib. Or.* 3.185–86, 596–600; *Tg. Ps.-J.* on Gen 39:1. Later rabbis disclaimed even suspecting this behavior for Israelites (*y. Qidd.* 4:11, §6).

claims as examples of Nero's moral madness; as polygamy was illegal and Nero married heterosexually as well, these other unions were not taken in the same way. Later rabbis mythically depict ancient Israel's enemies as involved in such marriages (*Sipra A.M.* par. 8.193.1.7), but without relying on genuine historical information. Apart from rare exceptions like these (most of them meant to evoke horror), however, ancients thought of marriage as heterosexual unions designed especially to produce legitimate heirs, regardless of their views toward homosexual behavior. With a few exceptions, "marriage" by definition involved both genders (and an economic agreement between families).[98] Those who engaged in homosexual romance, even in the rarer cases when it involved long-term sexual relationships into adulthood, would not have used the title "marriage" to describe it.

Most readers today would share Paul's revulsion against the dominant forms of homosexual practice in his day: pederasty in both its voluntary and involuntary forms. Some scholars (especially Scroggs) argue that Paul opposed merely pederasty or other kinds of sexual exploitation. Critics of this proposal sometimes too readily dismiss the evidence for it: as we have observed, pederasty was in fact the dominant expression of homosexual activity in the ancient Mediterranean world.

But did Paul limit his criticism to simply those forms that remain most offensive in Western culture today? The dominant practice was not the only practice, and the word "pederast" was already available. More importantly, as most commentators (e.g., Jewett, Byrne) point out, he specifies lesbian as well as male homosexual behavior, and it is the same-sex element of the behavior that he explicitly targets.

The same criticism may be leveled against the view that Paul merely rejects homosexual behavior in the way that some philosophers did, as a failure to control one's appetites (comparable to gluttony). Rather, Paul's rejection of homosexual behavior belongs to his larger Jewish sexual ethic, which rejects all sexual behavior outside heterosexual marriage. His "against nature" argument echoes philosophic arguments that other Diaspora Jews had already applied to homosexual behavior in general. Readers today may agree or disagree with Paul, but some modern attempts, no matter how valiant, to make him more palatable to certain Western liberal values have failed to persuade a number of commentators, including this one.

98. See Keener 2000d: 685.

At the same time, we must not exaggerate what Paul is saying. He uses the examples of idolatry and homosexual behavior because Jewish people recognized these as exclusively Gentile vices. This recognition plays into Paul's strategy to expose *all* sin as deadly (1:28–32), hence all persons as sinners (3:23). Paul is not providing pastoral counsel here to believers struggling with homosexual temptation, and he is certainly not granting license to abuse those who practice homosexual behavior. (Nor would he grant license to denounce this vice while tolerating heterosexual behavior outside marriage, a condemnation that consumes considerably more space in his letters.) Given how common bisexual practice was, Paul undoubtedly worked closely with many believers who had come from this background (some of whom were still tempted by it; cf. the likeliest interpretation of *arsenokoitēs* in 1 Cor 6:9–11). Paul's message here would be more analogous to a preacher appealing to an audience on the basis of their shared values regarding homosexual behavior— then leading them to consider their own vices.

Various Vices (1:28–32)

For the third time (cf. 1:24, 26), in 1:28 Paul repeats the refrain that God "gave them over" to their own ways through their minds being corrupted (cf. 1:21–22). They did not "approve" (from *dokimazō*) God in their knowledge, so God gave them "unapproved" (*adokimos*) minds to do "unfitting" things.[99] For Paul, humanity's distortion of the truth about God's character leads to their distortion of the purpose of human sexuality, and ultimately to every kind of vice. As he will point out later, though, retaining true knowledge about God's standards by the law makes one responsible for sin, rather than saving one (2:20; 7:23–25; 8:5–8).

Paul then lists examples of the "unfitting" things produced by this depraved mind, what he will later call the perspective of the flesh (8:5–8). Ancient moralists commonly used vice lists,[100] sometimes arranged with repetitions to rhetorically drive home the point. Paul's is longer than aver-

99. Paul's "unfitting" may reflect Stoic terminology, alluding to people acting against nature (1:26–27); but the particular examples of "unfitting things" here unfold in 1:29–31.

100. E.g., Ezek 18:6–8, 11–13; Philo *Posterity* 52; *Sacrifices* 32; Plato *Laws* 1.649D; Aristotle *Eth. eud.* 2.3.4, 1220b–21a; Cicero *Pis.* 27.66; idem *Cat.* 2.4.7; 2.5.10; 2.10.22, 25; Seneca *Dial.* 9.2.10–12.

age, though far briefer than some. His rhetorical repetition and variation makes the list all the more effective: "filled with" four basic evils; "full of" five sins; a summary of eight kinds of sinners; and deficiency in four positive traits (1:29–31).[101] Whereas Jewish people could relegate idolatry and homosexual intercourse to the corrupted ideologies of Gentiles, the present sins also appear in lists of Jewish misbehavior: envy, strife, gossip, slander, arrogance, disobedience to parents, and so forth. By the end of his list, Paul has inductively convicted both Jews and Gentiles as being under sin (he might do so deductively in 3:9–19), paving the way for his argument in ch. 2.

Paul shows that humanity rightly stands under the sentence of death (1:32). For though they technically should know better (1:19–20; cf. 2:14–15), they do what they know to be worthy of death (the way of the fleshly worldview, which yields death, 8:6).[102] Those who refused to approve God in their thinking (1:28) now approve others who share their own behavior (1:32). God's "righteous standard" or "requirement,"[103] however, demands capital punishment for all transgressors, whether idolaters or gossipers and (most relevant for Paul's continuing argument in 2:17, 23; 3:27, albeit with different terminology) boasters.

---

101. Lists could either use repeated conjunctions (e.g., "and . . . and"; 1 Cor 6:9–10; 2 Cor 12:21; Acts 15:20) or no conjunctions (asyndeton), as here (cf. Gal 5:19–23).

102. Even from the era of the "beginning" (1:20) they knew (cf. Gen 3:3) that human death was the consequence of humanity's sin (Rom 5:12, 14, 17, 21; 6:16, 21, 23; 7:5, 13). This was even more true for knowers of the law (cf. 2:26; 8:4). Jewish teachers also believed that God had given commandments to humanity before the law (*Jub.* 7:20–21; Ps.-Phoc. passim; what the later rabbis called Noahide commandments, e.g., *Mek. Bah.* 5.90–94; *Sipre Deut.* 343.4.1).

103. *Dikaiōma.* God's righteous character is thus also revealed in his wrath (1:18), though especially in the gospel where he puts people in the right (1:17); the tension is resolved especially in 3:26.

ROMANS 2

MADE RIGHT BY TRUSTING CHRIST (1:18—5:11), *cont.*

God's Impartial Judgment (2:1–16)

In this section (and some others, most obviously 3:1–9; 9:14–24) Paul employs a lively rhetorical style called diatribe, commonly used for teaching. This style typically includes an imaginary interlocutor, who may or may not be explicitly identified, who raises objections. These objections allow the speaker or writer to develop the argument, demolishing the objections one at a time while holding the audience's attention.[1] Scholars debate whether Paul begins addressing a specifically Jewish interlocutor here (2:3) or only at 2:17 (where it is explicit); most likely he implicitly addresses the Jewish interlocutor throughout the chapter, since what "we know" (2:2), what the interlocutor should know (2:4), and the continuity of subject matter (cf. 2:9–10, 12–15; with 2:25–29) all suggest a Jewish hearer. Nevertheless, Paul remains subtle in the first section, springing his rhetorical trap only gradually as he shows that Jew and Gentile alike are condemned. Singling out a hearer (rhetorical "apostrophe"), as Paul does with "O man" (2:1, 3; cf. 9:20), was a common rhetorical device,[2] again effective for holding audience attention.

Because those who commit all kinds of sins (1:29–31) recognize that such behavior merits death under God's standard (1:32), they deserve divine judgment (2:3, 5). Whether they (like morally lax Gentiles) excuse or (like strict Jews) condemn such behavior, they are condemned (2:15). In 1:32 they excuse it, and in 2:1 they condemn it, but both approaches of sinners are inexcusable (1:20; 2:1–5).

1. On the style, see Stowers 1981: 122–33.

2. E.g., Isa 22:17; Mic 6:8; Epictetus *Disc.* 1.1.23 and passim; Marcus Aurelius *Med.* 5.36.1; 11.15. For the interlocutor including Jews, see e.g., Augustine *Exp. prop. Rom.* 7–8 (Bray 1998: 52).

Paul develops this condemnation of those who piously denounce sin by means of a syllogism: they commit these sins (2:1), we know that such sins merit God's judgment (2:2; cf. 1:32), therefore they will not escape God's judgment (2:3). Most people recognized and condemned such inconsistency,[3] a point to which Paul returns in a more explicit challenge to a Jewish interlocutor in 2:17–25. Paul prepares his audience far in advance for his warning against judging culturally different believers in Rom 14:3–4, 10, 13.

If anyone wishes to appeal to God's mercy, Paul is clear (against some of his detractors, 3:8) that God's mercy gives space for repentance. That is, God's mercy brings about righteousness, rather than simply blessing sinners in their sin (2:4). Jewish hearers would understand that the kindness of God was what led people to repentance (2:4);[4] some also thought of treasuring up rewards in heaven (cf. e.g., Tob 4:9–10)—though what is stored up here is wrath (2:5)![5]

Continuing his lavish display of effective literary devices, Paul now reinforces his point with inverted repetition, what is called a chiasm (2:6–11):

A God repays each according to their works (2:6)

   B To those who do good, seeking glory and honor[6] (2:7)

      C But wrath to those who disobey the truth (2:8)[7]

      C′ Suffering to those who do evil (2:9)

   B′ But glory and honor to those who do good (2:10)

A′ Because God is impartial (2:11)

In this passage Paul argues for God's ethnic impartiality.[8] Contrary to Jewish expectations, God will judge both Jew and Gentile (2:9–10), both

---

3. E.g., Matt 7:1; Polybius 12.23.1, 3; 12.24.5; Seneca *Dial.* 4.28.6–8; Juvenal *Sat.* 2.9–10, 20–21; *b. Roš. Haš.* 16b.

4. Cf. *Let. Aris.* 187–88; Wis 11:23; 12:10, 19; the fifth benediction of the *'Amida*.

5. The connection is uncertain, since "treasure up" did not always carry its originally literal sense (see e.g., Prov 1:18; 2:7; 16:27 lxx).

6. Roman culture valued seeking honor and glory, but the glory Paul emphasizes here is eternal (8:18; 9:23), equivalent to God's praise at the judgment (2:29). On the honor sense of "glory" (and seeking only honor from God, as in 2:29), see the information in Keener 2003b: 885–86; for other aspects of "glory," see ibid., 410.

7. Cf. those disobeying the truth about God (1:25) facing wrath (1:18).

8. On divine impartiality, see most thoroughly Bassler 1982. God not discriminating

those with the law of Moses and those with only natural law (2:12–15)—
and he will hold those with greater revelation more accountable! Judging
people in accordance with their deeds was one way of speaking of God's
impartiality;[9] the surprise is that, instead of God's own people being favored, they are judged more strictly because they have a fuller knowledge
of right and wrong (2:12–15; 3:20; 7:7–11; cf. Amos 3:2).

In view of the lostness of all humanity in this section (3:9, 23), scholars debate whether those who do good works for eternal life[10] represent
a real but small class of people (the way some Jewish people thought of
"righteous Gentiles"); a hypothetical class of people (posited perhaps
for rhetorical purposes) (cf. 10:5; Gal 3:11);[11] or Christians (cf. 2:29).
Especially both latter proposals may have some merit: in principle it is
the righteous who will be saved, and in practice it is those who are in
Christ who can live righteously (8:2–4). Yet Paul's *focus* at this point is
not on Christians, but on the principle of God's ethnic impartiality (also
the point of all humanity being under sin in 3:9). Paul is digressing on
the point precisely to explain how those who fancied themselves morally
superior were treasuring up *wrath* for themselves (2:5). It served Paul's
point to note that Gentiles would at least sometimes do morally right
actions, whereas Jews would sometimes not do them. Nevertheless, apart
from Christ, the natural law of conscience innate in human beings functions like the external law of Moses, identifying sin but not transforming
people to be righteous (2:14–15). Comparing the passage with other passages in Romans allows us to see that while it focuses on the potential
righteousness of any person, Paul would only aver that those transformed
by Christ would live thus:

---

between Jew and Gentile is a theme of Romans (cf. 3:30).

9. E.g., Sir 16:12; Paul here echoes Ps 62:12; Prov 24:12.

10. For one synthesis of how judgment by works and justification only by faith fit in
Paul's concern for reaching Gentiles, see insightfully Boers 1994: 221–24. Those with the
law within fulfill righteousness (8:2–4; Gathercole 2002: 223), and are still evaluated for
works (14:10; 2 Cor 5:10).

11. One could debate whether his rhetoric is hypothetical here or hyperbolic in
3:9–23 (where he seems to place every individual under sin), his objective being merely
to show that both *groups* (Jew and Gentile) need Christ. But it is doubtful that he thought
of morally sentient adults who had not sinned, of Adamites who did not need to be in
Christ (5:12–21), or of people of flesh who did not need the Spirit for life (8:2–10).

The righteous do good works (2:7)	These cannot be Jewish law-works (3:20, 27–28)
The righteous endure (2:7)	Believers endure (5:3–4; 8:25; 12:12; 15:4–5)
The righteous "seek" for glory (2:7)	No one "seeks" for God (3:11); one must not "seek" righteousness the wrong way (10:3, 20)
The righteous seek glory and honor (2:7, 10)	Humanity lost God's glory (3:23), but glory awaits believers (5:2; 8:18, 21; 9:21, 23)
The righteous receive eternal life (2:7)	Believers in Jesus receive eternal life (5:21; 6:22–23; cf. 8:13)
The righteous will have peace (2:10)	Humanity does not know peace (3:17), but believers will have it (5:1; 8:6; 14:17)
The righteous do "good" (2:7, 10)	The wicked do not do good (7:18–19; cf. 3:10); believers should do what is good (12:9, 21; 13:4; 15:2)
Doers of good include both Jews and Greeks (2:10)	Both Jews and Gentiles are under sin (3:9); the community of believers includes both Jews and Gentiles (1:16; 9:24; 10:12; cf. 3:29)

Thus while Paul is focusing on God's ethnic impartiality rather than on believers here, when he later addresses such issues he seems to assume that it is believers in Jesus who are able to fulfill the role of the righteous. Christ comes not merely to forgive unrighteousness but to empower for righteous living.

Scholars again differ as to whether the law in obedient Gentiles' hearts by nature (2:14–15) refers to Christians or to conscience in all humans. In practice, it those in whom the Spirit dwells (Jew or Gentile) who fulfill the heart of God's law (8:2–4; Jer 31:31–34).[12] There may be an element of such emphasis here, preparing for 2:29. Nevertheless, Christians also had access to the written law, so in 2:14–15 Paul probably focuses more generally on a natural law innate in humanity. He has already spoken of God's revelation in creation (1:20), including within humans (1:19), and he also

12. They even have the Spirit "testifying" like the conscience here (8:16), while apparently retaining conscience's testimony as well (9:1).

45

appeals to the Greco-Roman notion of "conscience" (9:1).[13] Although employing it in a wide range of ways, Greco-Roman sources (including Jewish ones) speak widely of a law of nature,[14] and even Palestinian Jews outside this widespread tradition seem to have believed that God had given laws to Gentiles' ancestors in the time of Noah.[15] Such a morally informed person's divided thoughts in 2:15 may presage the morally divided person in 7:15–23 (who, however, knows more specifically Moses's law and hyperbolically appears incapable of doing any good).

Indicting Hypocrisy (2:17–24)

Paul's diatribe uses rhetorical exaggeration, common in polemic, to hold attention. The evildoing Jewish interlocutor here is hyperbolic, perhaps even reduced to the absurd.[16] Certainly most Jewish people did not commit adultery or rob temples! Paul's graphically rendered point is simply that Jewish ethnicity or possession of the law cannot guarantee moral superiority to Gentiles. (Paul will maintain the sin of all Jews with a biblical argument in 3:9–20.) Because of the general law of nature, some Gentiles might do what is morally right (2:14–15), even while this hyperbolic Jewish objector, who three or four times reiterates dependence on the law (2:17, 18, 20, 23), dishonors God by breaking it (2:23).

Torah study was central to Pharisaic and presumably other Jewish teachers' piety (2:17–20), but intellectual and spiritual proficiency risked generating pride in one's accomplishments, then as now. Certainly today some have used such proficiency to diminish their concern with corresponding failure in the area of praxis. This Jewish teacher's fundamental problem, twice repeated, is finding security in or "boasting" in the law (2:17, 23; cf. Sir 39:8). Ancients often considered unqualified boasting ob-

13. Already used in Greek-speaking Judaism (e.g., Josephus *Ant.* 16.103, 212; idem *J.W.* 4.189, 193; *T. Reu.* 4:3; Wallis 1974–75; idem 1975).

14. In moral senses, e.g., Xenophon *Mem.* 4.4.19; Aristotle *Rhet.* 1.15.6, 1375ab; Cicero *Inv.* 2.22.65; 2.53.161; Seneca *Ben.* 4.17.4; Musonius Rufus 16, p. 104.35–36; Epictetus *Disc.* 2.16.27–28; Horsley 1978. Philo viewed Moses's law as a written version of the law of nature (Najman 2003).

15. E.g., *Jub.* 7:20; *t. ʾAbod. Zar.* 8:4–8; *b. Sanh.* 56a, bar.; *Pesiq. Rab Kah.* 12:1; *Gen. Rab.* 34:8.

16. *Reductio ad absurdum* was a familiar line of argument (cf. e.g., Lysias *Or.* 4.5–6, §101; Seneca *Ep. Lucil.* 83.9; 113.20; Heath 1997: 93–94).

noxious to begin with,[17] but for Paul boasting in one's works as opposed to God's activity is sinful (3:27; 4:2; 5:2–3, 11; 15:17).[18]

Ancient rhetoric was fond of repetition, which cumulatively reinforces the overall effect of one's words. Paul cites about eleven pious Jewish claims for his interlocutor in 2:17–20, whose righteousness he then challenges with five rhetorical questions (as often in prosecuting or defensive rhetoric) in 2:21–23.[19] The latter cases each use antithesis and the literary device of starting and ending with parallel language (x . . . y/x . . . y) to drive home the point. Evoking prophetic biblical critiques throughout,[20] Paul finishes off the hyperbolic hypocrite with an explicit text in 2:23–24. Ironically, the righteousness this interlocutor claims in the law of Moses is available only to those in whose hearts the law is written by the Spirit (8:2–4):

The name "Jew" (2:17)	True Jews (2:29), children of Abraham (4:12, 16–17), and those grafted into Israel (11:17)
Boasting in God (2:17, 23)	Boasting in God the right way (5:11; cf. 5:2–3)
Knowing God's will and approving the good (2:18)	Knowing God's will and approving the good (12:2)
A light to those in darkness (2:19)	People of light rather than darkness (13:12)
Teacher of law (2:20)	Right use of teaching (6:17; 12:7; 15:4; 16:17)
Having knowledge and truth in the law (2:20)	Having knowledge of truth (15:8, 14)

17. See discussion in Forbes 1986; Watson 2003; Keener 2005b: 221–22.

18. On boasting here, cf. Gathercole 2002: 162–88, 215. Given possible allusions to Isa 42:6–7 here, it is not impossible that this Jewish "instructor" is also seeking to reach (and circumcise) Gentiles (cf. Isa 42:6; those in darkness in Rom 1:21), not unlike the teacher in Josephus *Ant.* 18.82. But this leader of the blind was himself blind and in darkness (cf. Rom 11:8–10).

19. Cf. analogous challenges to hypocrisy in antiquity, e.g., Seneca *Controv.* 2.6.5; and many other cases of accumulating rhetorical questions, e.g., Lysias *Or.* 10.22–23, §118; Cicero *Phil.* 3.6.15; Musonius Rufus 11, p. 80.22–25; 13B, p. 90.13–16; 15, p. 98.25–27; Lucian *Tyr.* 10. These add rhetorical force (see Dionysius of Halicarnassus *Dem.* 54).

20. See e.g., Jer 7:9; Grieb 2002: 32; cf. 1QS 1.23–24; CD 4.16–18; 8.5–8.

Ancients considered temple robbery (2:22) the epitome of impiety.[21] Many Gentiles suspected Jews of this crime because they knew that they did not regard pagan temples as sacred,[22] though Jewish apologists emphasized that good Jews would do no such thing.[23] Here Paul's hyperbolic opponent, far from abhorring idols, apparently finds their sale lucrative. Profaning God's name (2:23–24) was among the most heinous of offenses.[24] The sort of hypocritical Jew who discredited God and his people depicted here could be familiar enough to Paul's audience: a generation earlier, one Jewish charlatan, who professed to teach Moses's laws but did not obey them, had exploited Roman women, leading to scandal in Rome (Josephus *Ant.* 18.81–84).

As at some other points in Romans (e.g., 3:10–18), Paul uses the Scriptures in what may be a deliberately unexpected way. In the context of Isa 52:5 God's name was blasphemed among Gentiles because of his people's suffering; here, Paul complains, God is blasphemed because of their sin! They were exiled to begin with, however, because of their sin (cf. Ezek 36:18–20). Paul might connect this passage with many of his people's rejection of the good news of Isa 52:7 (cited in Rom 10:15.)

Inward Jewishness (2:25–29)

Responding to one boasting in his Jewish ethnicity and virtues (2:17–24), Paul counters that Jewishness (here embodied in circumcision) is valuable only if one truly keeps the covenant. Gentiles who follow the moral demands of the law, even if they lack knowledge of the written law (or are uncircumcised Godfearers attached to the synagogue), will be reckoned more within the covenant than Jews who break the law. Although Paul again speaks in principle of any Gentile, in practice those who could fulfill this standard, from Paul's perspective, are those who are in Christ, since they are the ones who have the Spirit (cf. 2:29 with 7:5–6; 8:9).

21. E.g., Xenophon *Apol.* 25; Cicero *Quint. fratr.* 1.1.8.25; idem *Fin.* 3.9.32; Lucian *Hermot.* 37; *Vit. Aes.* 127–28; Hermogenes *Progymn.* 6, On Commonplace, 12.

22. Cf. Acts 19:37; Josephus *Ag. Ap.* 1.192–93, 248–49; for Jewish assault on pagan shrines, cf. Exod 34:13; Deut 7:5; 12:3; Philo *Embassy* 200, 202.

23. E.g., Josephus *Ant.* 4.207; idem *Ag. Ap.* 2.237; Philo *Moses* 2.205.

24. Cf. Lev 22:32; *Sipre Deut.* 328.1.5; Moore 1971: 2:101; Urbach 1979: 1:357; Keener 1999: 219.

Scripture supported Paul's contention that those who violated God's law were uncircumcised in heart (Rom 2:25; Lev 26:41; Jer 4:4; 9:25–26); Paul goes beyond Scripture simply in arguing the converse, namely, that those who keep God's law are circumcised in God's sight (Rom 2:26). Physical circumcision was a dividing issue; many Roman Gentiles criticized Jews for this practice, and it remained a primary barrier for Gentile men desiring to join God's people. Most Jews did not believe that Gentiles needed to be circumcised to be saved; they needed it only to become members of Israel's covenant.[25] Paul thus prepares here for his later argument about Gentile believers being grafted into Israel's heritage alongside Jewish believers (4:16; 11:17).[26]

Literal circumcision appears in far fewer biblical texts than one would expect from its later emphasis (although it is crucial in most of these, especially Gen 17; Ex 4:26; Lev 12:3; Josh 5:2–8);[27] but Jewish people emphasized it especially rigorously in the centuries before Paul's day as a significant distinctive of national identity. Without rejecting physical circumcision, Paul regarded spiritual circumcision (Deut 10:16; 30:6; Lev 26:41; Jer 4:4; 9:25–26; cf. Ezek 44:7, 9) as essential and more crucial than the physical covenant "sign." Physical circumcision remained acceptable for Jewish believers, but the imposition of circumcision on Gentile believers risked alienating people from the covenant needlessly (cf. 1 Cor 7:18–19; Gal 5:6; 6:15).[28] For Paul, the promised gift of the Spirit (2:29) confirmed God's acceptance of Gentiles into his new covenant, obviating the need for a mere symbol of the covenant that simply pointed to it.[29]

25. For Jewish views of Gentiles, see Donaldson 1997b: 52–74.

26. The Gentile practitioner "judging" the Jewish nonpractitioner may involve merely being a comparison standard for God's judgment (see e.g., Matt 12:41–42/Luke 11:31–32; *Lev. Rab.* 2:9; *Pesiq. Rab.* 35:3; comparable scenarios involving other kinds of figures in *'Abot R. Nat.* 6A; 12, §30B), but some Jewish eschatological scenarios did involve the righteous judging the wicked (1 *En.* 91:12; 95:3; 98:12; 1QpHab 5.4; 4Q418 frag. 69, 2.7–8; *Sipre Deut.* 47.2.8).

27. That it was symbolic identification rather than ontologically efficacious is clear from where it had been omitted (Josh 5:2–8; cf. Exod 4:25).

28. Some other individuals allowed this concession, at least in some extraordinary cases (Josephus *Ant.* 20.41; see further Watson 2007: 75–78); but this would be a minority view in Jerusalem and probably even in most Diaspora synagogues.

29. Generally, when Paul contrasts "flesh" and "Spirit," as in 2:28–29, he refers to God's Spirit (see e.g., 1:3–4; 8:4–9, 13; cf. Gal 3:3; 4:29; 5:16–17; 6:8; Phil 3:3). The Spirit is the foretaste of the future age (Rom 8:23; 2 Cor 1:22; 5:5), and the symbol is irrelevant compared to the new creation (Gal 6:15).

The genuine Jew, Paul says, seeks his or her praise from God (2:29), like the righteous people of 2:7, 10. Paul might be offering a wordplay that some of his audience would recognize: the name of the Jews' ancestor "Judah" meant "praise" (though translated differently in Gen 29:35; 49:8). For the contrast between Spirit and letter, see the comment on 7:6.

ROMANS 3

Made Right by Trusting Christ (1:18—5:11), *cont.*

God's Faithfulness (3:1–8)

It is not God who has broken the covenant, Paul insists (3:1–8). Ancient writers often used rhetorical questions, and some of these, like some of the questions here, could be objections supplied by an imaginary interlocutor, a straw man to be refuted.[1] The interlocutor here raises the obvious objection to Paul's argument: if ethnic Jewishness and outward circumcision did not guarantee covenant membership (2:25–29), what was the value of these matters (3:1)?[2] Paul replies that Israel's benefit is a greater *opportunity*, although this opportunity also entailed (as Paul has been noting, 1:16; 2:9–10) greater responsibility. The opportunity involved their role in salvation history (a role Paul continues to assign to ethnic Israel, 9:4–5; 11:12, 15) and their greater access to God's clearest revelation in Scripture (an access today shared also with Christians). God "entrusted" them with his oracles (3:2). (Although Paul says "first" in 3:2, he does not get beyond this initial benefit here [cf. 1:8]; many think he

---

1. Scholars debate exactly which rhetorical questions imply an interlocutor; indeed, one could simply anticipate potential objections (e.g., *Rhet. Alex.* 18, 1432b.11—1433b.16; 36, 1442b.4–6; Cicero *Rosc. Amer.* 18.52) or answer one's own questions (Cicero *De or.* 40.137). Though "What, then?" (Rom 3:1, 9) could belong to interlocution (e.g., Cicero *Tusc.* 3.20.46; Seneca *Dial.* 3.6.1; 3.8.7), it sometimes offered a summation or advancing of the argument (e.g., Musonius Rufus 5, p. 50.21; Dio Chrysostom *Or.* 31.55, 60; Menander Rhetor 2.1–2, 376.4). Nevertheless, we need not doubt the presence of an interlocutor in at least some of them. There can be no question that ancient sources used unmarked interlocutors as well as marked ones (e.g., Cicero *Sull.* 19.54—20.56; 22.62; idem *Scaur.* 9.18; 18.41; idem *Phil.* 3.6.15, 16; Virgil *Aen.* 10.67; Dio Chrysostom *Or.* 23; 31.12). See here e.g., Stowers 1994: 162–66, 232; idem 1984: 707–22.

2. Considering the benefit or profit of a matter was a primary consideration both in rhetoric and ethics (e.g., Musonius Rufus 8, p. 60.10–12; Arius Didymus *Epit.* 2.7.5d, pp. 28–29.17–29; for a number of sources, see Keener 2003b: 856).

picks the subject up in 9:4–5. Certainly he revisits the present issues more fully in chs. 9–11.)

The interlocutor again objects in 3:3: surely Israel's lack of faith does not negate God's faithfulness to his covenant, does it? (Unbelief and faithfulness in this verse are both cognates of "entrusted" in 3:2.) Indeed, some Jewish teachers were at great pains to show that no matter how Israel behaved, God always counted them as his children.[3] Paul exclaims, essentially, "No way!" (3:4).[4] But he identifies God's covenant faithfulness with his righteousness (see comment on 1:17), and insists that it is God as Israel's judge, rather than disobedient Israel, who will be shown righteous.[5] (That his righteousness and faithfulness also include a continuing plan for Israel will be clarified later in 11:1–32, esp. 11:25–32.)

"Everyone is a liar" (3:4) comes from Ps 116:11 (115:2 LXX), anticipating Paul's texts for human sinfulness in 3:10–18 (esp. 3:13). Because it comes from the "Hallel" psalms used in festivals (at least in Jerusalem), its wording may have been familiar. But Paul more explicitly cites Ps 51:4, where the psalmist admits his guilt and God's righteousness. Because the current version of the psalm already identified it with David's repentance, Paul probably anticipates here God's forgiveness of David without works in Rom 4:6–8.

Reducing the now desperate objections of his imaginary interlocutor to the absurd, Paul poses the objection that since Israel's sin and falsehood reveal God's righteousness and truth,[6] such misbehavior ought not

3. R. Meir (against R. Judah) in *Sipre Deut.* 96.4.1 (cf. similarly *Sipre Deut.* 308.1.2). These rabbis taught in the late second century, but may reflect earlier ideas.

4. Like interlocutors, such a negation is familiar in diatribe, with this phrase in the late first-century Stoic Epictetus (Malherbe 1989: 25–26; also Demosthenes *Aristog.* 1.30; Gen 44:7, 17; Josh 22:29; 24:16); but in other language also elsewhere (e.g., Plato *Charm.* 175A; Cicero *Rosc. Amer.* 1.2; Seneca *Ep. Lucil.* 94.32; Dio Chrysostom *Or.* 55.3).

5. Cf. *Ps. Sol.* 8:23, 26; perhaps Gen 18:25; Sir 18:2. That God is "true" (cf. Pss 25:10; 31:5) means that he is "faithful"; the same Hebrew conception stands behind both Greek terms (the Hebrew term elsewhere translated "faithful" is rendered "true" in the Greek version of Psalms; so Dunn 1988: 1:133; e.g., Ps 40:10–11). For theodicy arguing that deity is not responsible for sin, see e.g., Jas 1:13–14; Aeschines *Tim.* 190. "What shall we say?" (3:5; cf. 4:1; 6:1; 7:7; 8:31; 9:14, 30) was a common expression (e.g., Fronto *Ad M. Caes.* 3.17).

6. These contrasts echo the contrasts between Israel's faithlessness and God's faithfulness in 3:3, and their deception and God's truth in 3:4 (see Hays 2005: 54). On *reductio ad absurdum*, see the note on Rom 2:17–24.

be judged harshly (3:5, 7).[7] But God, who is righteous to judge the world (i.e., all nations; 3:6), is also righteous to judge his disobedient people. (Even the interlocutor accepts the premise that God will judge the world.) In fact, one who tries to justify sinners on account of God's glory may as well argue, "Let us commit evil because the result will be good" (3:8). But God's glory would be displayed in his righteous judgment of such sinners, not by exonerating them![8] Presumably by twisting Paul's argument about justification by faith, some had insisted[9] that Paul essentially taught that one may as well sin—a perversion of the doctrine also popular today. This conception entirely misses Paul's point, as his letter will go on to make clear: one truly "righteoused" by faith is not only put in right relationship with God, but now has new power to live righteously (by faith that God has made them share Christ's victory over sin; Rom 6; cf. Gal 2:17–21; 5:5–6, 24).

All under Sin (3:9–20)

While God has been faithful to the covenant (3:1–8), Israel has not (3:9–20). Paul graphically underlines the sinfulness of Jews as well as Gentiles, but the point he makes by itself would not be controversial. Jewish sources concur that all, or virtually all, sinned.[10] What is striking about Paul is the

---

7. One could argue that a good outcome mitigated one's wrongdoing (Hermogenes *Issues* 38.20–25), or occasionally even declare sinners righteous because God brought their acts about (*Tg. Neof.* 1 on Gen 38:25). Moralists would demur (e.g., Seneca *Ep. Lucil.* 87.22, 25).

8. Their behavior in fact causes God to be blasphemed (2:24), not glorified.

9. Both Jewish and Gentile sources denounce slander as a terrible sin; it appears in Paul's list in Rom 1:30. Rumors apparently spread about Paul in the Jerusalem church (Acts 21:21). Attributing the slander to "certain persons" might follow the common practice of damning some opponents with anonymity. That sin "demonstrated" God's righteousness (3:5) may be a perversion of Paul's teaching that God "demonstrated" love toward sinners (5:8).

10. 1 Esd 4:37; 1QS 11.9–10; 1QH 4.29–30; 16.11; cf. *Jub.* 21:21; Moore 1971: 467–68; Bonsirven 1964: 114. Greeks also regarded genuinely good persons as few (Epictetus *Disc.* 2.19.26–27; Dio Chrysostom *Or.* 13.13; Lucian *Tim.* 25; Diogenes Laertius 1.88; Malherbe 1989: 17; cf. Rom 5:7). Some held that only *virtually* all sinned, sometimes exempting some famous patriarchs (Pr Man 8; *T. Ab.* 10 A; Bray 1998: 149 cites Theodoret of Cyr *Interp. Rom.* on Rom 5:19) or others (*'Abot R. Nat.* 14A); some others attributed sin even to the patriarchs (e.g., *T. Ab.* 9, Rec. A).

conclusion he draws: those who sin are lost, even if they belong to the chosen people.

One could not counter Paul's argument in 3:1–8 with the objection that Jews were morally superior[11] to Gentiles (3:9). While on points like sexual immorality Jews generally *were* morally superior, Paul holds those with greater knowledge of the law to a higher standard (2:12), and includes sins of the heart (cf. 2:16), which are stirred all the more by repressing them (7:7–8). Paul notes in 3:9 that he has already established that both Jews and Gentiles are under sin; there was little point claiming to be superior to another when both were under sin's dominion. While Paul has already offered a general argument to this effect based on a hypothetical Jewish sinner (2:17–29), he now argues more generally from Scripture.[12]

In 3:10–18 Paul piles up texts (most of them from the Psalms) about the common sinfulness of humanity.[13] Apart from a few collections of ancient texts (such as at Qumran), few directly linked texts at such great length as here, and even the longer collections often addressed sections of Scripture rather than topics, and rarely "blended" diverse texts into a medley. Yet just as Jewish midrash regularly linked texts based on a common key word or concept, Paul links all these texts not only by their reference to sin but by other means as well. First, some of these texts allude somehow to death (3:13ac, 15–17), a theme that will recur (5:12, 14, 17, 21; 6:16, 21, 23; 7:5, 10, 13, 24; 8:6).[14] Second, most allude to body parts: eyes (3:18), feet (3:15–17), and perhaps appropriately first and at greatest length, the mouth (3:13–14).[15] Mention of parts of the body might

11. Technically, Paul's use of the middle here probably signifies protecting oneself rather than superiority, hence might involve the notion of protection from God's wrath (*BDAG*). Alternatively, if read as a passive, the interlocutor objects that Paul's argument puts Jews at a *dis*advantage, but Paul equalizes all.

12. Others also used quotations to argue that sin was widespread (Seneca *Ben.* 5.15.3; *Nat.* 4.pref. 19), though Paul's argument here seems more forceful. An argument claiming "all" when it proved only "most" could be technically defective (*Rhet. Her.* 2.20.32), though hyperbole would stand in both diatribe and polemical rhetoric.

13. In rhetoric, repeating a thought reinforced it.

14. Graves' uncleanness might also suggest defiling speech; on the danger of tongues like serpents, e.g., Pliny *Nat.* 18.1.4; *Rhet. Her.* 4.49.62; perhaps Ps 58:3–4.

15. Paul has just mentioned slander (3:8)! Significant for rhetorical effect, Paul also links some texts with an initial "there is not" (six lines) and a closing "their" in Greek (four lines; Jewett 2007: 254), though in some cases he adapts the wording slightly (as was common) to fit the rhetorical pattern.

prepare for Paul's later treatment of "flesh" (cf. 6:6; 7:5, 24–25; 8:10, 13; Col 3:5).[16]

Paul first quotes Ps 14:1–3 (13:1–3 LXX); because it has two identical lines ("there is no one who does kindness," 14:1, 3), Paul changes the first to "no one righteous" (probably based on Eccl 7:20), underlining the link with his own larger argument.[17] Then Paul quotes Pss 5:9; 140:3; 10:7; Isa 59:7–8; and finally Ps 36:1. Only Paul's use of Isa 59:7–8 in Rom 3:15–17 in its original context applied to Israel as a whole (at least in Isaiah's generation); perhaps the midrashic linking of these texts allows Paul to apply that principle to the other references as well. While the psalm texts contextually addressed the psalmist's enemies, Paul uses them to indict Israel as a whole on the principle that Scripture proclaims these matters to those who are under the law (3:19). Again, it especially indicts those who have the greatest knowledge and responsibility (cf. Amos 3:2).

Because the law condemns those under it,[18] every mouth, including Jewish ones, will be silenced (3:19). Like the rest of the world, the hypothetical objector of 3:5–8 will have nothing to argue in the day of judgment, when God will be shown righteous in his judgment (3:4, 6, 8).[19] The law is not meant to transform sinners into righteous people (cf. 8:3), but to reveal God's righteous standard (3:20; though see also comment on 3:21; 8:2). That is, the law shows people their sinfulness, as Paul has just exemplified in 3:10–18. Paul's words also allude to Ps 143:2, which pleads for God's mercy because "no one living [here, no flesh] will be reckoned righteous" in his sight.[20]

16. Cf. this use of body parts in Maximus of Tyre *Or.* 7.7; Porphyry *Marc.* 33.506–7; Amoraim in Urbach 1979: 1:473. In the rhetorical figure synecdoche, a part could stand for the whole (Anderson 2000: 112).

17. Some manuscripts of our current Greek translation of Ps 14:3 are considerably longer than a normal verse and essentially include the rest of Paul's quotation, in contrast to the Hebrew version; but this expanded version presumably reflects Christian scribes' knowledge of Paul's quotation here.

18. The law's speech reflects the rhetorical device *prosōpopoiia*.

19. Cf. also the mouths in 3:13–14 (and slander in 3:8), but the silencing of humanity before God's judgment is a wider motif (Isa 41:1; Zeph 1:7; 2:13; cf. Beale 1999: 446–52). The view that Paul addresses only Gentiles here runs precisely counter to Paul's point (3:9, 19–20).

20. As Hays (1989: 51–52) points out, the context in Ps 143:1 appeals to God's righteousness and faithfulness, relevant to this context (Rom 3:3, 5), and especially to Scripture revealing God's righteousness in Rom 3:21 (see also Hays 1980: 114–15).

Scholars today debate the precise sense of "works of the law" in 3:20. Some argue that it indicates specifically Jewish identity markers such as circumcision (cf. chs. 4, 14), while others contend that the phrase should include obedience to all the law unless specified otherwise. (The precise sense of the parallel phrase in the Qumran text 4QMMT is similarly debated; cf. 1QS 6.18.) Given biblical texts about "doing" the law, "works" of the law presumably may encompass the whole.[21] Nevertheless, Jewish distinctives would emphasize Paul's case particularly well, as his point here is to emphasize that the written law does not make Jewish people more righteous before God than Gentiles (3:9, 22–23, 29–30). It is also such distinctives that Gentiles joining Israel in the traditional way would be most compelled to adopt (as exemplified in the emphasis on circumcision in Gal 2:3–12; 5:2–11; 6:12–15), advantages Jews inherited as part of their culture.

God's Solution for All (3:21–31)

Humanity has sinned and merited judgment (3:9–20), but God remains faithful and righteous (3:21–31; cf. 3:1–8), so that people can also be set right with him through faith. The law revealed sin but did not make people righteous (3:20). We should not take this limitation to mean that the law itself is bad (7:7, 14). The problem is not the law, but using it in a way that it was never intended to be used. The law teaches right from wrong but does not provide, nor does it claim to provide, self-justification by one's own religious achievement. The law and the prophets do in fact teach the right way to be put in right relationship with God and made righteous (3:21): not by boasting in one's achievement, but by faith, i.e., depending on God (3:27, 31). Paul will go on to specify that at this stage in salvation history the faith must be in God's ultimate work, Jesus the Messiah (3:26).

Paul has been addressing God's righteousness to some degree since the key statement in 1:17, where God's righteousness was also "revealed" (despite the different term) in terms of faith.[22] His development of the concept will, however, cluster here (3:22, 25, 26); repetition was a stan-

21. Cf. Gathercole 2002: 92–93, 238; Watson 2007: 19, 128, 212.

22. Paul's likely conclusion suggests that Gentiles' salvation is an important part of God's righteousness now revealed from Scripture (16:26), inverting traditional expectations of what his righteousness involved (3:3–5).

dard way of driving home a theme. The cognate verb *dikaioō* also appears repeatedly (3:24, 26, 28, 30), providing an alternative for the lack of justification provided by works of the law in 3:20. Paul shows how at this juncture in salvation history ("now," 3:21) God's righteousness has been revealed through faith (in contrast to attempts to be "righteoused" by law; 3:20).

God's righteousness is through the "faith of Jesus Christ" (3:22; also 3:26)—an expression that has occasioned enormous debate. The Greek construction can mean Jesus's own faith(fulness), or it can mean faith in Jesus, and scholars have offered compelling arguments for both positions. Greek authors before and after Paul felt free to use genitives both subjectively (i.e., here "faith *of* Jesus") and objectively (i.e., here "faith *in* Jesus").[23] In favor of it referring to Jesus's own faith(fulness)[24] is the centrality of his work (3:24–25); the parallel expression regarding God's faithfulness earlier in the chapter (3:3); and most compellingly, the precisely parallel expression to believers being of the faith of Jesus (3:26) and the faith of Abraham (4:16).

In favor of the reading, "faith in Jesus" (the objective genitive),[25] the noun is plainly connected with the verb in 3:22, where it involves believers' faith (also Gal 2:16).[26] Although cognate nouns and verbs do not always carry the same significance, it seems likelier than not that they do here (the verb appears six times in ch. 4), and in Romans Jesus is always the object of this verb rather than its example. In forty-two uses of the verb in Romans we regularly read of believers' faith in Jesus, yet we nowhere in unambiguous terms read of Jesus's own faith. Although Paul could have written "faith *in* Jesus" more obviously, the genitive construc-

---

23. Harrisville 2006; objective genitives are more common with God's name. Thus, e.g., "knowledge of Jesus" is objective in Phil 3:8, allowing the same approach to "faith of Jesus" in Phil 3:9 (Schreiner 1998: 183); but subjective genitives with faith dominate the context of Rom 3–4 (3:3; 4:12, 16).

24. See e.g., K. Barth, J. Dunnill, J. Gager, K. Grieb, R. Hays, M. Hooker, L. Johnson, L. Ramaroson, S. Stowers, C. Talbert, S. Tonstad, N. T. Wright.

25. See e.g., Origen, Augustine, Abelard, T. Aquinas, M. Luther, B. Byrne, J. Dunn, J. Fitzmyer, A. Hultgren, R. B. Matlock, D. Moo, T. Schreiner, T. Tobin; cf. F. Watson. Some believe that Paul included both senses, though inclining toward the objective reading (e.g., A. Schlatter, L. Morris, M. Reasoner, R. Jewett); another option is a genitive of origin (faith enabled by Christ; D. Rusam; cf. Gal 2:20). For one history of views, see Reasoner 2005: 7, 24, 27, 30, 38.

26. Far from being superfluous on the objective genitive reading, it is emphatic (in Rom 3:22; Gal 3:22; Phil 3:9).

tion allowed for a more obvious contrast with "works of law." The church fathers, many of whom knew the language particularly intimately, also generally understood this particular phrase as an objective genitive.

In light of such evidence, I am currently inclined to agree with the conventional "faith in Jesus" understanding, despite the popularity of and many strong arguments for the currently more fashionable "faith of Jesus" interpretation. Because for Paul such faith also entails obedience (cf. 1:5), however, "faith in Jesus" need not be as far from the theological convictions of "faith of Jesus" as some interpreters have contended.

In any case, the emphasis on faith (3:22) rather than dependence on the law (3:20) annuls a distinction between Jew and Gentile with respect to salvation (3:22; cf. 10:12): all have likewise sinned (3:23), hence they can receive righteousness solely through God's gift in Christ (3:24–25). The aorist tense of "sinned" in 3:23 need not allude specifically to Adam (2:12, where both Jew and Gentile also sinned), but Paul later unfolds this idea in terms of Adam's fall (5:12, 14, 16). Humanity formed in God's image lost his glory through Adam's fall (cf. 1:23; 1 Cor 11:7; Ps 8:5), and it would be restored in Christ (Rom 8:18, 21, 29). (Most commentators here cite the Jewish tradition of Adam's glory lost at the fall; the present tense here could denote continuing effects of that fall. On what Adam lost, see comment on 5:12–21.) Most Jewish people agreed that virtually all have sinned (see comment on 3:9).

Many scholars take some or all of Paul's comments about the solution in 3:24–25 to be Paul's adaptation of an early Christian tradition (typically a creed or a hymn).[27] While it would be precarious to rule out the possibility (there are many terms rare in Paul), we should note that the grammatical elements cited by NT scholars as characteristic of such creeds characterize exalted prose more generally, and could simply signal Paul's rhetorical shift. In any event, the passage reflects Paul's view, whether or not it is original with him.[28]

Believers are set right and made righteous as a gift (3:24; through the new Adam in 5:15, 17) by grace (3:24; contrasted with works of the law in 4:4, 16; 11:6; associated with the new Adam in 5:15, 17, 20, 21). For an ancient audience, the mention of either "gift" or "grace" (favor

27. E.g., Hunter 1961: 120; Meyer 1983: 198–208; Stuhlmacher 1994: 58; Dunn 1988: 1:163–64. Talbert (1966) even viewed it as an interpolation (though this is no longer his view).

28. See Haacker 2003: 108–9; Talbert 2002: 106–8; Young 1974.

or generosity) would imply benefaction; their coupling here underlines the emphasis on the divine initiative on which believers can depend. The content of the benefaction involves "redemption," a term denoting the liberation of slaves, as in the exodus.[29] (The cognate verb in the LXX sometimes, but not always, includes a ransom price, as typically in earlier Greek; the context here might suggest Jesus's blood as such a price.)[30] This experience of redemption is completed in the future (Rom 8:23; cf. Eph 1:14; 4:30; Luke 21:38; 1QM 15.1–2), but here involves what Christ has already done, filled out in the freedom from slavery image of 6:6–23 (cf. 7:25; 8:15, 21).

God's righteousness attested by Scripture (3:21) and involving faith in Jesus (3:22) was demonstrated in Jesus's redemptive death (3:24–25). Whereas God had previously displayed mercy, he now demonstrated his righteousness by being both righteous (or just) and by putting believers in Jesus right with him (3:25–26; see comment on 1:17).

Paul then appeals to a different biblical image, namely, the cover of the ark of the covenant (*hilastērion* in 3:25; see Exod 25:17–22 and elsewhere in the LXX; Heb 9:5), a translation earlier recognized by Origen, Luther, and Tyndale, among others. God "planned"[31] Jesus as the "mercy seat" or ark cover. But what is the point of Paul's comparison? Granted, Jesus is the locus of the divine presence, but, as many have noted, the following mention of his "blood" strongly suggests an allusion to the annual consecration of this holy place through sacrificial blood on the Day of Atonement (Lev 16:14–15).[32] By Jesus's own blood, God consecrated

---

29. In 1 Cor 1:30 Paul may associate redemption with other salvific concepts; the different term in Gal 3:13 and 4:5 might carry a similar sense, except emphasizing the cost. Eph 1:7 and Col 1:14 (which I treat as Pauline, and which are otherwise our earliest extant interpretation of Paul) associate redemption with forgiveness.

30. Cf. redemption by Jesus's sacrificial blood in Heb 9:14–15; 1 Pet 1:18–19; perhaps Rev 1:5; 5:9. Many church fathers viewed Christ's death as a ransom from the devil, but this interpretation seems inconsistent with the sacrificial connotations of Jesus's death in this context (which they also could recognize).

31. The same term appears with this sense in Rom 1:13; Eph 1:9; the term also means "display publicly." Although some suggest levitical connotations (Exod 29:23; 40:4, 23; Lev 24:8; 2 Macc 1:8), it has a broader sense.

32. Cf. Jesus's death and cognate atonement language in Heb 2:17 (in view of Heb 7:27; 9:26; 10:10–12); 1 John 2:2; 4:10. It might also allude to the eschatological re-consecration (Ezek 43:20). Against Dodd and those who have followed him, who doubt that the LXX used cognate language for genuinely propitiating God's wrath, as in pagan Greek, Scripture spoke both of God's wrath and of particular offerings propitiating it, a nuance

Jesus as the place where forgiven humanity can meet God. Crucifixion was not always bloody, and the Gospels use "blood" not to describe the event itself but its significance.[33] In an image related to the tabernacle, "blood" likely connotes sacrificial death, as elsewhere in early Christian meditation on the point of Jesus's death, both regarding atonement and purification (1 Pet 1:2, 19; 1 John 1:7).[34] Paul's image would be intelligible; an extant Hellenistic Jewish source suggests that some others used *hilastērion* figuratively, as Paul did. For them, it was a figure for atonement itself, specifically the atonement offered by a human death turning away God's wrath from the people (4 Macc 17:22).[35] In a context replete with mentions of God's wrath (Rom 1:18; 2:5, 8; 3:5; 4:15), this function is significant: Jesus's blood elsewhere turns away God's anger (5:9–10) and his death may be sacrificial in 8:3.

Previously God "passed over" his people's sins rather than punishing them justly (*paresis* in 3:25 means "postponing" or "neglecting" punishment),[36] but now he was revealing or proving his righteousness by showing that he was both righteous and the one who would put his people right with him (his people here being those with Jesus-faith). If we take the two elements as contrasts, God was just to punish sin, yet put his people right with him by executing the sentence on another (Jesus's atoning death being viewed like that of martyrs in Maccabean literature).[37] If they are coordinated, God's righteousness includes covenant faithfulness to put people right with him (see comment on 1:17). Because God's righ-

---

probably evoked here (see Rom 5:9; 8:3; cf. Gosling 2001).

33. The covenant sacrifice (Mark 14:24) and blood guilt (Matt 23:35/Luke 11:50–51).

34. For Jesus's sacrificial blood inaugurating a covenant, in light of Exod 24:5, 8, see 1 Cor 11:25; Mark 14:24; Heb 9:18–20; 10:29; 12:24; 13:20.

35. This image also connects with ransom (4 Macc 17:21), hence perhaps with "redemption" (Rom 3:24); without this term, martyr-atonement also appears in 2 Macc 7:37–38; 4 Macc 6:27–29. Scholars also point to Josephus *Ant.* 16.182; Gen 6:16 Symm. While less compelling, they reinforce the observation that the LXX term's cognates had influenced its figurative application.

36. For God overlooking sins, at least temporarily, cf. Wis 11:23; Acts 14:16; 17:30.

37. When not enforced, laws could be said to lose their validity (Aeschines *Tim.* 36, 192). Later rabbis portrayed God's attributes of justice and mercy competing (Urbach 1979: 1:448–61; cf. Jas 2:13); Paul may resolve such tension here.

teousness likely includes both justice and covenant faithfulness (1:17–18; 3:3–8) we may be able to accommodate both alternatives.[38]

In light of the foregoing explanation in 3:22–26, then (*oun*, "therefore"; 3:27), self-boasting has no place. One might boast in one's merit if one interpreted the goal of the law as works; but instead the law teaches the way of faith (3:27; cf. 9:31–32), as is clear throughout Paul's argument here.[39] The law attests God's righteousness, not humanity's (3:21–23), and faith establishes the law (3:31). Paul's message about Jesus in fact draws on analogies in the law that make this point, such as redemption and atonement (3:24–25). Thus, one is righted by depending on God, not by merit (3:28). (Paul also contrasts approaches to the law in 8:2; 9:31–32; 10:5–8.)

Paul has never lost sight of the reason he is making this case for faith in Romans: the point that Jew and Gentile must come to God on the same terms, rather than a Jewish person starting with the advantage of knowing the law (3:9, 22). If there is one God—and that was the basic cornerstone of Judaism (Deut 6:4)[40]—then he must be God for all humanity, not only for Israel (Rom 3:29–30). Instead of using God's supremacy to argue for Israel's sole (end-time) exaltation, as many of his contemporaries did, he uses it to argue that God cares about all humanity. Does Paul, however, envision separate means of righting for these groups, Jews "by" or "from" faith(fulness) and Gentiles "through" faith(fulness) (3:30)? "By" and "from" may simply reflect stylistic variation, which was important in rhetoric.[41] Paul has already been clear that for both this faith must be Jesus-faith (3:22), not dependence on law-works (3:19–20). Being God of all humanity means that God does not care only about those to whom he gave the Torah.[42]

38. Paul's repetition of "demonstrate his righteousness" might be rhetorical reinforcement (by anadiplosis); it is surely rhetorical commitment to maintain the clarity of syntax (by dilogia). See Anderson 2000: 18, 37; idem 1999: 228.

39. Insofar as "law" translates *tora*, it can include all of God's gracious instruction in Scripture, or focus more narrowly on that instruction in the Pentateuch. Translating "law" here as "principle" (NIV; omitted altogether in NLT), however, ignores the obvious context (3:19–21, 28, 31), perhaps in favor of theological bias.

40. For its regular recitation, see e.g., *m. Ber.* 1:1–4; 2:1, 3; *Tamid* 5:1; and the earlier Nash papyrus.

41. Cf. Campbell 1992.

42. Some ancient writers did emphasize God as God of all humanity (e.g., Josephus *Ag. Ap.* 2.193), but the emphasis on God caring about Gentiles, while present in some

In 3:31 Paul both concludes a line of argument and foreshadows what is to come.[43] The law supports the faith-way of God's righteousness (3:21–22); Paul will demonstrate this point more fully in a foundational example from the Torah, namely Abraham, in 4:1–25.[44] (Paul is not using technical hermeneutical terms here, although other Jewish teachers sometimes contrasted "breaking" or "annulling" the law with "establishing" it.)

---

ancient sources, is far more pervasive in modern Judaism.

43. Ancient writers could use transitions (e.g., *Rhet. Her.* 4.26.35).

44. See especially the approach of Rhyne 1981 (e.g., 75).

ROMANS 4

Abraham Righted by Faith (4:1–8)

Having claimed in 3:31 that the way of faith establishes the teaching of the law (cf. also 3:21), Paul now goes on to demonstrate this by means of a midrash on a foundational passage for Israel's history. Revealing the biblical foundations for the points that he has just been making, he will establish that even Abraham could not boast in his works (3:27; 4:2); that even he was put right with God by trust rather than merit (3:28; 4:3–5); and that God had a purpose for uncircumcised Gentiles as well as circumcised Jews (3:29–30; 4:9–12, 16–18).

Abraham was the defining ancestor of Israel (4:1; though not only of Israel; 9:7–13), so his support for accepting uncircumcised Gentiles among God's people would outweigh any other Jewish objections.[1] Not only was Abraham the model for Israel,[2] but later rabbis considered him the model Gentile convert to Judaism and affirmed his and Sarah's witness to Gentiles. Those who appealed to the model of Abraham often appealed to his works, with faith among them.

But however much Abraham's faith was expressed in obedience and righteousness, it is clear that faith was the foundation for these other elements. Scripture specifically announced that God counted Abram as righteous when he believed God's promise (Gen 15:6; quoted in Rom 4:3).

---

1. Later rabbis also claimed the benefits of the patriarchs' merits (e.g., *m. 'Abot* 2:2; *Mek. Pisha* 16.165–68, with other opinions in 16.169–72; *Besh.* 4.52–57; *Sipra Behuq.* pq. 8.269.2.5; *Sipre Deut.* 8.1.1). We lack space to engage the competing arguments regarding the syntax of Rom 4:1 (e.g., Hays 1989: 54; idem 2005: 64–73; Gathercole 2002: 234).

2. For Abraham receiving the covenant through obedience, Talbert (2002: 98) cites Gen 26:2–5; *Jub.* 15:3–4; Sir 44:19–21; CD 3.2. For a history of early Jewish approaches to Gen 15:6, see Oeming 1998: 16–33. For why Paul focuses on Abraham rather than Sarah here, see Grieb 2002: 51.

Abram's faith was far from perfect: God had essentially promised both land and seed (Gen 12:1–2), but even after God assured Abram he would receive both, he requested confirmation regarding the land (15:7–8), and soon he and Sarai resorted to Hagar as a surrogate mother (16:2). Abram's faith is much greater years later when he offers up Isaac apparently without question (22:2–3), but this initial, somewhat rudimentary faith is sufficient to be reckoned righteous, analogous to even those initially entering the Christian faith.

Reading his key text for all it is worth, as midrashic expositors typically did, Paul contrasts the text's words with his construction of righteousness by obeying the law (what a Gentile Godfearer might feel necessary to become a full convert to Judaism). God was not paying Abraham his due for righteous deeds,[3] but "reckoning" his faith as if it were righteousness (4:4–5); Paul highlights this term "reckon," using it eleven times in this chapter.[4] Paul's claim that God "acquits" or "makes right the ungodly" (4:5) is deliberatively provocative,[5] for it sounds like injustice (cf. Ex 23:7). Paul backs up this claim, however, with his following citation. Jewish midrash also linked together texts based on a common key term or phrase, and Paul in 4:6–8 cites the favored state ("blessing," in many translations) of another whose behavior was "reckoned" by God's favor rather than his works (Ps 32:1–2). Having produced Abraham as a witness, he now cites David, who was held to be the author of many psalms (especially in the early Psalter). The psalmist had clearly sinned (Ps 32:3), yet God did not "reckon" the sin to him.

Father Also of Gentiles Who Believe (4:9–12)

In 4:9–13 Paul returns to the issue that prompted (both in Romans and Galatians) his heavy emphasis on being made right by faith: God puts both Jews and Gentiles right with him by the same means. As we noted above, Jewish people regarded Abraham as a model Gentile convert. Paul

---

3. Just "wages" for human behavior, in fact, are death (a different term in 6:23), though the present term appears more positively in 1 Cor 3:8, 14; 9:17–18.

4. Cf. finding "favor" (*charis*, "grace") in the Lord's eyes in Gen 6:8; 18:3 (the LXX's first two uses of the term).

5. The Greek terminology would sound even worse to those unfamiliar with the LXX (Anderson [1999: 209] speaks of "lexical shock").

uses context[6] to point out that Abraham was put right with God by faith in Gen 15:6—over thirteen years before hs circumcision (since it preceded Ishmael's conception, 16:4; and Ishmael was thirteen at the circumcision, 17:25). "This blessing" (4:9) of which David spoke (4:6–8)—of being "reckoned" righteous not by works but, as in Gen 15:6, by faith (4:3)—applied to Abraham before he was circumcised.

People spoke of both ethnic and spiritual ancestry; spiritual ancestors were those in whose ways one walked, i.e., those one imitated as if parents.[7] Those who have faith, like Abraham did, are his spiritual heirs more than those who simply practice the outward seal of circumcision (4:11–12).[8] Some Jewish teachers appealed to ancestral merit for blessing, a benefit unavailable to Gentile converts,[9] but Paul allowed Abraham only as a model.

At this point, a Jewish interlocutor could have replied, "Abraham was counted righteous as a Godfearer, but joined the covenant by means of circumcision" (cf. Gen 17:10–14). Paul's response is that God gave Abram even the promise of the land while uncircumcised, and certainly centuries before the law (Rom 4:13). Circumcision was merely an external "sign" or "seal" of his already-existing faith (4:11), and is not inherently essential to that faith (here Paul may recall his own argument about spiritual circumcision in 2:25–29). A "seal" could function as a symbol (Exod 28:11, 21, 36); a "sign" of the covenant would be, like the rainbow in Gen 9:12–13, 16–17, a reminder of the deliverance that God had established, not the deliverance itself.

6. On the typical Jewish application of this principle, see e.g., Longenecker 1975: 118.

7. See Keener 2005a: 3; idem 2003b: 756–57. Many thinkers regarded shared character as a closer tie than birth (deSilva 2000: 194–95, 202–6; cf. Philo *Heir* 68–69).

8. Some later rabbinic sources treat circumcision as a seal (cf. *t. Ber.* 6:13; also *Barn.* 9.6), an idea presumably not borrowed from Paul; circumcision as a covenant "sign" recalls Gen 17:11 (*Jub.* 15:26). Some think Paul replaced circumcision with baptism (Lampe 1951: 3–5; Richardson 1958: 352–53), but Paul instead emphasizes faith (Barth 1974: 1:135–43; Dunn 1998: 454–55; Thrall 1994: 156–58). Paul's "seal" of the Spirit (2 Cor 1:22) also does not explicitly mention baptism (though cf. *Herm.* 93.2–4).

9. For ancestral merit, see e.g., *L.A.B.* 35:3; *T. Levi* 15:4 (if not interpolated); *3 En.* 1:3; *Sipra Behuq.* pq. 8.269.2.5; *Sipre Deut.* 8.1.1; for the exodus, *Mek. Pisha* 16.165–68; *Besh.* 4.52–54; for its unavailability to proselytes, see later *Num. Rab.* 8:9. Not all agreed (*Sipre Deut.* 329.3.1), and the application of such merit to individual salvation might be later. Circumcision (*Mek. Pisha* 16.169–70) and faith (*Mek. Besh.* 7.135–38) were also meritorious.

The Promise through Faith (4:13–25)

Constructing again his antithesis between God's original plan of promise and the Israel-specific law (Rom 4:13–15; cf. Gal 3:17–19), Paul argues that if righteousness came by faith in the promise, the law (like the circumcision that prefigured it) is not what is needed to achieve it. Various Jewish thinkers highlighted some biblical covenants while playing down others, so Paul's treatment of Moses's law as a phase between the Abrahamic promise and the new covenant was no more idiosyncratic than some other treatments of the day.[10] Scripture promised Abraham "the land" (*haaretz*), but in Hebrew this could mean either a specific land or the earth, and by Paul's day Jewish thinkers often applied the promise to the world as a whole, or even to inheriting the world to come.[11] When Paul speaks elsewhere of "inheriting," as here (4:13), he often uses it in the idiom of the life of the coming age (Rom 8:17; 1 Cor 6:9–10; 15:50; Gal 5:21).[12] Just as faith does not void law (Rom 3:31), so in 4:14 the law cannot void faith and promise, which would also threaten Scripure and God's covenant (cf. Gal 3:17–18). For Paul, law's function (in this context) is to reveal failures to meet God's standard rather than to reckon righteousness (Rom 4:15).

In 4:16 Paul again returns to the key issue that motivates his argument: God's one way of righteousness is not only for those who are of the law (circumcised Israelites), but those who are of faith like Abraham—all his spiritual descendants, both Jewish and Gentile.[13] While not citing the blessing of all nations in Abraham here (as in Gal 3:8; Gen 12:3; 18:18; 22:18), he cites Abraham as father of many nations (Gen 17:4–6; Rom 4:17). Although by itself that promise might mean father of Ishmaelites, Edomites, Midianites and other ethnic descendants,[14] Paul applies it to Abraham's spiritual heirs. Not all those physical descendants would really inherit the covenant (Gen 17:7–8; cf. Rom 9:6–13, 25–29), whereas God

10. See Talbert 2002: 17, with sources; cf. Knox 1925: 135.

11. With many commentators (e.g., Byrne 1996: 157; cf. *Jub.* 32:19).

12. A common Jewish formulation (e.g., *1 En.* 40:9; *4 Ezra* 7:96; *m. 'Abot* 3:11; for other sources, see e.g., Keener 1999: 167; and esp. Hester 1968).

13. Paul's wording in 4:16 may allow for God's continuing plan for ethnic Israel, anticipating his later argument in Rom 11.

14. *t. Ber.* 1:12 applies it to being "father" of all humanity, perhaps in the sense of his seed eventually ruling the world (cf. *t. Ber.* 1:13; *Mek. Besh.* 7.139–40).

would welcome those with Abraham's faith as he welcomed Abraham.[15] Paul reads Scripture not only for covenantal history, but devotionally for insight into and examples of a dynamic relationship with God.

Some have contrasted Abraham's model of faith with fallen humanity's apostasy in Romans 1:[16]

Rom 1:20–27	Rom 4:17–21
Humanity failed to recognize its creator (1:20, 25)	Abraham trusted the creator (4:17)
Humanity ignored God's power (1:20, using *dunamis*)	Abraham trusted God's power (4:21, using *dunatos*)
Humanity did not give God glory (1:21)	Abraham gave God glory (4:20)
Humanity dishonored their bodies (1:24)	Abraham found new strength in his body (4:19)
Humanity used their bodies in non-productive, same-sex relations (1:26–27)	Abraham and Sarah conceived a child (4:19)—miraculously being fruitful and multiplying

If Paul intends such a contrast, it would help prepare for the further contrast between Abraham's faith and Adamic humanity's fallenness in 5:12–21.[17]

The affirmation that God raises the dead and creatively calls things into being (4:17)[18] prepares for Paul's explanation of the relevance of Abraham's "resurrection faith" for later believers (4:19, 24). Abraham maintained hope despite the hopelessness of the situation (4:18), just as believers must (5:2–5; 8:24–25). The nature of Abraham's faith would instruct Paul's audience: whereas some of them were weak in faith (14:1–2), Israel's great ancestor Abraham was strong in faith (4:19–20);

15. Viewed in a broader context of the empire, Paul's portrait offers a striking contrast to the imperial subjugation of "the nations" (see Lopez 2008).

16. Wright 2004: 78.

17. Abraham also prefigures Christ in 5:12–21 in this respect, although I did not take *pistis Christou* in 3:22 as a reference to Christ's faith (parallel to Abraham's), as some do.

18. This is the contemporary Jewish language of creation *ex nihilo* (Byrne 1996: 159–60; Dunn 1988: vol. 1, 218; O'Neill 2002; *2 Bar.* 21:4); Paul already appealed to creation in Rom 1:20. God's "calling" that formed his people and would form them in the future appears in 8:30; 9:7, 12, 24–26. *Mē onta* appears also in 1 Cor 1:28.

as he was "fully persuaded" (4:21), so should they be (14:5); as he refused to doubt (*diakrinō*; 4:20), so should they (14:23). Likewise, he avoided unbelief (*apistia*; 4:20), in contrast to much of contemporary Israel (3:3; 11:20, 23). In contrast to those who refused to glorify God even after his works (1:21), Abraham glorified him before the fulfillment of his promise (4:20), counting his word as good as done (though he acknowledged fully his own physical state; 4:19). Abraham is thus a striking example of loyal, obedient faith, and this is the sort of faith that was counted as righteousness (4:22). Paul offers no comfort to those, in his day (3:8) or in recent centuries, who think that his view of saving faith is irrelevant to life, merely untested assent to a widely shared proposition.

The object of faith is also significant. The repeated theme of "promise" here (4:20-21; also 4:13-14, 16) might recall for Paul's audience the importance of trusting the promised Messiah (1:2-4). The promise of the "seed" (descendants; 4:18) may point to a key element in Paul's analogy. Most important in Paul's analogy is Abraham's faith in God's message to him, but that message foreshadowed the gospel in key ways. Just as the promise of inheriting "the world" (4:13) foreshadowed the kingdom (i.e., the expected reign of the Messiah), so the promised seed may have foreshadowed a more particular seed (cf. Gal 3:16). Isaac was the child of promise (9:8), but his lineage also included a later promise, the seed of David (Rom 1:3; cf. 2 Sam 7:12). Those in Christ would reign with him (Rom 5:17; cf. Dan 7:14, 22).

More specifically, in 4:19, his faith in the God who could surmount the "deadness" of his body[19] and Sarah's womb was resurrection faith (4:17).[20] Abraham modeled faith not simply abstractly, but by believing in a promised seed and in resurrection; these objects offered a concrete model for believers in Jesus's resurrection (4:24).

All along, Paul thus has in mind his objective of applying the text to his audience, and he says so plainly in 4:23-24. Events in biblical history may have *happened* for the sake of those involved in them, but they were *written* for subsequent generations to learn from their example (cf.

19. He was "about one hundred" when the promise was fulfilled, not when (many years earlier) it was given (unless one is rounding to the nearest half century). The "deadness" of his body also anticipates the resurrection of believers' "dead" (mortal) bodies (8:10-11). Cf. Heb 11:12.

20. The author of Hebrews, who focuses on Abraham offering up Isaac, also finds anticipatory resurrection faith there (Heb 11:17-19).

15:4; 1 Cor 10:11).[21] We have already noted how Paul shapes his telling of Abraham's story to prepare for resurrection faith in 4:24. In 4:25 Paul summarizes his gospel (grounded in Scripture, cf. 1 Cor 15:3–4). Paul may use parallel clauses here (*dia* + the accusative = "on account of") simply for rhetorical effect, even though the first clause notes the cause requiring Jesus's death and the second the goal (hence an ultimate, teleological cause) of his resurrection.[22] In view of his abundant allusions to Isaiah in Romans, his language in 4:24–25 may allude to the suffering servant of Isa 53:5–12.[23]

Paul's new term *paraptōma* ("transgression") prepares for the six uses of the term in 5:15–20, as Paul's use of the rare term *dikaiōsis* ("acquittal") prepares for his only other use of it in 5:18 (where it contrasts with *paraptōma*). Paul's teaching in the following units seems to flesh out more explicitly what Jesus's death on account of sin means, both in terms of Jesus's martyrdom turning away God's wrath (5:9) and his perfect obedience in death reversing Adam's disobedience (5:18–19).

21. Paul's approach here is to argue from analogy, not to "allegorize" like Philo, though he employs the same "on our account" in 1 Cor 9:10 (regarding a law; see e.g., discussion in Keener 2005b: 78–79).

22. Those who trust in Jesus's resurrection are righted in 4:24. God rights believers both because of Jesus's death (4:25) and his resurrection (5:9). Although his focus is more often on the resurrection, Paul emphasizes different aspects at different points for rhetorical balance.

23. Often noted: e.g., Hunter 1955: 54; Stuhlmacher 1994: 75; Dunn 1988: 1:241; Johnson 2001: 173–74; Byrne 1996: 161; Jewett 2007: 342.

ROMANS 5

MADE RIGHT BY TRUSTING CHRIST (1:18—5:11), *cont.*

Righted and Reconciled by Christ (5:1–11)

In 5:1, Paul reasons from what he has just established (hence "therefore," 5:1): believers have been righted (so 4:25) by faith ("those who believe" in 4:24). In light of this established point, Paul addresses believers having "peace" with God (5:1),[1] i.e., no longer being his enemies (5:10) but being reconciled to him (5:10–11). This reconciliation is accomplished through Jesus because of his death and resurrection (4:25).

In 5:2 Paul contends that Jesus has also ushered believers into grace by faith (for grace and faith, cf. 3:22, 24; 4:3–4, 16); the perfect tense of "stand" suggests that believers remain in this grace (cf. "stand" in contrast to "fall" in 11:20; 14:4). Whereas Paul has denounced one who falsely "boasts" (*kauchaomai*) in God or the law (2:17, 23), Paul notes that in Jesus believers can boast in hope (5:2), in the face of suffering confident that it leads to hope (5:3–5), and in God (5:11).[2] "Hope" here follows the example of Abraham's resurrection hope in the preceding paragraph (4:18), but in this case the focus is eschatological salvation (cf. 8:20, 24–25). Believers hope for sharing God's "glory" (8:18, 21, 30), what was lost in Adam (cf. 3:23; 1 Cor 11:7).

Like Abraham, however (cf. 4:19), Paul wants believers to trust God's promise even when they faced obstacles that made it appear un-

---

1. Scholars debate whether the original text of Romans says "We have peace with God" or "Let us have peace with God." Although the latter has significant textual attestation, the majority of commentators argue that the former makes more sense of the context, and the latter would be a natural scribal error (if the scribe heard a long ō for a short o).

2. We may debate whether 5:11 is a third case or a summary of the first two. If the former, it could be relevant that one might support a rhetorical thesis with three illustrations or points (Quintilian *Inst.* 4.5.3; cf. Cicero *Mur.* 5.11; Pliny the Younger *Ep.* 2.20.9).

realistic apart from God (5:3). They would thus boast not only in hope directly (5:2), but in affliction that ultimately reinforced their hope (5:3; cf. 8:24–25).[3] Paul employs the rousing rhetorical chain device of climax (or sorites) in 5:3–5.[4] Because affliction tests faith, it allows one to demonstrate endurance, which is a necessary expression of faith for those who would receive eternal life (2:7). (Paul most certainly did not regard faith as saving if it failed to persevere in Christ; cf. 11:22; 1 Cor 9:27; Gal 4:19; 5:4.) Affliction first produces "tested character" (*dokimē*, 5:4); one's faith was shown to be genuine through the pressures of life, and the genuineness and help of the Spirit (5:5) vindicate one's hope of eternal life (contrast *adokimos*, one who failed the test, in 1:28).[5]

Paul climaxes with hope (5:5). When one's hope proved false, one would be "ashamed"; the psalmist prayed that God would not let his hope in God cause him such shame (Ps 119:116). The object of believers' hope, however (sharing God's glory, Rom 5:2), would not put them to shame (5:5; cf. 1:16; 9:33; 10:11). The basis of Paul's confidence in the future was the divine sign of proven character already within believers, namely, the Spirit attesting God's love for them (5:5). Grammatically, "love of God" could mean believers' love for God or God's love through them, but in light of the following context it must mean God's love for them (5:8). That is, believers can be assured of the outcome of their sufferings because God's Spirit within them points to Christ's death for them,[6] as well as resurrection hope (5:8–10). That the Spirit is a *gift* (5:5), in contrast to some Jewish traditions,[7] also fits Paul's theology of grace in this letter.

3. Some philosophers (Cicero *Tusc.* 2.7.17 [Epicurus]; Seneca *Nat.* 3, pref. 11–15, esp. 12; Epictetus *Disc.* 3.8.6), apocalyptists (2 *Bar.* 52:6; cf. 1QS 10.15–17) and others (Sir 2:4–5; *Sipre Deut.* 32.5.5) encouraged joy during suffering. This applied especially to persecution (2 Macc 6:30; Josephus *J.W.* 2.152).

4. E.g., Demosthenes *Con.* §19; *Rhet. Her.* 4.25.34–35; Demetrius *Eloc.* 5.270; Maximus of Tyre *Or.* 16.3; Fronto *Ad M. Caes.* 1.6.4; Philostratus *Ep. Apoll.* 33; in Jewish circles, Wis 6:17–20; *Sipre Deut.* 161.1.3; *b. 'Abod. Zar.* 20b. Augustine recognized this (*Doctr. chr.* 4.7.11, in Anderson 1999: 17–18).

5. Similar ideas appear in Jas 1:2–4; 1 Pet 1:6–7, possibly reflecting a common early Christian source (Davids 1982: 65–66).

6. The idea may include Christ sharing humanity's sufferings (cf. 8:3) as his body (believers) should also share his (Phil 3:10), and the Spirit shares believers' "groanings" (Rom 8:26).

7. *m. Sotah* 9:15; *t. Sotah* 13:3; *Mek. Besh.* 7.135–39; *Sipre Deut.* 173.1.3; later *'Abot R. Nat.* 11, §28B; *y. 'Abod. Zar.* 3:1, §2; *y. Hor.* 3:5, §3; *y. Sotah* 9:16, §2; *b. Sukkah* 28a, bar.; see also Davies 1973: 98. But note the Spirit as gift in Wis 9:17 (like wisdom; cf. 8:21; Sir 1:10); *Sib. Or.* 4.46.

That the love is here "poured out" through the Spirit might evoke the promised outpouring of the prophetic Spirit in Joel 2:28–29 (cf. Isa 32:15; 44:3; Ezek 39:29), so that the Spirit here may speak to or inspire believers' hearts with God's love (cf. Rom 8:16).

Hope is secure because it rests on God's love (5:5), which is demonstrated in Christ's sacrifice (5:6–9). Paul has already noted that Christ was delivered for our transgressions (4:25); now he elaborates on humans' state as transgressors, and how committed God's love was to saving them. Normally a person would be reluctant to die for another person, although there would be some exceptions for a good person (5:6–7).[8] But Christ died for sinners (5:8), objects of God's wrath (5:9),[9] God's enemies (5:10). By his death he reconciled these sinners to God, overcoming the enmity, and those in solidarity with him would be saved eschatologically because of his resurrection (5:11).

These verses (5:6–11) help flesh out what Paul means about Jesus dying because of our transgressions (4:24), although Paul will also provide additional models of Jesus's death afterward (especially 5:18–19; 6:3–10). That Jesus's blood here propitiates God's wrath (5:9) fits some biblical and other ancient conceptions. Because crucifixion was not *primarily* bloody (in contrast to execution by decapitation),[10] the mention of blood is theologically significant.[11] While modern theology may be often uncomfortable with the idea of God's wrath, we ought not to suppose that Paul shared such scruples (cf. Rom 9:22; 1 Cor 1:18; 3:17; 10:8–10; 11:30–32;

8. On death for friends in Greek thought, see Epictetus *Disc.* 2.7.3; Diogenes Laertius 10.120; further Keener 2000a: 383–84. Jewish martyrdoms were for God (so also Origen *Comm. Rom.* on 5:7), and one should not even give to sinners (Sir 12:4, 7). A good man was thought to be rare (Diogenes Laertius 1.77, 88; 9.2.20; see Rom 3:23).

9. Salvation from God's wrath in the day of judgment, appears also in 1 Thess 1:10; 5:9; for this eschatological use of wrath in Romans, see e.g., 2:5; 9:22.

10. Although John 20:25 and probably Luke 24:39–40 (most mss) presuppose Jesus nailed to the cross, victims could even be simply tied to it. Crucifixion could be "bloody," but that was not primary; the language points instead to the theology of guilt for innocent blood (e.g., Matt 23:35) or of sacrifice (probably here).

11. With many commentators (albeit against others). For blood and atonement, see e.g., Exod 29:36; 30:10; 34:25; Lev 4:26; 16:27, 30; cf. 1 Sam 3:14; 2 Chron 29:24. Such atonement could appease God's wrath (Num 16:46). Sin offerings are often connected with atonement (Exod 29:36; 30:10; Lev 4:20; 5:6; 6:30; 7:7; 9:7; 10:17; 12:8; 14:19; 15:15, 30; 16:6, 11, 27; Num 6:11; 8:12; 15:25; 28:22; 29:5, 11; 2 Chron 29:24; Ezek 45:17), as are guilt offerings (Lev 5:6, 16, 18; 7:7; 14:21; 19:22). Vicarious atonement appears as early as Canaanite and Hittite ritual and was certainly widely understood in Paul's day, both in paganism and (contrary to some proposals) in Judaism (later, among Tannaim, cf. e.g., Kim 2001–5: summarized on 143–45).

Phil 1:28; 3:19; 1 Thess 1:10; 2:16; 5:3, 9), including in this context (Rom 1:18; 2:5, 8, 12; 3:5; 4:15). The context of such wrath, however, highlights the depth of God's sacrificial love here (apparently embodied in God's costly sacrifice for humanity, again against many modern theological conceptions).

Evoking 4:24–25, Paul indicates that hope is secure not only because Christ died for us, but also because he rose (5:9–10). In 5:11 Paul may summarize his point in this paragraph: believers can boast in God (see comment on 5:2) because Jesus's death has reconciled us to him.[12] We also boast in God alone because proven character and hope come by God's Spirit in our hearts rather than our own work (5:2–5). "Through our Lord Jesus Christ" (5:1, 11) frames the paragraph.

LIFE IN CHRIST AND THE SPIRIT (5:12—8:39)

Having addressed righteousness by dependence on Christ's work in 1:17—5:11, Paul now turns to the new life involved in being identified with Christ (5:12—6:11) and in the Spirit's indwelling (8:1–39). It is this new life in union with God, rather than mere human knowledge about God's righteous law (7:1–25), that produces true righteousness.

Because Paul often transitions from one thought to the next rather than following a neat hierarchical outline, scholars often debate whether Romans 5 belongs with the previous section on justification (1:16—4:25) or the following one on life (6:1—8:39).[13] In 5:1–11, however, Paul is applying to his audience principles exemplified by Abraham's model in chapter 4; in 5:12–21, Paul shifts from the figure of Abraham to the figure of Adam, and the new life in chapter 6 follows directly from 5:12–21. Thus, with a minority of scholars (e.g., Talbert), I believe that it might be simplest to assign 5:1–11 to the previous section and 5:12–21 to the following one. At the very least, the possibility of such a division invites us to take into account the importance of both the preceding and following contexts.

12. Cf. reconciliation in 2 Macc 5:20; for reconciliation and atonement, see Plutarch *Thes.*15.1; especially Fitzgerald 2001: 243, 252–53 (the most distinctive aspect here being that the offended party offers the payment, Fitzgerald 2001: 255). For reconciliation and friendship, see Fitzgerald 2003: 334–37.

13. For surveys of views, see e.g., Fitzmyer 1993: 96–97; Moo 1996: 291. Because Paul transitions gradually between points, scholars naturally find connections with both the preceding and following material.

Reversing the Fall (5:12–21)

In chapter 4, Paul has argued against depending on ethnic descent from Abraham. Now he reminds his biblically informed audience that all people are descended from Adam. A Jewish audience might concur with his condemnation of those in solidarity with Adam, provided he excluded those in ethnic solidarity with Abraham.[14] Yet for Paul, it is apparently behavior or choices, more than genetics, that identifies one's solidarity; he addresses those who believe like Abraham, who sin like Adam, or who are baptized into Christ (cf. 6:3). Paul affirms clearly that death entered the world through sin (5:12). Though he makes the contrast with Christ bringing life (5:15–21, esp. 18–19) only a few verses later, his never-completed "just as" (*hōsper*) in this verse betrays his plan to address that issue. Scholars debate the grammar in the last clause of the verse; most, however, conclude that it says that death pervaded humanity "because" all sinned (e.g., NASB; NRSV; TNIV).[15] Other Jewish thinkers agreed that while Adam introduced sin, and hence death,[16] each of Adam's descendants has replicated his sin (*4 Ezra* 3:21; *2 Bar.* 18:1–2; 54:15, 19).[17]

Paul digresses briefly regarding the law in 5:13–14. In 5:13 (cf. 4:15; 5:20) Paul must bring in the law's condemning function (i.e., the law as a righteous standard, hence a criterion of judgment) to prepare for his later

14. For the Jewish character of 5:12–21's content (though Genesis should make that sufficiently obvious in terms of the use of "Adam"), see e.g., Davies 1980: 36–57; Scroggs 1966: 18–58; Hultgren 2003.

15. Other possibilities abound (see Fitzmyer 1993: 413–17, who ultimately prefers "with the result that"). Dependent on Latin translation, Augustine in his later years (in contrast to earlier and later voices in the Greek church such as Origen, Chrysostom and Theodoret) thought that Adam's descendants sinned in him and his guilt was passed on to them. What seems likelier is that, the connection with God having been broken, all begin alienated from God hence susceptible to sin (cf. perhaps *4 Ezra* 3:20–22).

16. E.g., *4 Ezra* 3:7; 4:30; *2 Bar.* 17:2–3; 23:4; 48:42–45; 56:5–6; *L.A.E.* 44:3–4; *Sipre Deut.* 323.5.1; 339.1.2; cf. Gen 2:17. For Adam's death being a spiritual death "in passions," see Philo *Alleg. Interp.* 1.106. Through Scripture, Paul was thoroughly familiar with the ancient Israelite concept of corporate repercussions for sin (on corporate solidarity, see e.g., Davies 1980: 103–4; Longenecker 1975: 93–94; Grieb 2002: 67; in Adam, e.g., *m. Sanh.* 4:5). Whether he conceived Adam as an individual or "as the archetype of 'every-man'" (Dunn 1998: 94–95) is theologically less significant, since it was self-evident that human sin had been initiated long before and pervaded all humanity (cf. Ambrosiaster *Commentary on Paul's Epistles* on 5:12).

17. After blaming the fall on Adam (*4 Ezra* 7:118–19), a passage goes on to list their own sins (7:119–26); cf. *1 En.* 98:4.

association of the law with death in 7:9–11. Nevertheless, sin and death clearly go back to Adam (5:14). Sin brings death, even before the coming of the (Mosaic) law; the law simply allows sin to be reckoned, or counted (5:13).[18] Natural law already counted sin, but the more concrete Mosaic law invites fuller judgment (2:12–15). In mentioning those who did not sin like Adam (5:14), Paul might qualify (hence perhaps forestall objections against) his argument that all have sinned like Adam and sin brings death. Those before the law could not sin like Adam (who transgressed an express commandment), yet shared the mortality of humanity as a whole.[19]

Paul develops this contrast between Adam and Christ in 5:15–20. In Jewish traditions, Adam was the first-formed model for humanity,[20] full of "glory" before his fall (cf. 3:23).[21] (Some rabbis later than Paul even portrayed Adam as enormous, "filling the earth" by himself.)[22] If Adam lost his glory through sin, Paul expects a restoration through another Adam (cf. also 1 Cor 15:22, 45–49). The structure of Genesis already connected Noah and Abraham with Adam by means of two genealogies of roughly ten generations each, ending in three sons (Gen 5:6–32; 11:10–26; cf. also *m. 'Abot* 5:2). The accounts of each of these three patriarchs included blessings, a commission to multiply and subdue land, and curses (Gen 1:28; 3:14–15; 9:1–7, 25; 12:1–3). Noah (Gen 5:29) and Abraham were steps on the way back to paradise (cf. *Gen. Rab.* 14:6); but Paul looks ultimately to a second Adam.[23]

Ancient rhetoric made abundant use of comparison (*synkrisis*), but the objects compared did not need to be precisely equivalent (as Paul in-

---

18. A cognate of the term for "reckoned" with respect to righteousness by faith in ch. 4.

19. The same might be said of infants, who did not transgress like Adam (given the high rate of infant and childhood mortality in Paul's world, he could not but have known of such cases).

20. Wis 10:1; *L.A.B.* 37:3.

21. E.g., *3 Bar.* 4:16; *Apoc. Mos.* 39:2; *'Abot R. Nat.* 1 A; *Pesiq. Rab Kah.* 4:4; 26:3; cf. perhaps CD 3.20. For his primordial beauty, see *Sib. Or.* 1.24.

22. E.g., *'Abot R. Nat.* 8, §22; 42, §116 B. After the fall, however, he was cut down to one hundred cubits (*Pesiq. Rab Kah.* 1:1; 5:3; cf. *Sipra Behuq.* pq. 3.263.1.9).

23. This may reverse the expectation in some Diaspora Jewish interpretation, where the first man of Gen 1 was greater than the second man they inferred in Gen 2 (Philo *Alleg. Interp.* 1.31–32; 2.4–5). Many Jewish eschatological texts compared the future paradise with the beginning (e.g., *Sipra Behuq.* pq. 1.261.1.6).

dicates explicitly in 5:15a).[24] Paul's use of paired antithesis drives home the point more fully, stirringly building to a rhetorical crescendo (as is readily evident if one reads the letter aloud, the way Paul expected believers in Rome to hear it). Paul argues from lesser to greater (on the superiority of the "second man," see 1 Cor 15:45–47), a common Jewish argumentative technique (*qal vaomer*)[25] but one also common throughout the ancient world. Some patristic interpreters and many scholars today argue that Paul personifies Sin and Death, and personification was also a familiar rhetorical technique.[26]

The six uses of *paraptōma* in 5:15–20 recall 4:25, and might recall the transgression of Adam in Wis 10:1. The term also typically implies violation of a particular standard, hence it may prevent the hearer from losing sight of the recurring topic of violation of the law. The allusion back to 4:25 is most explicit in 5:18, which also repeats *dikaiōsis* (the only other use in the Pauline corpus or NT). This passage, then, continues to flesh out the meaning of the gospel summary in 4:24–25.

Emphasizing the superiority of Christ over Adam, Paul repeatedly stresses "grace" and the "free gift" (eight times in 5:15–17, and twice in 5:20–21). Righteousness is not earned, but bestowed; those who are in Christ should live righteousness, but because of God's gift rather than in order to achieve it. In contrast to death reigning through Adam's transgression, those who are in Christ will reign in life (5:17). This expression may refer to the eschatological kingdom,[27] and in the context of Adam might allude to regaining the role that he lost (cf. Gen 1:26–28; cf. the restoration of the image in Rom 8:29). "Life" (contrasting with Adam's legacy of death) appears in 5:17, 18, and 21, as in much Jewish usage as shorthand for the resurrected "life of the coming age" (see 2:7; 4:17; 5:10; 6:10, 22–23; 8:11, 13).[28]

24. Some later rabbis also expected God's benefit to the world through the righteous to exceed the multiplication of death through Adam (*Sipra VDDeho.* par. 12.65.2.4). For rhetorical reasons, Paul includes a series of *-ma* terms in the Greek of 5:14–16, especially 5:16.

25. E.g., Longenecker 1975: 117.

26. For death personified, see e.g., Hos 13:14; Sir 41:1–2; 2 *Bar.* 21:23; Horace *Sat.* 2.1.58; on personification generally, see e.g., *Rhet. Her.* 4.53.66. On sin as a power, see Gaventa 2004.

27. Cf. 4:13; Dan 7:22; 1QM 1.5; 12.16; *Jub.* 22:11–12.

28. Such life belonged properly to the righteous (1:17; 10:5), which here means those made righteous in Christ.

The deliberately lopsided contrast is developed more fully in 5:18–19. Adam's transgression introduced death to all humanity (all born as Adam's descendants, dependent on him as flesh). By contrast, Jesus's act of obedience and righteousness introduced righting, life, and righteousness to all who are in him (baptized into solidarity with him, 6:3; dependent on him through the Spirit, 8:1–11).[29] ("The many"[30] in this context refers to all who are defined by their relationship to either Adam or Christ.)

Jesus's act of obedience that reverses Adam's disobedience (5:18–19) alludes back to his death for us in the Father's loving design (5:6–10). Paul elsewhere defines Jesus's obedience in terms of humbling himself to the point of shameful execution on a cross, perhaps in contrast to Adam seeking divinity (Phil 2:6–8; cf. Gen 3:5). Adam, by seeking greater life, brought death, whereas Jesus by dying brought life. Just as Adam introduced sin, Jesus now introduces true righteousness (5:19) that stems from solidarity with his obedience. Paul's understanding is not that Jesus merely reverses Adam's punishment (although his accomplishment includes that),[31] but that Jesus came to form a new basis for humanity, enabling people to serve God fully from the heart (cf. 8:2–4, 29).

In 5:20 Paul returns to the role of the law that he introduced in 5:13: as God's righteous standard, it more visibly exposes sin to condemnation.[32] Because law did not transform Adamites from the heart, it merely intensified their problem. Because Jewish people believed that the law as moral instruction enabled them to be more righteous than Gentiles (cf. 6:15; 7:12, 14a, 16, 22), statements like this (and 6:14; 7:5, 8–9) were meant to shock them into paying attention. The law was perfect (7:12), but meant to inform rather than transform, unless written in the heart by

29. Some read these verses universalistically, in tension with statements about the eschatological destruction of some (2:5; 9:22; Phil 3:19; 1 Thess 5:3), but the context delimits the application of Adam's and Christ's work to those who are in each of them, remaining consistent with texts about destruction. The future tense of "being righteoused" here suggests completion eschatologically.

30. The phrase refers to the elect at Qumran (1QS 6.6–21; cf. Dan 12:3; Marcus 1956), but is here used also for the "many" in Adam (5:19a), parallel with "all humanity" (5:18); the phrase can refer to "the multitudes" (e.g., Epictetus *Disc.* 1.2.18; 1.3.4; 2.1.22). It is not impossible that Paul alludes to the justification of the "many" in Isa 53:11–12 (though "many" is frequent in the LXX).

31. Despite Paul's possible use of some cognates in this section for purposes of variation, *dikaiōsis* in 5:18 is clearly forensic, contrasted with the "condemnation" brought by Adam's sin.

32. Cf. 2 *Bar.* 15:5–6; see excursus on the law, preceding 7:7–13.

the Spirit (8:2). The contrast between the old and new covenant was that God's people would observe the new covenant, the laws being now written in their hearts (2:29; 7:6; 8:2; Jer 31:33). Flesh in Adam cannot fulfill this righteousness. What the law could not do—make people righteous—God had done in Christ (8:3). Climaxing his contrast between the fruits of Adam and Christ, Paul notes that the greater the sin, the greater the grace that countered it (5:20–21).

ROMANS 6

Life in Christ and the Spirit (5:12—8:39), *cont.*

Dead to Sin, Alive in Christ (6:1–11)

As Paul in 5:1–11 applied to believers' lives insights gleaned from Abraham's example in ch. 4, so in 6:1–11 Paul applies insights gleaned from the contrast with Adam in 5:12–21. Paul's detractors, who believe that Gentiles should keep the law, consider him antinomian (3:8; Acts 21:21), apparently fearing that his view of the law will generate more sin. Paul instead argues that by revealing sin law increased the level to which sin is knowing revolt against God (Rom 5:20a)—but that God provided grace more than commensurate with the sin (5:20b). Paul's focus on grace raises the objection: is Paul saying that one should sin all the more so all the more grace may be added (6:1)? Paul retorts that the opposite is true: grace delivers not merely from punishment, but from sin's power. It is empowering grace rather than law (as a standard), that transforms. It is thus God's gift rather than his standard that produces genuine righteousness from the heart.

Why does Paul suddenly shift to speak of having "died" to sin in Christ (6:2–11)? He has been pointing out how Adam introduced death to humanity, whereas Christ brought life (5:12–21). Those who are in Christ share his death (6:3–4), a death justly incurred by Adamic humanity's transgression (5:12, 15, 17, 21). But because Christ himself was righteous yet embraced Adamic flesh and death (8:3), he not only embodies death to the old way, but inaugurates a new way of righteousness and life for those united with him (5:18–19). Those who are in Christ are no longer in the sphere of Adam, hence are "dead" to their former sin (6:5–7) and even to death (6:8–10), at least in a proleptic way that will effect their resurrection someday (6:5, 8; 8:23); Christ does not need to die again (6:9–10). Thus the *palaios anthrōpos*, the "old person" crucified with

Christ (6:6), represents who humanity was in Adam. Those who are in Christ (in whom Adamic sin and death died) should no longer identify themselves with the toxic legacy of fallen humanity, but rather with their eternal identity secured by Christ.[1]

Whereas all people are born in solidarity with Adam, solidarity with Christ (hence his death and resurrection) begins through baptism into him (6:3-4). Elsewhere Paul uses analogous language for baptism into Moses (1 Cor 10:2), but baptism into Christ (Gal 3:27) or his body (1 Cor 12:13) seems a more organic metaphor involving transfer of not only allegiance but identity. Gentile converts to Judaism were immersed to wash away their former Gentile impurities;[2] they were being initiated into a new solidarity with the descendants of Abraham. Christians in such a context would understand baptism as an act of conversion—not that the water itself was holy or efficacious, but the act of obedience, demonstrating committed faith, offered an open demarcation of conversion. The divine side of conversion, however, initiates a new identity in the righteousness and life initiated by Christ (Rom 5:18-19), a solidarity with Christ and his body that includes sharing his death and burial to Adam as well as new life.[3]

"Glory" (6:4) may evoke the resurrection hope (8:18, 21, 30), a body raised in glory (1 Cor 15:40-43; Phil 3:21), resurrected by the Spirit (Rom 8:10-11; cf. 1 Cor 15:43-44). To "walk" (*peripateō*) in newness of life evokes especially OT and early Jewish language for how one behaves; it is identical here with walking properly (13:13), in love (14:15), and by the Spirit (8:4; Gal 5:16). God's Spirit provides the "newness" here that the law could not provide (7:6), and this new identity and role in Christ contrasts with the old person in Adam (6:6).[4] In 6:5 Paul indicates that believers

1. That "old person" alludes to Adam is clear also in other Pauline texts; thus in Eph 4:22-24 and Col 3:9-10 the "new person" is "created in God's likeness," as one would expect in the new Adam (cf. Gen 1:26-27; 1 Cor 15:49).

2. See Epictetus *Disc.* 2.9.20; Juvenal *Sat.* 14.104; *Sib. Or.* 4.162-65; *m. Pesah.* 8:8; other sources in Keener 2003b: 444-47. But Dunn (1988: 1:312) may be right to find the connection with Jesus's death in Mark 10:38-39; Luke 12:50. Apparently relevant comparisons with "dying and rising" gods are significantly later than Paul (see esp. Wagner 1967).

3. Just as identity in Adam transcended ethnicity, so does identity through baptism into Christ (1 Cor 12:13; Gal 3:27-28).

4. Both ancient (e.g., Cyril of Alexandria *Expl. Rom.* on Rom 6:6) and modern (e.g., Barth 1933: 197) commentators have recognized the connection here with Adam in the

live in a period of what some call "eschatological tension": already they walk in newness, delivered from sin, but they still await the resurrection of their bodies (6:5; 8:23). As suggested in 5:12–21, once believers shared the "image" or "likeness" of Adam (cf. 1:23; 5:14; 8:3; Phil 2:7; a cognate in Gen 1:26), but now they share the likeness (*homoiōma*) of Jesus's death and will also share his resurrection (Rom 6:5; cf. 1 Cor 15:49).

In 6:6, Paul introduces the slave metaphor, which he will develop in 6:12–21 (cf also 7:6, 25; 8:15).[5] Both slavery and manumission (freeing slaves) were extremely common in Rome. Slavery was a common metaphor; ancient thinkers often warned against being enslaved by passions or false ideologies.[6] Like manumission, death ended one's slavery (6:6), just as divorce (literally "freeing") or death ended one's being bound by marriage (7:2–3).[7] Sin was the source of death (5:12–21). Thus, because believers have been freed by Christ's death from sin (6:6–7), their union with Christ, who died once and now remains alive forever, guarantees them future resurrection and eternal life (6:8–10).[8]

In 6:11, Paul climactically evokes his earlier arguments about righteousness. Eleven times Paul speaks of God "reckoning" righteousness to someone's account in chapter 4. In 6:11, however, he summons believers to *agree* with God's perspective; as God has "reckoned" righteousness to them, they must reckon themselves righteous. They are righteous because they are in Christ, in whom they both died to their identity as sinners

---

preceding context.

5. *Dikaioō* in 6:7 may continue the image of freedom if it plays on both Paul's usual sense of the term (making one right) and another possible (albeit related) sense, to "free" one from claims against. Some note here a Jewish tradition that death cancels one's debts.

6. See e.g., the survey of metaphoric uses (with references) in Keener 2003b: 749–51. For ideologies, see e.g., Plutarch *Superst.* 5, *Mor.* 167B; Ps.-Crates *Ep.* 16; for passions or pleasure, see e.g., Xenophon *Apol.* 16 (Socrates on bodily passions); Plato *Phaedrus* 238E; Isocrates *Ad Nic.* 29 (*Or.* 2); *Let. Aris.* 277–78; *T. Jos.* 7:8; Josephus *Ant.* 1.74; idem *J.W.* 1.243; Philo *Heir* 269; for the body, Philo *Abraham* 241; for sin, see e.g., *T. Sim.* 3:4; *T. Jud.* 15:2.

7. Some point out how conversion, insofar as it effected a new identity, could theoretically effect manumission if not prevented (cf. *b. Yebam* 45b–47b; Bamberger 1968: 127; Buchanan 1970: 206; for broader discussion of slaves' immersion, see Hezser 2005: 35–41). Wright 1999: 28–29, citing 1 Cor 10:2 and the context of salvation history in Romans, views Rom 6 as related to the exodus (also Allen 1964: 31; Daube 1969: 59–60; for slavery and the exodus, see Hezser 2005: 363–76).

8. For martyrs "alive to God," cf. 4 Macc 7:18–19.

in Adam and were raised to a new master, God. They must view their identity as those who have died and been raised in Christ, and hence must live accordingly. Paul is simply demanding belief congruent with the truth he has explained in 6:2–10: in Christ, believers died to the sin of Adamic humanity and have new life. If they believe this, they will "walk" (6:4) accordingly.[9] If they can have faith that Jesus rose, having faith that they share this resurrection life should be a natural corollary. Some ancient commentators also recognized this approach. Origen comments, "Whoever thinks or considers that he is dead will not sin. For example, if lust for a woman gets hold of me or if greed for silver, gold or riches stirs me and I say in my heart that I have died with Christ . . . the lust is immediately quenched and sin disappears."[10]

Scholars often find in Paul a tension between the indicative and the imperative; Paul summons them to be what he declares they are. This may be because for Paul identity is determined by being in Christ, but the believer must still choose to believe the eschatological reality sufficiently to live accordingly. Through faith one receives a new identity, and through faith one must also continue to embrace and live in that new identity, so that obedient works become expressions of living faith.[11]

Do Not Serve Sin (6:12–23)

Having established that in principle believers are dead to sin, their identity defined by their union and future with Christ, Paul now exhorts them to live accordingly. If they are no longer slaves to sin (6:6), then sin must no longer reign (*basileuō*) in them (6:12; cf. 5:14, 17, 21) or rule

---

9. For the eschatological destruction of sin, relevant to believers foretasting resurrection life in Christ, see e.g., Jer 3:17; 31:32–34; 1QS 4.17–26; 5.5; *Jub.* 50:5; *1 En.* 5:8–9; 91:8–11, 17; 92:5; 107:1; 108:3; *Ps. Sol.* 17:32; *4 Ezra* 7:92; *T. Mos.* 10:1; *T. Zeb.* 9:8 (MSS); on the eschatological execution of the evil impulse in later rabbis, see e.g., *Pesiq. Rab Kah.* 24:17; *Pesiq. Rab. Kah. Sup.* 3:2; *b. Sukkah* 52a. Evil desire ceases after death in *L.A.B.* 33:3.

10. Origen *Comm. Rom.* on 6:11 (Bray 1998: 162).

11. Engberg-Pedersen 2000: 55, 65, 233, helpfully compares a similar conceptualization about belief in Stoicism, though the conceptual pattern may have existed somewhat more widely (Pindar *Pythian Odes* 2.72; Pliny *Ep.* 1.3.5; see comment on Rom 8:1–11), perhaps even (in a more general way) in Scripture (Rosner 1999: 86–89; cf. Sir 7:16; Josephus *Ant.* 3.44–45). Many believed that the mind and correct beliefs could overcome passion (e.g., Cicero *Off.* 2.5.18; idem *Leg.* 1.23.60; idem *Inv.* 2.54.164; Stowers 2001: 92; 4 Macc 1:1, 9); Paul rejects mere human mental power (Rom 7:22–23; 8:6), here stressing rather faith in Christ and solidarity with him.

(*kurieuō*) them (6:14; cf. 6:9; 7:1; 14:9). They must be slaves who obey God and righteousness rather than sin (6:16–22).[12] Jesus had preached the impending reign of God; Paul's explanation of the new life in Christ and by the Spirit shows how he believes that God reigns in believers in the present (cf. 14:9, 17).

In 6:12 Paul warns against following the passions or illicit "desires" (cf. 1:24; 7:7–8; 13:9, 14) of the body destined for death. Whatever else "flesh" means (see the excursus after 7:14–25), it has some association with the body's susceptibility to following its passions rather than deliberate submission to Christ. Bodily members can be used for evil (1:24; 6:6; 7:24; 8:10, 13), but they can also be presented to God's service (6:13, 19; 12:1), presumably as members of a greater body (7:4; 12:4–5).[13] The presenting of bodies to God as his "instruments" (6:13) and slaves (6:16) could perhaps evoke weapons for battle, a very common meaning of the term here for "instruments" (*hopla*; see 13:12; 2 Cor 10:4). Reckoning themselves new (6:11), believers must no longer view themselves as under death (6:12), but rather, as alive from the dead (6:13).

Paul again shocks the sensibilities of his audience by reversing traditional expectations. It is those under the law rather than those under grace who are prone to sin (6:14–15), which he will soon identify with lawlessness (6:19). Those of us in societies lacking many moral boundaries may appreciate the helpfulness of external laws,[14] but Paul demands an inner transformation that yields a desire to submit to God's will (8:5–9).[15] One must serve either sin or righteousness (6:16–20). (Paul sometimes mixes his contrasts, e.g., sin leading to death versus obedience leading to righteousness in 6:16, but rather than weakening his antitheses Paul is strengthening the moral dualism established in 5:12–21, with everything bad on one side of the ledger and everything good on the other.) The "teaching" they obeyed (6:17) at least includes the gospel (16:17), which

12. The transference of slavery to another master occurred in sacral manumission (to temples), but Paul probably has the more general slave image in mind. Like slavery in general (see comment on 6:6), *kurieuō* could be used for evil (e.g., *T. Dan* 3:2; 4:7) or good (Marcus Aurelius *Med.* 5.26) ruling one.

13. On some philosophers' warnings about bodily passions, see comment at 7:7–13.

14. Probably even Paul would have also accepted the value of laws for societies (cf. 13:1–7), following the philosophic dictum that the truly wise or righteous were the only ones who needed no external law (Gal 5:23; cf. 1 Tim 1:9–10).

15. Even if others did not press it as far as Paul, the idea that grace and a God-given identity generates righteousness should have been intelligible (cf. Wis 15:2–3).

they embraced in conversion expressed in baptism (6:3–4). "Obeying" that teaching meant that they had left their past way of life, in which they used whatever freedom they had to serve their own interests, and now recognized a new lord and master over their lives, namely Christ (cf. 6:23; 10:9–10; 14:8–9).[16]

Paul admits that his depiction of the rule of sin and righteousness in terms of slavery is merely a human analogy (6:19a),[17] but it is, nevertheless, a very intelligible one for his audience. A former slave of a bad master would not want to return to that master; in the same way, no sensible person would want to return to a lifestyle the fruit[18] of which was death (6:21). Paul has already established that sin brought death just as Christ's obedience inaugurated righteousness (5:12–21). Why then would someone choose sin when they have the choice to embrace life? In 6:23 Paul shifts or reverts to an economic metaphor: household slaves often on the side earned some "wages" (though this term is often a military one). Wages were not a matter of grace, but of what one deserved (4:4, though using a different term). Sin merited death, but God's free gift (*charisma*, 5:15–16) in Christ was eternal life, the life of the resurrection (cf. Dan 12:2).

16. This differs from the common emphasis on self-mastery (e.g., Epictetus *Disc.* 1.11.37; 4 Macc 13:1), but thinkers could speak of being slaves of philosophy (Seneca *Ep. Lucil.* 8.7) or of God (Philo *Cherubim* 107).

17. Later rabbis argued that Scripture used "ordinary language" to convey divine truth (*Sipra Qed.* par. 4.206.1.1) and sometimes noted that they were using human analogies (*Song Rab.* 1:1, §10; Johnston 1977: 519–20).

18. "Benefit" (NASB; TNIV) or "advantage" (NRSV) here is *karpos*, also meaning "fruit" or "product" (or "profit"; Musonius Rufus 14, p. 92.23). Paul will soon associate the law even with arousing passions bearing fruit for death (7:5). The natural product of the Spirit's activity is very different (Gal 5:22–23). In an economic context, *karpos* also meant "profit" or "gain" (hence flows naturally into "wages" in Rom 6:23).

ROMANS 7

Life in Christ and the Spirit (5:12—8:39), *cont.*

Freed from Law (7:1-6)

Paul has been addressing believers being freed from enslavement to sin (6:12-23), and now addresses their liberation from the law (7:1-6).[1] Though Paul by no means equates sin and the law (7:7), he views the latter as an instrument that magnified the responsibility for, hence power of, the former.

He begins by comparing the believer to a widowed wife. He grants that the law rules a person so long as one lives (7:1), but is building on the case that believers have died (6:2-11).[2] The husband's death "frees"[3] the wife from the "law" of her husband (7:2-3). Some Jewish traditions portray the Torah as God's daughter, Israel's bride;[4] Paul may shift such an image slightly here to accommodate believers' union with Christ (cf. 2 Cor 11:2). It is not believers' husband that has died, but believers themselves have died (Rom 6:2-11), hence are no longer married to the law. They died with Christ, and as his body (cf. Rom 12:4-5) are his bride. Although spelled out explicitly only in Eph 5:28-31, Paul probably already inferred the identity of bride and body from Gen 2:24, where husband and wife

---

1. Paul employs *katargeō* (to abolish or render ineffective) in both sections (6:6; 7:2, 6; cf. 2 Cor 3:7-14), as well as cognates of *eleutheros* (6:18, 20, 22; 7:3).

2. Many comment that later rabbis viewed death as annulling the law's jurisdiction.

3. Language used both for widowhood (cf. 1 Cor 7:39) and divorce (cf. 1 Cor 7:15; *m. Git.* 9:3; *CPJ* 2:10-12, §144) in ancient Jewish sources, though Paul is interested only in the former analogy here. Those who try to prohibit divorce from this passage misappropriate Paul's general language; the law (the point in question here) explicitly did accept divorce (Deut 24:1-4). That Greek-speaking husbands typically ruled their wives in antiquity (see Keener 2000d: 687-91) also allows for the idea of the law's domination here, since it might be taken for granted; nevertheless, analogies were limited in what should be pressed from them.

4. E.g., *Sipre Deut.* 345.2.2; *Pesiq. Rab Kah.* 12:11; 26:9.

constitute one flesh. Thus he elsewhere uses the language of Gen 2:24 for the believer's spiritual marriage to Christ (1 Cor 6:16–17). Paul's analogy does not neglect the issue of how a dead wife can marry; believers, dead with Christ to Adamic existence, are united with the risen Christ. Instead of producing physical offspring, this union results in fruit (*karpophoreō*) for God (7:4), as opposed to bearing fruit for death (7:5; cf. the *karpos*, "fruit" or "outcome," of life and death in 6:21–22).

Paul argues that believers are no longer "in the flesh," ruled by death-bearing passions working in their bodily members (7:5). This is because they have died and now belong to a different "body," the risen body of Christ (7:4). (Paul is building on the notion of solidarity with Christ in 5:12–21 and 6:3–11.)[5] Believers freed from law are still servants, but servants of God (cf. 6:22) who "serve" (*douleuō*) in "newness" (7:6). This "newness" clearly evokes believers' newness of life with Christ in 6:4; it contrasts with "oldness" (7:6) that evokes the old life in the old Adam in 6:6. The "new" way conflicts with the values of the present age (12:2).

The new life in 7:6 is empowered by the Spirit rather than the "letter," a contrast Paul will develop further in 8:2–4 (where believers fulfill righteousness by God's Spirit empowering them rather than by external regulations). Paul uses "letter" for the mere written details of the law (Jewish teachers could focus even on details of spelling) as opposed to its heart (2:27, 29).[6] Another context where he raises the contrast (2 Cor 3:6–7) suggests that Paul denigrates the old covenant only by way of comparison with the new covenant, in which the promised (eschatological) Spirit would write the laws in the hearts of God's people (blending Jer 31:31–34 with Ezek 36:26–27; cf. Rom 8:2).[7] In 7:5–6 Paul lays out the contrast that he will develop between life under the law and death in the flesh (7:7–25; as in 7:5), and life in the Spirit (8:1–17; as in 7:6).

---

5. That the link between these "bodies" is more than coincidental is suggested by the collocation of both in close contexts in Rom 12:1, 4–5; 1 Cor 11:24; 12:12–27; Col 1:22–24; 2:11, 19, 23; 3:5, 15. The movement is from Adam's seed, dependent on him for their identity, to Christ's body, dependent on him.

6. Ancient legal interpreters also differentiated what we would call the mere letter of the law from its intent (Hermogenes *Issues* 40.6–19; 80.10–13; 82.4–5; 83.20; cf. Cohen 1966: 39–62).

7. For this argument in 2 Cor 3:3–6, see e.g., Keener 2005b: 167–68. In some ancient comparisons, both objects of comparison were positive (see sources in Keener 2003b: 916–17).

Excursus: Paul and the Law in Romans

In 5:12–21 and 8:2–9, Paul contrasts life in Adam and in the flesh with life in Christ and in the Spirit. In these and other passages, Paul employs antithetical sets, sometimes mixing elements of one set randomly with other elements of the set in his antitheses.

Adam's transgression → death (5:15)	Jesus's grace → grace and gift (5:15)
(Adam's transgression) → judgment, condemnation (5:16)	(Many transgressions) → free gift, justification/acquittal (5:16)
Adam's transgression → death's reign (5:17)	Jesus → (grace, gift of righteousness) → those in Christ reign (5:17)
Adam's transgression → condemnation (5:18)	Jesus's righteous act (i.e., obedient death) → justification/acquittal, life (5:18)
Adam's disobedience → "the many" became sinners (5:19)	Jesus's (act of) obedience → many are brought to be righteous (5:19)
Law increased the transgression (5:20)	Yet grace increased all the more (5:20)
Sin reigned in death (5:21)	Grace reigned through righteousness to eternal life (5:21)
Do not present your members for sin (6:13)	Present your members for righteousness (6:13)
Law (6:14–15)	Grace (6:14–15)
Sin → death (6:16)	Obedience → righteousness (6:16)
Slaves of sin (6:17)	Obedient to the teaching (6:17)
Slaves of sin, free from righteousness (6:18, 20)	Slaves of righteousness, free from sin (6:18, 20)
Presented members as slaves to uncleanness and lawlessness → lawlessness (6:19)	Present members as slaves to righteousness for consecration to God (6:19)
Death (6:22–23)	Consecration to God → eternal life (6:22–23)
Dead to former spouse, the law (7:3–4)	Married to Christ (7:4)

Fleshly passions worked in body via law → fruit for death (7:5)	Fruit for God (7:4); released from/ dead to law (7:6)
Oldness of the letter (7:6; cf. old humanity, 6:6)	Newness of the Spirit (7:6; cf. newness of life, 6:4)
Law of sin and death (8:2)	Law of the Spirit (8:2)
Law could not deliver from sin (8:3)	God delivered from sin (8:3)
Flesh (8:3–9)	Spirit (8:3–9)
Fleshly perspective is death (8:6)	Spirit-perspective is life and peace (8:6)
Body is dead on account of sin (8:10)	Spirit is life on account of righteousness (8:10)
Those who live according to the flesh must die (8:13)	Those who kill the works of the body will live (8:13)
Spirit of slavery (8:15)	Spirit of adoption (8:15)

Thus Paul contrasts sin and righteousness, death and life, condemnation and acquittal, and slavery and freedom (though this pair can be inverted).

Yet he also occasionally mentions law in this contrast, and places it on the sin/death side of the ledger. It is no surprise that the shocked interlocutor objects, "Is the law sin?" (7:7). But the written law is good; it was simply a partial solution for humanity in Adam, however, until its fuller substance could be inscribed on transformed hearts (8:2). God gave the righteous law's stipulations to identify and restrain sin, but on their own they would not change the heart. The law was not sin, but merely a catalyst that amplified sinfulness (4:15; 5:13, 20; 6:14; 7:5, 7); sin exploited it. Without Christ, the law could only inform, but the Spirit would transform.

For Paul, the law is good (7:12, 14); the problem is not the law but flesh, which law was designed to control, not transform (8:3).[8] Nevertheless, the regulations of the law pointed God's people to his righteousness. When approached the right way, as God's message and witness rather than a standard to achieve, the law supported the truth of the gospel (3:31; 10:6–8). Thus the law must be approached by faith rather than works (i.e., trust in God instead of flesh, 3:27; 9:31–32). Its content must be inscribed on the heart by the Spirit rather than depending on efforts of the flesh (8:2–4). Paul teaches not only moral truths, but even the way of the gospel itself, from the law. This

8. Sanders 1983b argues that Paul treats the law's purpose differently in different arguments, but remains consistent in his thesis that all are saved only through Christ.

"faith" approach to the law differs, however, from attempts to achieve righteousness by works (10:3, 5–8). The status of the law appears problematic so often in Romans precisely because it is the abuse of the law that is most at issue. Had that abuse actually represented God's intention, it would have left new Gentile converts at a severe disadvantage vis-à-vis Jewish people raised with the law.

Paul sometimes uses deliberatively provocative statements about the law (even more so in Galatians than in Romans) for his rhetorical purpose. We should not use such statements to sum up Paul's whole theology of the law (or even assume that, from his occasional letters, we *have* his entire theology of the law). Still less should we discard all insights that we might arrive at inductively through studying the Pentateuch, based on Paul's approach in specific polemical or pedagogical contexts. Nevertheless, Paul's point is critical: merely knowing and, as best as possible, following the letter of biblical precepts does not make one righteous. Rather, the heart of Scripture teaches about the God who graciously makes righteous by his own saving acts. Jew and Gentile must thus come to God on the same terms, through God's saving acts, which now are available to both in Christ. The law is not meant as a vehicle for self-improvement; it is meant as God's revelation that points us to his way of righteousness (3:21).

The Law and Sin (7:7–13)

Paul's larger argument about one way of salvation for Jew and Gentile (1:16) requires him to give central place to the law in his argument, which divided Jew and Gentile (2:12–14, 17, 26–27; 3:27–31; 4:16; 9:30–32). Paul thus often addresses the law (2:12–27; 3:19–21, 27–31; 4:13–16; 5:13, 20; 6:14–15; 9:31—10:5; 13:8–10), but nowhere in as much detail as here.

Paul's analogous treatment of freedom from sin (6:12–23) and the law (7:1–6) raises the obvious objection: is Paul identifying the law with sin (7:7)? Paul emphatically rejects that equation, emphasizing the goodness of the law (7:12, 14). The problem is not the law, but the flesh's inability to fulfill it (7:5, 14, 18, 25; 8:3–8). The law's role is to identify sin, and in 7:7 Paul offers as a key example the one commandment in the decalogue that specifies motives: "you shall not covet."[9] (Philosophers and moral-

---

9. Despite the first object of the prohibition in Exod 20:17 and the most prominent temptation for an adolescent (cf. Rom 7:9), the designation of "covet" is not exclusively

ists emphasized controlling passions and avoiding pleasure,[10] and some Diaspora Jewish intellectuals applied this commandment accordingly.)[11] Those raised with the law might obey most of its precepts from upbringing and habit, as part of their culture, but only those in whose hearts the law was written would always *desire* to keep the commandments. (The objects of coveting specified in Exod 20:17 are also objects of commandments against theft and adultery.) Once the law identified sin, the person committing the sin was violating God's will more knowingly, rendering sin the more heinous and the sinner the more culpable (7:7-8).

God designed the law to grant life to those who obeyed it (7:10; 10:5),[12] but because sinful humans would disobey it, it produced death (7:9-10; cf. 7:5). While Paul earlier mentioned that Adam brought death into the world (5:12-21), it was under the law—a divine standard of moral truth—that sin became most evident, exposing humanity's complicity with it (5:13, 20; cf. 2:12; 3:20; 4:15). The law thus became a further agent of death, validating that those who sinned merited this sentence (cf. 1:32). (Some associate receiving the law with the tradition of *bar mitzvah*, at adolescence; but Paul probably refers to a moral consciousness that begins much earlier, before an understanding of the law's moral demands.)[13]

Scholars debate whether Paul is the primary speaker in these verses, or whether he is "impersonating" someone else (a common rhetorical device; I discuss the question of persona again at 7:14-25). Certainly his background in the law now informs his description, though he interprets

---

sexual. The evil impulse sometimes had sexual connotations (*b. Sanh.* 45a; *b. Qidd.* 30b), but not always.

10. E.g., Xenophon *Mem.* 1.2.23-24; 4.5.3; Seneca *Ep. Lucil.* 59.1; Musonius Rufus 1, p. 32.22; Epictetus *Disc.* 2.1.10; Dio Chrysostom *Or.* 1.13; 3.34; 8.20; Arius Didymus *Epit.* 2.7.10, pp. 56-57.6-30; 2.7.10b, pp. 58-59.17-18; pp. 60-61.1-2; 2.7.10e, pp. 62-63.20-23. In Jewish sources, e.g., Ps 106:14; Sir 18:30-32; *T. Ash.* 3:2; 6:5; *T. Jud.* 13:2; *Apoc. Mos.* 19:3; Philo *Creation* 157-59.

11. See Tobin 2004: 231-32 (citing esp. 4 Macc 2:4-6; Philo *Decalogue* 142-53, 173-74; *Spec. Laws* 4.79-131); Stowers 2003: 532.

12. See e.g., Deut 4:40; 8:1; Bar 3:9; 4:1-2; *Ps. Sol.* 14:2; *L.A.B.* 23:10; 2 *Bar.* 38:2; *m.* 'Abot 2:7; 6:7.

13. *Bar Mitzvah* is first attested in the medieval period, although (on the analogy of coming-of-age ceremonies in surrounding cultures, at which one assumed full legal accountability, Gaius *Inst.* 3.208) something like it had probably long existed. It was from this passage that Augustine inferred what became an age of accountability (Reasoner 2005: 71; in Judaism, cf. *Gen. Rab.* 26:1-2; 63:10). But some knowledge of law (e.g., hyperbolically, *m.* 'Abot 5:21) and moral consciousness (Musonius Rufus 4, p. 46.35-36) were held to begin much earlier.

it from a Christian perspective. Nevertheless, he is not writing an auto-biography, but highlighting an experience meant to communicate a truth to his audience; if he depicts life under the law, he depicts an experience more widely shared. Because he describes life under the law in 7:7–13, what he depicts is not intended as his current experience; because his verbs are past tense in these verses, most commentators agree on this point (somewhat more controversial are 7:14–25, treated below).

If Paul is writing in another persona, who is the persona? Two proposals are most common, and both have some merit. Many see Adamic humanity here. Whether there is any deliberate echo of the fall here,[14] the emphasis on Adam bringing death in the recent pericope 5:12–21 presumably does inform this passage. Others, given the prominence of the law, highlight Israel as the background of the speaker here, and whatever else the speaker represents, it involves human experience under the law (i.e., Israel's experience, far more than Adam's, 5:13).[15] Israel sought to establish their own righteousness by the law rather than relying on God to put them right with him (9:30–32; 10:3). The verbal echoes are not compelling for either approach, but the context may be suggestive. Most importantly, whatever the particulars, we may concur that Paul depicts life under the law without God's gift of righteousness.

The Flesh and Sin (7:14–25)

Whereas most commentators recognize that 7:8–13, which uses past tense verbs, does not refer to Paul's present state, they are somewhat more divided in their assessment of 7:14–25.[16] Nevertheless, most do recognize that Paul speaks in a voice other than his own present person here;[17] the

14. To retain continuity with Adam, some compare "deceived" in 7:11 to Eve's deception (2 Cor 11:3; Gen 3:13; Josephus *Ant.* 1.48), although the term appears in many other settings. Deception is at best a faint echo (and the "commandment" applies better to the "Israel" interpretation), but Paul has already linked "death" to Adam (5:12, 14, 17).

15. Cf. Paul's shift from plural to singular in 3:5, 7 (as in 7:5–6; 7:7–25). Zion speaks in the first-person singular in Lam 1:11–22. Cf. Moo 1986.

16. Reacting against Pelagians, the later Augustine came to depict Rom 7 as the Christian life (with most Latin fathers); most church fathers, however, especially in the east, viewed it as non-Christian (see Bray 1998: 189–99; Reasoner 2005: 67–84). The medieval Western church, Luther, and Calvin followed the dominant Western tradition; Erasmus, Wesley and Pietists followed the tradition of the Greek fathers.

17. For a hypothetical or rhetorical "I," see e.g., 1 Cor 10:29–30; 13:1–3, 11–12; Seneca *Dial.* 7.11.1; 8.5.1; cf. "we" in Rom 6:1; "I" in 1 Cor 8:13; Gal 2:18–21. Various

contrasts with the larger context are simply too great to fit the Christian life as he describes it, even had Paul thought himself an unusually weak Christian.

Rom 7:7–25	Believers in the context
Law, sin, and death (7:7–13)	Freed from law (7:4, 6; 8:2), sin (6:18, 20, 22) and death (5:21; 6:23; 8:2)
I am fleshy (7:14)	You are not in the (sphere of) flesh, if Christ lives in you (8:9); no longer in the flesh (7:5)
I have been sold[18] under (as a slave to) sin (7:14; cf. 7:23)	Believers have been freed from enslavement to sin (6:18, 20, 22); they are "redeemed" (3:24)
Knowing right (in the law) without the ability to *do* right (7:15–23)	Power to live righteously (8:4), not conferred by external law (8:3); contrast 2:17–24
Sin dwells in (and rules) me (7:17, 20)	The Spirit dwells in believers (8:9, 11)
Nothing good dwells in me (i.e., in me as flesh; 7:18)	The Spirit dwells in believers (8:9, 11)
The law of sin dominates his bodily members (7:23)	Believers are freed from the law of sin (8:2)
Sin wins the war and captures "me" as a prisoner (7:23)	(Believers should win the spiritual war, cf. 2 Cor 10:3–5)
I want freedom from this "body of death" (body destined for death; 7:24)	Believers who do not live for their own bodily desires (8:10–13) are freed from the way of death (8:2), in contrast to those who follow the flesh (8:6, 13)
A slave to the law of sin in his flesh, vs. his mind (7:25)	Believers are freed from the law of sin (8:2; cf. 6:18, 20, 22); the mental perspective either belongs to the Spirit or the flesh (8:5–9)

scholars (e.g., Stowers 1994: 264–68; idem 2003: 537; Tobin 2004: 10, 226–27) compare the rhetorical technique of *prosopopoiia* (or, more technically, *ēthopopoiia*; Hermogenes *Progymn.* 9, On Ethopoeia, 20–22), writing a speech as if someone else, an approach at least as old as Origen, though tentatively (Reasoner 2005: 69).

18. Cf. God "selling" Israel into captivity for their sins (e.g., Judg 2:14; 3:8; 4:2; 10:7;

The present tense verbs, then, would simply serve to accentuate rhetorical vividness, something like the use of the historical present in narrative.[19] Essentially Paul already outlined this contrast before depicting it: the past life "in the [sphere of] the flesh," when the law stirred the body for death (7:5), differs from current freedom from the law in living by the Spirit (7:6). Ideally, Paul's depiction cannot refer to a believer, least of all to one who embraces Paul's theology of new life in Christ. That is not to claim that no believer would ever share any elements of the description, but any believer who did so would be thinking in a manner incompatible with Paul's teaching on the law. For Paul, anyone struggling to be made righteous by following God's standard, rather than relying on God's transforming gift of righteousness, might experience the sort of tension between knowing right and being right described here.[20] Paul's description here, however, is hyperbolic (as in 2:17–24): *complete* inability to do right and involuntarily compulsion to do wrong (7:15–20) sounds like possession rather than mere moral frustration!

The sort of struggle depicted in 7:14–25 would resonate with many people in antiquity. Some philosophers depicted the struggle between reason and the body's passions,[21] an image relevant here (especially 7:22–23). Judaism spoke of an evil impulse (*yetzer*),[22] and later teachers argued that learning Torah would strengthen one's good impulse to defeat the evil im-

---

Isa 50:1), and "delivering" them afterward (e.g., Judg 2:16, 18; 3:9).

19. E.g., Mark 1:12, 21, 37, 40, 41, though not consistently; Cicero *Quinct.* 4.14; 5.20; more consistently, Caesar *Bell. civ.* passim. For using present tense for vivid depiction, see Rowe 1997: 143–44. Speeches-in-character sought to vary tense (from present to past to future in Hermogenes *Progymn.* 9, On Ethopoeia, 21–22, though this differs from here).

20. For both assurance of righteousness and consciousness of sin appearing together in some early Jewish texts, see e.g., Talbert 2002: 199–200 (though before Paul's conversion the former seems to have predominated for him, Phil 3:4–6).

21. E.g., 4 Macc 1:1, 9, 29; 2:18–22; 3:2–5; 13:1–2 (cf. further Krieger 2002: 87–88); Seneca *Ep. Lucil.* 66.32; Arius Didymus *Epit.* 2.7.10a, p. 56.24–30; Maximus of Tyre *Or.* 33.3; cf. Sallust *Bell. Cat.* 51.3; the continuing struggle in Seneca *Ep. Lucil.* 20.6; Maximus of Tyre *Or.* 38.6; the Aristotelian theory in Engberg-Pedersen 2000: 52; idem 2003: 612; Platonic theory in Stowers 2003: 529, 537–38.

22. 1QS 5.5; CD 2.15–16; 4Q417 f1.ii.12; *Jub.* 35:9; 4 *Ezra* 7:92; *m. 'Abot* 2:11; *Sipre Deut.* 32.3.1; 45.1.3; cf. Gen 6:5; Sir 37:3. The evil *yetzer* was not strictly associated with the body (Urbach 1979: 1:472), though it affected the body (*'Abot R. Nat.* 16A; *Pesiq. Rab Kah. Sup.* 3:2).

pulse.[23] Some Diaspora Jews also argued that the law enabled one to rule one's passions.[24] Here, by contrast, evil so dominates the person that the law known to the mind cannot stave off sin's exploitation of the law in the flesh. Some of Paul's language fits the portrayal of pathetic enslavement to passion in Greek sources (most often compared with wicked Medea's or Phaedra's submission to passion rather than reason).[25] Paul's application of the language in this context, however, shockingly applies to a pious Jew trying to observe God's law.

The mind and inner person recognizes what is right, knowing God's law (7:16, 22–23).[26] But whereas many ancient thinkers (especially Stoics) felt that proper knowledge would produce transformation,[27] Paul denies that knowledge apart from God's Spirit can produce righteousness (cf. 8:2–4). Righteousness must be God's gift alone (4:11; 5:17; 10:3), and humans cannot boast in their own righteousness before God (3:27; 4:2).

The inability to submit to God's law in this passage is summarized as characteristic of the mental framework dominated by the flesh in 8:5. While the mind and inner person of 7:22–23 knows what is good, it is dominated by issues raised by the bodily members (7:23), hence is the mindset of the flesh (8:5). Like one enslaved by sin in 6:16–20, the mind here is defeated in battle (contrast 6:13; 13:12) and made a prisoner of war.[28] Prisoners of war were normally enslaved if they were not ran-

23. E.g., *Sipre Deut.* 45.1.2; *'Abot R. Nat.* 16A; *b. Qidd.* 30b, bar.; *Tg. Qoh.* on 10:4; for the law vs. sin, cf. also *m. 'Abot* 4:2; *m. Qidd.* 1:10. God's help was needed (e.g., 4Q436 f1a+bi:10; *Sipre Num.* 40.1.3).

24. 4 Macc 2:21–23. One destroys the evil impulse by good works in *T. Ash.* 3:2.

25. See e.g., Euripides *Med.* 1077–80; Seneca *Med.* 926–30, 988–90; see more extensively Renehan 1973: 24–26; Gill 1998: 121, 137; Stowers 1994: 260–63; Tobin 2004: 232–34. Given the denigration in some ancient sources of the feminine as irrational (cf. Gemünden 1997), the analogy would be all the more shocking.

26. The more positive portrayal of the inner person in 2 Cor 4:16 (cf. also Eph 3:16) depicts Paul's state as a believer (in contrast to here); on the background of "inner person," see the views in Aune 2001: 220–22; Markschies 1994; Betz 2000.

27. Cf. Epictetus *Disc.* 1.28.6; 2.17.21–22; Tobin 2004: 235; but note Arius Didymus *Epit.* 2.7.10a, pp. 56–57.24–33; Musonius Rufus 6, p. 52.15–17. Stoics also affirmed the value of law (Arius Didymus *Epit.* 2.7.11d, p. 68.1–7; 2.7.11i, p. 76.30–37).

28. If 6:16–20 involves self-enslavement, as many commentators think, the experience under the law here might be more brutal. Others also employed the image of waging war with the passions (Xenophon *Mem.* 1.2.24; Dio Chrysostom *Or.* 8.20; Ps.-Diogenes *Ep.* 5, 12; cf. *m. 'Abot* 4:1; Schechter 1961: 272–73) and passions taking one as an enslaved prisoner (Maximus of Tyre *Or.* 36.4), including of war (Dio Chrysostom *Or.* 32.90;

somed. The anguished persona in this text cries out, "Wretched person that I am!"[29] needing deliverance from the "body of death" (a body under the sentence of and destined for death, 7:24; 8:10).[30]

The answer, no less exclamatory, comes in 7:25. Paul often says, "Thanks be to God!" when commenting on freedom from sin or death (6:17; 1 Cor 15:57; cf. 2 Cor 2:14; 8:16; 9:15),[31] and sometimes when concluding a section, as here (1 Cor 15:57; 2 Cor 9:15), but the addition of "through Jesus Christ our Lord" sounds like an implied answer to the lament of 7:24. Before treating this victory, however (in 8:1–17), Paul summarizes the state of affairs: the mind may serve God's law, but the flesh submits to the law as exploited by sin (7:7–9). His mention of the mind serving God's law probably points to its unfulfilled desire to do right (7:16, 22–23), hence still refers to the perspective dominated by the flesh (8:5–7); alternatively but less likely, it might refer to the perspective of the Spirit that contrasts with the fleshly perspective (8:5–7).

Excursus: The "Flesh" (*sarx*) in Romans

Neoplatonic and gnostic dualism absorbed by later Christianity denied that the body was good,[32] and many scholars today, reacting against this conception, argue that Paul's use of *sarx* bears little relation to *sōma*, "body." Some

---

Iamblichus *Pyth. Life* 17.78).

29. Characteristic of tragic laments (e.g., Aeschylus *Ag.* 1260; cf. Ovid *Metam.* 9.474; Apuleius *Metam.* 3.25); some applied "wretched" to the bodily state (Epictetus *Disc.* 1.3.5–6; 1.9.12).

30. Some envisioned the soul as a prisoner within the body, hence death as a release from suffering or limitation (Cicero *Tusc.* 1.31.75; Epictetus *Disc.* 1.9.16; Maximus of Tyre *Or.* 7.5; Heraclitus *Ep.* 5, who describes the body as "dead"; cf. Philo *Alleg. Interp.* 1.108); cf. "this dead body" in Epictetus *Disc.* 2.19.27 (cf. Marcus Aurelius *Med.* 10.33.3). Some answered the question, "Who will release me?" with suicide (Diogenes Laertius 6.18, 21).

31. The phrase is not, however, uniquely Paul's (Epictetus *Disc.* 4.4.7; Ps.-Crates *Ep.* 33; Ps.-Diogenes *Ep.* 34).

32. Cf. Philostratus *Vit.Apoll.* 7.26; Iamblichus *Pyth.* 31.205; Plotinus *Enn.* 1.8; 2.4; 3.6.6–7; Porphyry *Marc.* 10.176; 13.227–29; 14.242–50; 25.394–95; 33.506–9; Manichaeans in Augustine *Contin.* 10.24. Earlier, see concerns regarding bodily appetites, in Plato *Phaedo* 66CD; Seneca *Dial.* 7.8.2; idem *Ep. Lucil.* 8.5; Epictetus *Disc.* 1.3.3; Dio Chrysostom *Or.* 4.115; Plutarch *Isis* 78, *Mor.* 382F; Maximus of Tyre *Or.* 7.7; 11.10.

translations (such as the NIV) even poorly translate *sarx* simply as "sinful nature" (which for some Christian traditions also evokes a dualism of two natures
struggling within the believer).

Paul certainly believes that the body can be used for good (12:1)—but
also for evil (6:13). The body as such is not evil, but if the body's desires
rather than God's Spirit dominates one's existence, one readily comes into
the power of sin.[33] Paul speaks of the "passions" (1:24; 6:12; 13:14) and
"desiring" what is not one's own (7:7–8; 13:9). Impure hearts lead to defiling
bodies sexually (1:24); the old life in Adam involves the "body of sin" (6:6);
one should avoid obeying the desires of the mortal body (6:12); the existence
of moral defeat is characterized by the "body of death" (7:24; cf. 8:10–13).

Paul connects the term "flesh" with the body. Ultimately this is not an
anthropological dualism between two parts within a person (in 7:23, the mind
remains subject to the flesh), but humanity as *sarx* contrasted with God's
Spirit (8:4–9; Gen 6:3).[34] The OT employed the equivalent Hebrew term *basar*
for humans (or other animals) in their limited creatureliness, including their
mortality.[35] By Paul's day, some Jews employed the term for human weakness
in its susceptibility to sin.[36] *Basar* and its Greek translation *sarx* were not
inherently evil, but as "human weakness" were susceptible to sin. Flesh was
not meant to lead human life, but to be the arena in which life should be lived
in obedience to God. Paul could use "flesh" also for the outward existence
(Rom 1:3; 2:28; 4:1; 9:3, 5, 8; 11:14), again what is merely human (though
not intrinsically evil) rather than empowered by God (he sometimes contrasts
flesh with the Spirit or the promise).

Despite these observations, flesh had an inescapable bodily dimension.[37]
Contrary to the views of a large proportion of NT scholars, mostly following
secondary sources, Diaspora Jews by Paul's day commonly did distinguish

33. John Chrysostom contends that the problem for Paul is the unregenerate mind's
abuse of the body (*Hom. Cor.* 17.1; cf. *Hom. Rom.* 11).

34. Cf. 1QS 4.21; Flusser 1988: 64–65. For material vs. immaterial, cf. Isa 31:3; *1 En.*
106:17.

35. Often, e.g., Gen 6:3, 12–13, 17; 7:21; elsewhere, e.g., Sir 28:5; *Jub.* 5:2; *T. Job*
27:2/3.

36. Often in the Dead Sea Scrolls, e.g., 1QS 4.20–21; 9.9; 11.9, 12; Flusser 1988: 62–63;
also *T. Jud.* 19:4; *T. Zeb.* 9:7; Philo *Giants* 29–31 (though Philo often uses *sōma*). For the
Hellenistic idea, see e.g., Epictetus *Disc.* 2.23.30; Marcus Aurelius *Med.* 2.2.

37. See e.g., 1 Cor 6:16; Col 1:22; 2:11. See further discussion in Keener 2008a:
215–19.

soul and body, often expecting immortality for the former even when affirming resurrection for the latter.[38] In 7:5, sinful passions working in the body's members characterize being "in the flesh." In 8:13 one is either destined for death in the flesh or resurrection by putting to death the body's deeds. Flesh is also linked with the body in 6:19; it contrasts with the mind in 7:25; the law working in one's bodily members (7:23) is the law of the flesh (7:25).

The conflict between the law of sin in the members and the law in the mind in 7:25 was not the basis for the verdict of "no condemnation" in 8:1, as if God would overlook physical sin provided one's mind harbored good motives. Far from it: 8:1–13 contrasts those who serve the flesh with those who serve God by the Spirit! Paul's goal is a way of thinking dominated not by the flesh (hence by one's physical desires, which have a legitimate place, but not in ruling life), but a way of thinking dominated by the Spirit (8:5–9). This new way of thinking involves a renewed mind (12:2). This renewed mind teaches believers how to present their bodies in the service of the larger body—the body of Christ (12:1, 4–5). Such a mind is no longer self-centered, but Christ-centered; no longer seeking full autonomy, it now submits gladly to the greater good of God's purposes. "Flesh" is the localized self in contrast both to dependence on God (through the Spirit) and the corporate interests of Christ's body. Life ruled by the flesh is, at root, human selfishness and self-centeredness (or sometimes centered in one's group), rather than genuinely altruistically sharing God's interests. Paul's goal is not to annihilate self, as in some religions, but to connect it to the service of a greater purpose (cf. 12:1–8; Matt 6:33). Paul was no gnostic, but neither was he a hedonistic Western individualist who keeps religion in its subjective place.

---

38. Many references are listed in Keener 2003b: 553–54, but see more fully Gundry 1976. Even some later rabbis distinguished the heavenly soul and earthly body (*Sipre Deut.* 306.28.2).

ROMANS 8

LIFE IN CHRIST AND THE SPIRIT (5:12—8:39), *cont.*

Living by the Spirit (8:1-17)

In 8:1-15 Paul contrasts the new life in Christ with the best that law-informed flesh could do in 7:7-25. As 7:7-25 reflected life under law in the flesh introduced in 7:5, so 8:1-17 reflects the new life of the Spirit introduced in 7:6. Paul paints this contrast graphically, in the binary terms standard in his culture. Thus, for example, Jewish wisdom divided humanity into the righteous and the wicked, the wise and the foolish; likewise, Stoic philosophers divided humanity into those who were perfectly wise and those who were foolish.[1] Yet all Jews recognized that most or all people sinned (see comment on 3:9), and even "advanced" Stoic philosophers recognized that they did not perfectly conform to the ideal wise person.[2] In other words, Paul uses the familiar imagery of ideal types.[3] The issue is not that a person of the Spirit might sometimes succumb to fleshly temptation. Rather, the issue is that a person either had God's Spirit in them, hence lived a life oriented toward God, or a person had nothing more than themselves to depend on, hence could live only according to the flesh.

Whereas the person in bondage to sin in 7:15-25 recognizes that the law is good and thus that the person stands justly condemned for sin,

1. E.g., Seneca *Dial.* 7.11.1; Arius Didymus *Epit.* 2.7.11i, p. 78.12-18. This Stoic idealization occasioned criticism (e.g., Cicero *Fin.* 4.24.66-68; Lucian *Hermot.* 76-77). Stoics, however, spoke of life according to nature or wisdom, not according to the eschatological Spirit.

2. E.g., Seneca *Ep. Lucil.* 87.4-5; idem *Dial.* 7.18.1; Erskine 1990: 74; Engberg-Pedersen 2000: 61-62, 72-73; cf. similarly Confucius *Analects* 14.30.

3. See Keener 2008a: 211, 213-15 (also noting the same division in Qumran, 214; cf. Flusser 1988: 64-65; additionally new life in CD 16.4-6). One might speak even of two races of humanity (see e.g., Arius Didymus *Epit.* 2.7.11g, p. 72.5-18; Philo *Alleg. Interp.* 2.4).

there is no condemnation in Christ (8:1). This lack of "condemnation" recalls how condemnation belonged only to those in Adam, not to those in Christ (5:16, 18), for God took care of condemning sin in Christ in our stead (8:3). In Christ one is freed from the body of death (7:24), for one ruled by the life-giving Spirit rather than by the flesh (8:4–13) will be raised (8:2, 10–13).

After addressing the inadequacy of the law to make flesh righteous in 7:7–25, in 8:2 Paul shows how the law can be involved in making people righteous. The law of sin and death from which one is freed (8:2) refers to the law of sin working in one's body (7:23, 25). This was Paul's graphic way of saying that the law amplifies sin (7:8), hence brings death (7:5). Merely having the law in the mind made one conscious of, but did not free one from, sin (7:16, 22–23). Liberation would come only by the law of the Spirit (8:2), the promised Spirit of God that would inscribe God's law in the hearts of his people so they would keep his ways (Ezek 36:27). The Spirit was the "Spirit of life," who would raise the dead (Ezek 37:14; Rom 8:10–13).[4] (As noted earlier, Jewish people sometimes used "life" as shorthand for the life of the coming age.) Those who are in Christ share in his death and resurrection, and by the fruit of the indwelling Spirit fulfill the moral intention of the law (8:4; cf. 7:4; Gal 5:18, 22–23).[5]

The heart of the problem with the law (8:3) was what it was not designed to do: it righteously teaches right from wrong, but it does not transform a person to be righteous, to undo the power of sin Adam introduced into humanity. It was "weak" because it depended on "flesh" to fulfill it—and flesh could never fulfill God's righteousness (see the excursus on "flesh" after 7:14–25). Only Christ by dying could introduce righteousness (see 5:17–19). Although "concerning sin" need not be meant so narrowly, it probably evokes the biblical language of the levitical sin offering (over 80 percent of LXX uses of the phrase) to depict Jesus's mission (cf. 3:25; 5:8–9). For God to "condemn sin in the flesh" was for him to execute judgment on it in Jesus's person (cf. Jesus "becoming" sin in 2 Cor 5:21). By Jesus identifying with Adam, God destroyed sin in Jesus's

4. Cf. *T. Ab.* 18:11A; *m. Sot.* 9:15; perhaps *Sib. Or.* 4.46; *Jos. Asen.* 16:14/7–8; still, the same wording could apply to Gen 2:7 (*T. Reu.* 2:4). See especially Philip 2005: 137–38; Raharimanantsoa 2006: 393–96.

5. For the Spirit enabling righteousness, though not as strongly as here, cf. 1QH 4.29–32 (in contrast with flesh); 16.11–12; but the primary background is Ezek 36:27.

crucifixion, raising him as head of a new humanity,[6] i.e., his body (see comment at 7:4; 12:5).

What flesh could not accomplish, however, God did in Christ; the Spirit within believers would cause them to live out righteousness (8:4). That Paul attributes this empowerment to the law of the Spirit is not surprising, for the new covenant differed from the old covenant precisely in that God's people would now obey it (Jer 31:32–33) by God's own Spirit (Ezek 36:27). Contrary to his detractors (3:8), Paul is not antinomian; he expects the righteous life attested in the law, but expects it by depending on God's Spirit rather than human flesh. (Paul is thinking not of all individual commandments but of the righteous character that such commandments were intended to inculcate and point toward in an ancient Israelite context.)

In contrast to the law-informed mind defeated by the flesh in 7:22–23, Paul speaks here of a "frame of mind" (habitual way of thinking) guided by the Spirit (8:5–7). Philosophers spoke of focusing the mind on divine matters rather than bodily passions; Paul speaks of a new perspective on reality informed by God's Spirit active in one's life rather than dependence or obsession with one's own ways (8:5).[7] For Paul, the mind-frame of the flesh produced death (8:6); that is, the mind dominated by bodily desires (7:23) stood under the body's sentence of death (7:24). But the frame of mind dominated by the Spirit involves life and peace (8:6): both eternal life (5:21; 6:23) and peace with God (5:1) established through Christ. Paul would also know that the mind trusting in God has "peace" in the Hebrew version of Isa 26:3.[8]

The fleshly mind was at enmity with God (8:7), i.e., not reconciled through Christ (5:10). The *inability* to submit to God's law (8:7) has already been summarized in 7:16–23. The inability of the flesh to please God (8:8)

6. Sending Jesus in the "likeness" (cf. 5:14; 6:5) or image of sinful humanity (cf. Phil 2:7) probably suggests (in a manner consistent with 1 Cor 8:6; Phil 2:6–8) that Paul views Jesus as preexistent (Hurtado 2003: 196; cf. Byrne 1997); in Paul's theology, Jesus was fully human, but was himself sinless (2 Cor 5:21). To paraphrase Athanasius, in this context Jesus came in humanity's likeness (8:3) so humans might ultimately share again the divine likeness (8:29).

7. See Keener 2008a: 215, 219–21; on the mind in philosophy, see 212–13; its openness to the divine in 219–21; for the mind in Romans, 225–29. Cf. e.g., Philo *Unchangeable* 111 on the pleasure-enslaved mind that loves the body and the passions.

8. Keener 2008a: 224; for philosophers' perspectives on the mind with regard to death and peace, see Keener 2008a: 222–24.

challenged attempts to succeed by merely human works (cf. the conjunction of law, flesh and sin in 7:7–25); God is holy, and whatever works are not born from God's own Spirit cannot not satisfy his holiness.

Lest his audience misunderstand his point, Paul emphasizes that all who belong to Christ have the Spirit dwelling in them, hence are "in the [sphere of the] Spirit" rather than "in the [sphere of the] flesh" (8:9). "In the flesh" here does not simply mean "in the body" (as in Gal 2:20), but walking according to the flesh (8:4–8, 12–13). All who are in Christ have the Spirit (the "Spirit of Christ"),[9] hence they are able to live righteously (8:2–4, 13–14).

In 8:10–11, Paul shows that believers can trust God for the raising of their mortal bodies just as Abraham trusted in God's resurrecting power at work in his own "dead" body (4:19). Their bodies might be "dead" (under sentence of death,[10] 7:24) because of sin, but the Spirit is life (as in 8:2, 6) because of the righteousness brought by Christ (5:17, 21) and expressed in believers' lives (8:4). (The contrast here is not between the body and human spirit, but between depending on one's physical, mortal self and depending on God, as in 8:2–9.) Since the Spirit dwells in them (as noted in 8:9), the Spirit through whom the Father raised Jesus would also raise them (8:11; Ezek 37:9–14).

Those who follow the way of flesh will perish, as flesh does; by living like the old way of flesh has been crucified with Christ, however, believers have confidence that they will be raised (8:12–13; cf. 6:2–11; Gal 6:8).[11] Some ancient thinkers advocated that concern for bodily things tied the soul down to mortality, but meditation on heavenly matters prepared the soul for its life after separation from the body. Paul may borrow such language, but for him it is not the mind of itself (cf. Rom 8:5–7) but God's

9. The label certainly implies Jesus's deity (vs. later sources like *Gen. Rab.* 2:4, even Isa 11:2 refers to the divine Spirit; cf. Acts 16:7; Turner 1994: 436). Fee 1994a: 331, finds proto-Trinitarianism in 8:9–11. Some philosophers spoke of deity dwelling in humans (Epictetus *Disc.* 1.14.13–14; 2.8.14), but sometimes in pantheistic terms; Paul's imagery is more Jewish (cf. e.g., *T. Sim.* 4:4).

10. For "dead" meaning about to die, cf. Gen 20:3; *b. Pesah* 110a; even "half-dead" meant apparently or nearly dead (Luke 10:30; Callimachus *Hymn.* 6.59; Cornelius Nepos *Generals* 4.5.4; Livy 23.15.8; Quintus Curtius 4.8.8; Suetonius *Aug.* 5).

11. In light of the preceding context of Romans (see 5:15–21), each person chooses solidarity with Adam or with Christ: living according to the flesh inherited from Adam leads to the death that Adam introduced, whereas sharing the way of Christ's obedient death leads to resurrected eternal life. One puts to death bodily deeds by recognizing one's death with Christ (6:3–4, 11).

Spirit that is the agent of life, and the hope is not disembodiment but finally bodily resurrection.

To be "led" by God's Spirit (8:14) means at least partly to have the Spirit-inspired perspective that produces righteousness and life (8:4–6, 13; cf. Gal 5:18 with 5:16–23). Undoubtedly it also means that God's Spirit speaks to one, assuring one of one's relationship to God (8:15–16). The wording may particularly evoke the image of the exodus: God not only gave his people the law (8:2), but "led" them by his glory in the wilderness.[12] He led them in this way during the interim period between their redemption from Egypt and their entrance to their "inheritance" in the promised land, language he further evokes here (8:17).[13] Believers can trust God to lead their lives (not only morally, but more generally) in this period of interim existence.

The spirit of slavery (8:15) contrasts with the Spirit of the exodus just evoked in 8:14. As God adopted Israel in the exodus (9:4; Exod 4:22), so in 8:15–16 the Spirit assures believers (including Gentile believers) that they are God's children.[14] The Spirit is associated with believers as God's children in the future, because the Spirit will raise their bodies (8:10–11), hence revealing them as God's children (8:19–23, especially 23). But the Spirit provides believers a foretaste of that destiny (8:23), confirming their state as God's children in the present. Because the Spirit was often associated with prophecy,[15] the Spirit of Christ both inspires believers to cry out with Christ in their relationship to the Father in him (8:15), and inspires them to hear God's fatherhood toward them (8:16).[16] It seems doubtful

12. E.g., Exod 13:21; 15:13; Bar 2:11; Wis 10:17–18; *1 En.* 89:22; *Sib. Or.* 3.255; *4 Ezra* 14:4. For the Spirit and the exodus, cf. Isa 63:11; Hag 2:5; *Mek. Besh.* 3.82–83.

13. For exodus language in this paragraph, see e.g., Keesmat 1999. After Paul's day it became clear that the interim between Jesus's comings may have stretched longer than that between stages of salvation in the exodus; nevertheless it offered an analogy for an interim time.

14. A traditional title of Israel (e.g., Hos 11:1; *Ps. Sol.* 17:27; *Sib. Or.* 3.702–4; *Sipre Deut.* 43.16.1; 45.1.2; 96.4.1; 308.1.2); for the language of God's children in Jewish and other sources, see Keener 2003b: 400–2.

15. Menzies 2004: 49–101; idem 1991: 53–112; Turner 1996: 86–104 (including inspired wisdom and praise); Keener 1997: 10–13, 31–33. On the Spirit "inspiring" the "Abba" cry and other speech here, see Dunn 1999: 82, 85–87, 89–91.

16. Given the context of inheritance, "witness" might evoke witnesses to a will (Gaius *Inst.* 2.104–8), but in any case constitutes strong assurance, and may be conventional early Christian language (cf. Heb 10:15; 1 John 5:7–8; John 15:26; Rev 19:10), which Paul also associates with conscience (Rom 2:15; 9:1).

that Paul is simply teaching Aramaic to Greek-speaking Christians in Rome in reciting, "Abba"; rather, he is evoking Jesus's own prayer (*perhaps* even the specifically preserved one, as Jesus faced suffering; Mark 14:36). Those who have been baptized into Christ (6:3–4) share his sonship, hence his inheritance (8:17).[17] They confirm that status by sharing his sufferings, guaranteeing that they will also share his resurrected glory (8:17). (If one side of the cross involves Jesus taking believers' sin, the other side involves them sharing his sufferings for righteousness.)

Fusing the Horizons: Faith and Righteousness

When Paul opposes "law-works" to "Jesus-faith," he is not against obeying the law. It is in fact Jesus-faith that he claims produces true righteousness from the heart. The problem is not obeying the law, but seeking to be made right with God by it, apart from dependence on God's mercy. In fact, most Jewish thinkers would have agreed with Paul that people depended on God's mercy, although they did not usually radically contrast this appearance with human merit the way Paul did.

Jesus-faith means that believers must depend on (and be loyal to) what God has accomplished in Jesus to make them right with him. God has accounted such dependence as righteousness, so that those loyal to Jesus are acquitted and in right relationship with God. But just as God "accounts" or "reckons" such faith as righteousness (eleven times in ch. 4), those who trust Jesus should learn to trust enough to believe God's verdict, and "reckon" righteousness to their own account (Rom 6:11). They should believe their new identity in Christ and live accordingly.

When Christians do not live out the character of God's Spirit living in them (cf. the "fruit of the Spirit" in Gal 5:22–23), we fail to take saving faith to its logical conclusion. We do not do righteousness to get God's gift; rather, righteousness *is* God's gift in Christ, and we demonstrate active faith in Christ as we live accordingly. We do not stop sinning in order to be "saved"; rather, we are "saved" from sin through faith. To the extent that we really believe, however, we should live accordingly. While Paul usually presents this ideal in terms of two contrasting options (e.g., Spirit versus flesh, 8:3–11), the

17. On eschatological "inheritance," see Hester 1968; comment on 4:13. Paul's repetition of "children" from 8:16 is anadiplosis (for rhetorical reinforcement); on the relationship between adoption and inheritance, see e.g., Walters 2003.

life of Abraham shows that the faith through which he was initially reckoned righteous (Gen 15:6) was imperfect (e.g., 16:2). Nevertheless, over the years it grew to the place where he could offer up the promised seed in obedience to the God he trusted (22:10–12). Initial justification and transformation is obviously crucial, but it is only the beginning of God's plan to display his righteousness in those who depend on him.

Zeal in itself is no guarantee of pleasing God (cf. 8:8; 10:2–3). Even actions offered by one generation or person in sincere devotion to God can become for another routine legalism once severed from the motivation of the Spirit. That is why churches born out of passion for God can become legalistic or complacent in the next generation when they continue their forebears' behavior without cultivating their relationship with God.

Many are skeptical of Paul's claim here. Church history reveals that the church, at least on a large-scale political level, has often lived no differently than nonbelievers (and in some cases worse). But then, Paul's theology may have been largely untested because it has been largely untaught; emphasizing either moralism or justification without transformation truncates Paul's message of unity with Christ. Western Christendom today has imbibed the radical Enlightenment's skepticism of the supernatural, suspicious of miracles and other divine interventions. For Paul, however, the genuine Christian life is "supernatural" (i.e., divinely empowered) from start to finish, a life by God's own Spirit. Apart from acknowledging and embracing the Spirit, the best imitations of Pauline religion are just "flesh."

Present Suffering, Future Glory (8:18–30)

The sufferings of the present age[18] were not comparable with the future glory (8:18), which would somehow be proportional to it (cf. 2 Cor 4:17).[19] The glory could evoke God's presence in the wilderness (cf. 8:14; 9:4);[20] it especially involves God's eschatological revelation of glory (Isa 66:18–19), particularly the glorifying of his people (Rom 5:2; 8:21, 30; 9:23; 1 Thess 2:12; Isa 55:5; 60:1–2; 62:2).[21] Paul elsewhere describes the resurrection

18. Paul thinks of the "birth pangs" of the coming age (8:22), probably related to the Jewish expectation of suffering before the end (see comment on 8:22).

19. For the principle, cf. also Wis 3:4–5; 2 *Bar.* 15:8; 19:7; 48:50; *m. 'Abot* 5:23; *Sipre Deut.* 307.3.2–3; 310.4.1.

20. Exodus depicts the pillar and cloud (Exod 13:21–22), but Jewish tradition spoke also of God's "glory" (*1 En.* 89:22) and "presence" (*shekinah*; *Mek. Shir.* 3.67–70).

21. Cf. also *Sib. Or.* 3.282; 4 *Ezra* 7:98.

body as involving "glory" (1 Cor 15:40–43; Phil 3:21).[22] It may also imply the restoration of Adam's lost glory (3:23; 1 Cor 11:7), i.e., complete restoration to God's image in Christ (Rom 8:29; 1 Cor 15:45–49). As wrath would be "revealed" to the wicked (2:5), so would glory be "revealed" in the righteous (cf. Isa 40:5; 1 Pet 4:13; 5:1).

Paul elsewhere speaks of eager longing for events designated for Christ's return (8:23, 25; 1 Cor 1:7; Gal 5:5; Phil 3:20). In 8:19, however, all creation awaits that time; creation has suffered since Adam abdicated his role as God's vizier and caretaker of creation (cf. 8:20; Gen 1:26–28).[23] Creation longs for God's "children" to be revealed (8:19); in what sense is this yet to happen? The Spirit testifies to believers that they are already God's children (8:15–16), but this reality will be consummated when the Spirit resurrects their bodies (8:11–13). (Rhetorically, Paul includes three *apok-* words in 8:19, two of them also including *d* and *k* sounds.)

Whether we think that God or Adam "subjected" creation here, Paul's earlier emphasis on Adam's sin probably informs the cosmic effects of the fall here.[24] This is especially likely if "vanity" or "futility" (*mataiotēs*) refers back to humanity rebelling against the creator in Rom 1:20–21.[25] When God's children are restored, this subjection to vanity will be reversed. Though created in God's image (Gen 1:26–27) to govern the earth (Gen 1:28), humanity corrupted God's image through idolatry (Rom

22. In 1 Cor 15:40–41, he evokes the image of heavenly bodies as understood among his contemporaries (see discussion in Keener 2005b: 131).

23. Although Paul may personify creation here, its label "creation" sanctifies the cosmos by relating it to its creator (as Jewett notes) rather than the Gentile approach of treating earth as "mother" (though Paul does allow it "birth pangs," 8:22). Stoics spoke of nature's "sympathy" or working together (Murray 1915: 43); if Paul uses any element of the idea, he adapts it to reflect God's sovereignty.

24. Cf. e.g., Gen 3:17; *Jub.* 3:28; *4 Ezra* 7:11–12; *Sipre Num.* 18.1.1. For God as subjecter (cf. Pauline usage in 1 Cor 15:27–28; Phil 3:21), see e.g., Schreiner; for Adam, e.g., Talbert; for both, Byrne.

25. The only other use of a cognate in Romans. Since that context involves idolatry (1:23), a common use of "vanity" in Scripture (e.g., 1 Kgs 16:13, 26; 2 Kgs 17:15; Isa 44:9; Jer 2:5; 10:3, 15; Jonah 2:8; Wis 13:1; 15:8) and early Jewish sources (3 Macc 6:11; *Sib. Or.* 3.29, 547–48, 555), the idea may be that instead of recognizing God's greatness in creation (Rom 1:20), fallen humanity worshiped it, making images from it (1:23). With humanity's restoration to God's image in Christ (8:29), creation would also resume its rightful role. Creation's "corruption" (*phthora*, 8:21) might echo the wrong worship of "perishable" (*phthartos*, the only other cognate in Romans) created things (1:23).

1:23). When the image would be fully restored in Christ (8:29), those in the new Adam would be better stewards of the new world (4:13; 5:17).[26]

Perhaps the dependence of creation's restoration on the revelation of God's children means partly that just as Israel's restoration would signal the world's salvation (11:12), it was only Christ's return for his people that would transform the cosmos (cf. Isa 65:17–18; 66:22).[27] The glorification and liberation of God's children (8:21) would also liberate creation from "corruption" (8:21), i.e., mortality (cf. 1 Cor 15:42, 50; Gal 6:8). Adam introduced death into the world; Christ's redemption brought life (Rom 5:17–18), and the effects are to be cosmic.[28] "Slavery" (also 8:15) reflects the old order in Adam, including slavery to sin (6:6, 12–21) and perhaps the law (7:6, 25).

Longing for this liberation from perishability, creation's present sufferings (8:18) are in a sense birth pangs of the future world (8:22). As Israel "groaned" because of slavery, a groaning God counted as a prayer for redemption (Exod 2:23), so in the present age creation (8:22), believers (8:23), and the Spirit (8:26) groan in the face of sufferings for the redemption of the body (8:23).[29] "Redemption" refers to the freeing of slaves; the goal of freedom here was liberation from death (7:24), accomplished at the resurrection (8:11).[30] But this image of groaning also links with the image of travail (8:22) here; travail was a common image for suffering in Scripture, also applied to the sufferings of the end time.[31] Many Jewish

26. In a context addressing creation, even "glory" (8:21) may allude to transformation into Christ's "image," since Paul employs it as something of a synonym for image in 1 Cor 11:7 (cf. 2 Cor 3:18; 4:4; 4Q504 f8R:4).

27. See also 2 Pet 3:13; Rev 21:1; *1 En.* 72:1; 91:16; *Jub.* 1:29; 4:26; *2 Bar.* 44:9. In Paul's theology, believers have proleptically entered the new creation (2 Cor 5:17; Gal 6:15).

28. Many ancients thought that the heavens were imperishable, an image naturally transferable to the future age. Livable conditions would not exist in our universe without entropy and decay, and advanced life depends on the death of other life, all of which preceded humanity. Aside from such information being unavailable in Paul's day, however, he was speaking theologically of the sort of restoration depicted in figurative language in Isa 11:6–7; 65:17–18, 25; 66:22.

29. "Groaning" is not limited to exodus or childbirth contexts (see e.g., *Sib. Or.* 3.417, 438, 558, 602, 752), but the present context suggests these allusions.

30. For end-time redemption, see e.g., 1QM 1.12; 15.1–2; 18.11.

31. Cf. 1QH 3.3–18; *1 En.* 62:4; later, *b. Sanh.* 98b; *Shab.* 118a; possibly 1 Thess 5:3. For judgment imagery more generally, see e.g., Ps 48:6; Isa 13:8; 21:3; 26:17; 42:14; Jer 4:31; 6:24; 13:21; 22:23; 30:6; 31:8; 48:41; 49:22, 24; 50:43; Hos 13:13. Against the supposition that its common figurative use deprived the image of its original strength for

people compared the expected end-time tribulation with birth pangs for the new world. For believers living between the Messiah's first and second comings, that era of eschatological suffering was present (cf. Mark 13:7–8; Rev 12:2–5).[32]

Just as the messiah and his kingdom both had come and remained yet to come, believers are already adopted (8:15) and redeemed (3:24), yet in 8:23 they await the application of this reality to their bodies. Waiting for what is yet unseen exercises hope (8:24–25; cf. 2 Cor 4:18), which is deepened through tribulation and consequent endurance (Rom 5:3–4).[33] The hope is not simply imagination, however, for it is grounded in a firm guarantee: just as the "first fruits" was the actual beginning of the harvest, so the Spirit within believers is their initial experience of the future age (8:23; cf. 8:11).[34]

Not only do creation and believers groan with eagerness for liberation, but Christ's own Spirit groans with believers in their suffering, eager for their deliverance (8:26).[35] Whatever the other benefits of the Spirit's intercession (8:26–27), the Spirit works within believers during their sufferings to prepare them for conformity with the image of the crucified and resurrected Christ (8:28–29), i.e., to share his glory (8:30). The Spirit "helps"[36] believers in the weakness of their current bodily state (cf. 6:19; 8:3; 2 Cor 12:9); just as Israel's groans in suffering counted as prayers (Exod 2:23), so the Spirit offers an inarticulate prayer when believers are pressed by the hardships of the current age.[37] The prophetic Spirit leads

---

Paul, see Gal 4:19, 27.

32. The Qumran sectarians also apparently believed that they were living in the end-time tribulation, a period initially designated for a forty-year generation (CD 20.14–15) but that was then stretched to fit the duration of their exile (1QpHab 7.13–14).

33. Cf. possibly Hab 2:3, in the immediate context of Paul's controlling text in Rom 1:17.

34. For the Spirit and eschatology in Paul, see e.g., Cullmann 1956: 117; Dunn 1975: 308–18.

35. For God's eagerness for his people's deliverance, cf. Isa 30:18; *b. Sanh.* 97b.

36. The term "help with" applies to supporters to whom work is delegated in Exod 18:22; Num 11:17; in the latter, the Spirit enables this support. Probably more relevant are texts about God sustaining his people (e.g., Pss 3:5; 18:35; 40:11; 41:12; 119:116; Isa 26:3), perhaps especially Isa 42:1 (involving the Spirit). Paul employs an intensive form of the verb here; God is so worthy that only his Spirit can inspire adequately worthy worship and intercession (cf. Origen *Prayer* 4; Gregory of Nazianzus *Or. Bas.* 31.12).

37. Against some commentators, this is an experience different from tongues, which Paul values (1 Cor 12:10; 14:18) but regards as articulate. Some experiences were consid-

(8:14) and assures believers that they are God's children (8:16), and also inspires prayer to God (8:15), though the "prayer" in 8:26 may be one that believers do not always even recognize. As the Spirit intercedes within believers (8:26), Jesus intercedes for them at God's right hand (8:34).[38] The Spirit who knows God's heart (1 Cor 2:11) prays "according to God" (Rom 8:27), an idiom used elsewhere (cf. 15:5; 2 Cor 7:9–11) for what accords with God's will. Believers never have to worry about the efficacy of this intercession, because it is born from God's own presence within them (8:27), working to bring about his purpose (8:28). (Jewish people often spoke of God who "searches hearts.")[39]

Still holding in tension the present sufferings (8:18, 22) with the future glory (8:18, 21, 30), Paul affirms that God[40] causes all these present difficulties to produce good for those who love him (8:28). Some philosophers spoke of cooperating with fate or even maintaining happiness with it;[41] Paul goes beyond this, not resigned to impersonal fate but trusting the benevolent design of God, even when it seems hidden from external human experience of the present. Those who love him are special to him (cf. 1 Cor 2:9; 8:3; Deut 7:9; Sir 1:10). These are "called according to his purpose" (Rom 8:28),[42] and his purpose is to conform them to the image of his Son (8:29), thus bringing them to glory (8:30). The "good" that God seeks for those who love him, then, is above all their ultimate glory.

God uses his Son Jesus as the paradigm for making believers into God's children (8:29). Although Jesus was already God's Son before-

---

ered so sublime or sacred they were unutterable (cf. 2 Cor 12:4); Paul may transfer that sacredness to how God feels and responds to the sufferings of his children.

38. Cf. perhaps the *paraklētos* of John 14:16; 1 John 2:1; discussion in Keener 2003b: 956–61.

39. E.g., 1 Chron 28:9; *t. Sanh.* 8:3; on his full knowledge of hearts, *Ps. Sol.* 9:3; 14:8; *Let. Aris.* 132–33; Josephus *Ag. Ap.* 2.166; idem *Ant.* 4.41; Philo *Providence* 2.35; see further in Keener 2003b: 532.

40. "All things work" appears the likeliest reading, but no Jew would believe these "all things" were random (cf. Philo *Spec. Laws* 4.187; Josephus *Ag. Ap.* 2.294; *m. Ber.* 9:5; Eichrodt 1983: 19–20; even many philosophers believed that a divine Mind ordered "all things"). The context is clear that God is sovereign in working through the present sufferings; cf. also Gen 50:20 (although Paul's outcome in this context is esp. eschatological).

41. See e.g., Seneca *Dial.* 1.1.5; 1.2.4; 1.3.1; 1.5.8; 7.8.3; 7.15.4; idem *Ep. Lucil.* 96.1–2; 123.3; Musonius Rufus frg. 38, p. 136.1–8; Epictetus *Disc.* 1.14.16; 4.7.9; idem *Ench.* 8; Crates *Ep.* 35; Marcus Aurelius *Med.* 6.16; Diogenes Laertius 6.2.63.

42. The "called" include Gentiles (9:24–26), including the saints in Rome (1:6–7); the called will be glorified (8:30). God's "purpose" depends on his grace, not works (9:11).

hand (8:3), the title applied in a special way after the resurrection (cf. 1:4; Acts 13:33). The resurrection of believers will also display them as God's children in a new way (8:21–23); as the first to rise (1 Cor 15:20, 23), Jesus was the "firstborn" (Rom 8:29; cf. Col 1:18; Heb 1:6; Rev 1:5), also a designation of priority in honor. In conjunction with the context of present sufferings, being "conformed" to Jesus's image involves a present process through, among other things, sharing Christ's suffering (cf. 12:2; 2 Cor 3:18; Phil 3:10).[43] Nevertheless, it is the future consummation of that conforming, achieved with the glorification of the body, that Paul emphasizes in 8:29 (cf. 1 Cor 15:49; Phil 3:21). Like Wisdom or the "logos" in Hellenistic Judaism, Jesus is God's chief image through which God can stamp his image on others (cf. 2 Cor 4:4).[44] But Jesus is also the new Adam, restoring the divine image marred in Adam (cf. Gen 1:26–27). Glorification (Rom 8:30) also involves restoration of lost glory (cf. 3:23). In both cases, the description suggests that the restoration is greater than the fall (cf. 5:15–20).

When modern readers encounter terms like "chose" and "predestine" (Rom 8:29–30) we tend to read them in light of later theological debates, such as the Greek fathers' defense of free will against fatalism, Augustine's defense of God's sovereign grace against Pelagius, or the debates of the Reformation era.[45] Paul's own audience would think of Israel

43. The divine likeness in humanity could be intelligible to some philosophers (Seneca *Dial.* 1.1.5; Musonius Rufus 17, p. 108.15–16; Diogenes Laertius 6.2.51; Porphyry *Marc.* 13.233–34; 16.267; 26.413–14, 419–20; Iamblichus *Myst.* 7.4), but given Paul's many explicit biblical quotations, the dominant and nearest source Paul shares with his audience would be Scripture (see esp. Rom 5:12–21; cf. Sir 17:3; Wis 2:23; Philo *Creation* 69; 4 *Ezra* 8:44; *L.A.E.* 37:3; *Apoc. Mos.* 10:3; 33:5; *T. Naph.* 2:5; *m. 'Abot* 3:15). "Image" also connoted sonship (Gen 5:1–3; cf. Seneca *Dial.* 1.1.5; Menander Rhetor 2.6, 407.9; Philostratus *Hrk.* 52.2; Gregory of Nazianzus *Theo. Or.* 4.20).

44. See Wis 7:26; Philo *Creation* 26; idem *Spec. Laws* 3.207; idem *Planting* 18; idem *Dreams* 2.45. For the coalescing of this image with the first man, see Philo *Alleg. Interp.* 1.43; for the stamping of the first man's image on others, see *m. Sanh.* 4:5; *b. Sanh.* 38a.

45. Most ancient Jewish authors did not pit God's sovereignty against human choice (cf. e.g., Josephus *J.W.* 2.162–63; idem *Ant.* 18.13; *m. 'Abot* 3:16); a sovereign God could sovereignly allow much choice and still accomplish his purposes. Cf. also the balance in, e.g., Augustine *Simpl.* 10; Jerome *Pelag.* 1.5; for the change in Augustine's position, see e.g., Reasoner 2005: 97–100. In Scripture, God works in and around choices (see e.g., Exod 13:17; 1 Sam 9:8, 16). If God did not sovereignly make some choice possible, one might expect all people to follow his requirements and moral will; yet environment and genetics determine much, and any degree of choice might be impossible without God sovereignly enabling it.

as the people God had chosen,[46] and recognize that Paul's argument was designed to show that God was so sovereign that he was not bound to choose (with regard to salvation) based on Jewish ethnicity. Paul might ground predestination in foreknowledge (8:29) to allow that God takes faith into account (in advance) in salvation (a question much debated by theologians). Whether or not this is the case, he apparently refers to God's choice mostly to emphasize the initiative of God's grace rather than human works (9:11). Perhaps more importantly, Paul will use even the term "foreknow" for Israel (11:2),[47] thus connecting this claim with his larger argument. The specific formulation of Paul's discussion of God choosing people is still driven by his overall plan in Romans to argue that God saves Gentiles as well as Jews through Christ (see comment on 1:16).

In 8:30 Paul uses rhetorical climax (cf. 5:3–4) to point to the certainty of sharing Christ's glory based on what God has already accomplished. Paul presents all the elements in 8:30 as a *fait accompli*,[48] since from the standpoint of God's foreknowledge it is already done, though from the human standpoint glorification in particular remains clearly future (8:18, 21).

Secure in God's Love (8:31–39)

Before illustrating his point about God's gracious choice (8:29–30) from history (9:6–13), Paul in a rousing way gives the implications of his previous discussion. The present sufferings cannot be compared with future glory (8:18), and none of these sufferings can separate believers from God's love (8:35–39). Paul generates emotion in this passage with rousing rhetorical questions (8:31–35), affliction lists (8:35, 38–39), and a conspicuous chiasm (an inverted parallel structure, 8:35–39).

---

46. See e.g., Neh 9:7; Jer 33:24; Sir 46:1; 2 Macc 1:25; *Jub.* 1:29; 22:9–10; 2 *Bar.* 48:20. This should not be taken to exclude individual predestination (emphasized, e.g., in Qumran; for the righteous remnant, cf. 1QS 1.10; 2.5; 9.14; 11.7; 1QM 10.9–10; 12.1, 4; 15.1–2; 17.7), though most Jewish people did not treat the human and sovereign divine elements as mutually exclusive.

47. In Romans (cf. also *Jub.* 15:30); the terminology could also be applied more widely (*1 En.* 9:11).

48. Perhaps something like the completed action implied in the so-called "prophetic perfect" in Hebrew prophecy (e.g., Isa 53:4–6), although Hebrew tenses do not match English temporal tenses.

Believers need not fear external criticism against their relationship with God (8:31, 33), for example, for not keeping some external details of the law like physical circumcision (2:26–29). The confident question of 8:31 evokes especially Ps 118:6: God is for me, so what can humans do to me?[49] In 8:32, Paul echoes his earlier assurance that if God loved his people to the extent of Christ dying for them, how much greater would be the benefit of his resurrection (5:8–10)? He also echoes God delivering over Jesus (4:25; cf. 1 Cor 11:23; Gal 2:20),[50] believers being God's heirs (8:17), and perhaps believers' rule of the coming world (4:13; 5:17). In 8:33–34a Paul echoes Isa 50:8: God vindicates ("justifies," using *dikaioō*) me; who will contend with me? Who dares to bring a legal case against me?[51] If God as judge has already acquitted believers in Jesus (who died for them, and even more[52] rose), accusers raise accusations only at their own peril. The mention of God's "chosen" recalls 8:29–30 and emphasizes God's favor. Paul concludes 8:34 by showing that believers' vindication is surely settled, for Jesus (whose death and resurrection justified believers, 3:24; 4:25; 5:9) intercedes just as the Spirit does (8:26). Jesus's location at God's right hand indicates his exaltation (Ps 110:1), presumably including over hostile powers (Rom 8:38–39), and emphasizes his complete access to the one with whom he intercedes.

Now Paul offers a brief but fairly obvious chiasm:

A Nothing can separate believers from Christ's love (8:35a)

  B List of sufferings (8:35b)

    C Believers thoroughly overcome (8:37)

  B´ List of sufferings (8:38–39a)

A´ Nothing can separate believers from God's love in Christ (8:39)

49. More generally, God often affirms that he is with and for his servants (e.g., Gen 26:3, 24; 28:15; 31:3; Jer 20:11; cf. *T. Iss.* 7:7); God fights for his people in Exod 14:14, 25. In view of the quotation in Rom 8:33–34, cf. perhaps especially Isa 50:7.

50. Paul employed this verb *paradidōmi* earlier for Jesus's death in a context referring to Abraham, but not expressly mentioning the Aqedah. Many scholars, however, do see an allusion to Abraham offering up Isaac here; whether or not they are correct, such an analogy at the least displays the costliness of the sacrifice.

51. Paul changes LXX Isaiah's *krinō* to *katakrinō*, but he seems to have been using these interchangeably (cf. Rom 2:1, 3, 12, 16, 27; 3:4–7; 5:16, 18; 8:1, 3). Paul may use *hupophora* (where one asks what can be said against one's case; *Rhet. Her.* 4.23.33).

52. "Yea, rather" is not so much an afterthought but a common rhetorical technique (e.g., *Rhet. Her.* 4.26.36; Pliny *Ep.* 7.31.7; cf. Rowe 1997: 141). For the thought, cf. 5:9.

Paul emphasizes God's love in 8:35, 39, and Christ's love in 8:37 (which in Paul's thinking is linked with his death for others, Gal 2:20). Paul has already shown the great price God's love for humanity cost him in Christ (5:5, 8). Here the context involves God's eternal purposes for his children; nothing can thwart these purposes, which are already as good as done (8:29–30; cf. 9:11, 15–18). God justifies (8:33), so he will glorify (8:30); nothing can condemn believers (8:33–34). In some other contexts Paul enjoins perseverance and warns against falling away (e.g., 11:22; 1 Cor 9:27; 10:5–12; Gal 4:11, 19; 5:4; Col 1:22–23), but the rhetorical function of the present context is assurance in Christ.

Ancient writers used affliction lists for various purposes. Philosophers often used them, as Paul did for his own ministry (e.g., 1 Cor 4:9–13; 2 Cor 4:8–10; 6:4–10; 11:23–33), to demonstrate the integrity of their character exhibited in testing.[53] The present sufferings include deep poverty and persecution (8:35);[54] for the latter point (which will be a critical matter for the Roman church within a few years) Paul in 8:36 cites Ps 44:22, from a psalm of complaint (as in Rom 15:3). Whereas believers are "reckoned" righteous in God's sight (Rom 4:24), here they are "reckoned" as sheep for slaughter.[55] Whereas the experience of such wholesale slaughter bespeaks utter defeat, Paul in 8:37 declares that believers "prevail completely" (BDAG ὑπερνικάω), experiencing utter victory.[56] This is because even the harshest circumstances cannot dislodge believers from God's love and the incomparably greater hope of glory that awaits them (8:18; hope made firm through affliction, 5:3–4). They are special to God; he is with them and has a purpose for them, working even their sufferings for eternal glory (8:28).

53. See Fitzgerald 1988: 43–70; idem 2000: 16–17.

54. "Nakedness" could mean little-clothed (2 Cor 11:27; Tob 1:17; 4:16; Euripides *El.* 308; Livy 45.39.17; Epictetus *Disc.* 3.22.45–47). "Sword" can apply to execution (13:4) or war, but he probably applies the text in 8:36 to unjust, violent oppression (esp. for faith); later R. Akiba applied it to Jewish martyrs (Bonsirven 1964: 56; cf. more generally *Sipre Deut.* 32.3.4).

55. For sheep destined for slaughter, see e.g., Isa 53:7; Jer 25:34; Zech 11:4, 7.

56. For remaining unconquered in suffering, see Seneca *Ep. Lucil.* 27.3; 67.16; idem *Dial.* 7.8.3; Epictetus *Disc.* 1.1.23; 1.18.21–22; 2.18.31; for martyrs triumphing by martyrdom for truth, Xenophon *Apol.* 29 (Socrates); Rev 12:11; 15:2. Many contend that "overwhelming" conquest here alludes to sufferings not simply being vanquished, but working for good (Rom 8:28).

Having noted concrete afflictions like hunger and martyrdom, Paul turns now more generally to the powers and the cosmic dimension of the suffering. Because "rulers" (*archai*) and "powers" (*dunameis*) occur in the context of angels and other superhuman powers, many scholars believe that Paul refers here to heavenly ranks of spiritual authorities that stand behind the earthly ones.[57] Some have taken "height" and "depth" to refer to astrological[58] or, more simply, astronomical terms; in any case, the antithesis functions together as a Hebraic merism for all creation (Isa 7:11)—the greatest extremes could not separate God's presence (Ps 139:7-12, especially 139:8). Paul's climactic obstacle is "anything else created"—a reminder that if everything other than God is God's creation (Rom 1:20, 25) and if God is for his people, nothing can be against them. Indeed, creation itself longs for and will celebrate the deliverance of God's people (8:19-22).

Fusing the Horizons: Suffering

Paul's theological approach to suffering would encourage his Roman audience. They had faced the trauma of many of their number being expelled (49 CE), a situation that had ended perhaps less than five years earlier (54 CE), and would soon face deadly persecution (c. 64 CE). These believers also shared broader human experiences like grief for loved ones.

Suffering recalls our attention to God's faithfulness and promises. Believers in many parts of the world experience suffering on a dramatic level. Many have faced deadly persecution, such as (among many other possible examples) in northern Nigeria, Iran, and the Indian state of Orissa. Others have suffered from genocide and horrific ethnic conflicts, such as in the eastern Democratic Republic of Congo. Even in the face of such intense suffering, though, believers have often learned to cling deeply to God for hope (cf. 5:3-5). My wife was for eighteen months a refugee during war in Congo-Brazzaville, and her journal records her experiences of hope in God that gave her strength to face the anguish.

57. For angels of nations, see e.g., Dan 10:20-21; Deut 32:8 LXX; *Jub.* 15:30-32; *1 En.* 40:9; 61:10; 89:59—90:19; 1QM 14.15-16; 15.13-14; 17.5-8; *Mek. Shir.* 2:112ff. For angels over nature, see e.g., *Jub.* 2:2; *1 En.* 20:2; 60:12-22; 66:1-2; *2 En.* 19:3-4; 1QM 10.11-12.

58. E.g., Knox 1939: 106-7; MacGregor 1954: 23.

Moreover, the possibility of chaos is not far from any society. For example, an infrastructure collapse would threaten massive death in heavily urbanized, economically interdependent societies. Yet even without such large-scale catastrophes, all believers face suffering—the death of a family member, struggles with a severely autistic child, miscarriages, and so on.

Counselors warn against giving a glib assertion that "all things work for good" to a person who is suffering. Instead, we should begin to learn to trust Paul's message of God's sovereign care and destiny for us before we suffer. At times we may be content learning such ideas without incorporating them in our lives; when we face suffering, however, with only God to cling to, the genuineness of our faith is tested. Then, with God's help, we have opportunity to show our faith, to further develop an intellectual affirmation into a life of deeper trust.

ROMANS 9

ISRAEL'S ROLE AND SALVATION (9:1—11:36)

Some scholars in the past treated Rom 9–11 as a digression (or even an interpolation from another context), but few share that view today. Far from being a digression, these chapters pick up the issue of Israel addressed in 3:1–9 (from which Paul in a sense digressed to address the relationship between righteousness and the law). Paul has been addressing the relationship between Jew and Gentile in Christ throughout (1:16; 2:9–10, 13–14; 3:9, 29; 4:10–12), and now must deal with the biblical evidence concerning God's purposes in history concerning Israel and the covenant.

Israel Special and Beloved (9:1–5)

In 9:1–3 Paul shifts rhetorically from the height of celebration to the deepest lament. Once Paul has begun addressing God choosing people (8:29–30), he has reminded his audience that he has not left the Jewish-Gentile issue that has dominated his letter. If believers are adopted, promised glory (8:18, 21, 30), and have the law in their hearts (8:2), what shall one say about ethnic Israel, to whom such blessings were already promised (9:4–5)? If nothing can tear the objects of God's love from him (8:35–39), what has happened to Israel, who has occupied this position historically? Paul answers abundantly from Scripture—in fact, over 27 percent of explicit citations in extant Pauline letters appear in Rom 9–11.

Perhaps Paul's lament in 9:1–3 includes some hyperbole, or perhaps it reflects Paul's mood before his perilous journey to Jerusalem (15:31); he elsewhere speaks much of rejoicing (12:12, 15; 14:17; 15:13, 32; 16:19; Phil 1:18; 4:4). Paul's understanding of emotion allowed him to combine both elements (2 Cor 6:10).[1] What we can feel secure in saying is that Paul

---

1. Sorrow and tears could be used rhetorically to stir an audience (e.g., Cicero *Mil.*

deeply loved his people and sorrow for the resistance of most of them
to his gospel deeply wounded him. Along with his passion for reaching
Gentiles, in fact, his experience of his people's rejection of the one that
he was absolutely convinced was their rightful deliverer informed his approach in this letter as a whole. In 9:3 Paul offers himself for Israel, like
Moses of old[2] (and more than Elijah in Rom 11:2–3), and in so doing
he incidentally exemplifies the sort of spirit of self-sacrifice he invites in
12:1.

In 9:4–5 Paul elaborates the special benefits God has provided Israel
(finally following up on a theme he introduced only briefly with "first"
in 3:2).[3] Several of these reflect benefits he has already associated with
believers, including Gentile believers (whom he will soon show have been
"grafted into" Israel's heritage, 11:17): adoption as children (8:15, 23), glory (8:18, 21, 30), and the law (8:2, 4). Although there is a sense in which
these belong particularly to ethnic Israel (11:28; 15:8), all believers also
lay claim to the patriarchs (4:16–18)[4] and promises (4:13–16), as Paul will
soon show again (9:6–9). He will also show later that believers participate
in spiritual service or worship (*latreia*, 12:1; cf. 15:16).[5] Finally and most
importantly, the Messiah comes from Israel in a physical way (cf. also
1:3–4). Given the parallel to Paul's doxology in 1:25, "who is . . . God
blessed forever" in 9:5 most likely applies to the Christ who is over all,

---

38.105; idem *Cael.* 24.60; in letters, Cicero *Fam.* 14.3.1; 14.4.1; Pliny *Ep.* 5.21.6; 2 Cor
2:4; Phil 3:18); for *pathos* in Roman rhetorical appeals, see Kraftchick 2001: 52–56 (more
generally, see Olbricht and Sumney 2001); for weeping with others, e.g., Cicero *Fam.*
14.3.1; 14.4.1. Some Stoics may have disapproved (Engberg-Pedersen 2000: 96–97; Arius
Didymus *Epit.* 2.7.10, p. 56.6–16; 2.7.10a, p. 58.11–16; 2.7.10b, p. 58.26–27; 2.7.11e, p.
68.17–18), but in practice cf. Ps.-Heraclitus *Ep.* 5; Fitzgerald 1988: 199.

2. Exod 32:32 (with Schoeps 1961: 134, and many others); for the limits of such inter-
cessors' effectiveness, cf. Jer 15:1; Ezek 14:14, 20. Roman Gentiles respected citizens who
offered themselves for their people (Valerius Maximus 1.5.2; Plutarch *Cam.* 5.6), so they
could understand the sentiment.

3. Paul's rhetorical sensitivity is clear in 9:4: making the list sound fuller by polysyn-
deton (explicit conjunctions), Paul also chooses nouns ending in -*thesia*, -*a*, -*ai*, -*thesia*,
-*a*, -*ai* (Paul must break the pattern in 9:5 with two masculine nouns). The present tense
verb reveals God's continuing activity with regard to ethnic Israel (Piper 1983: 8).

4. The phrase (also in 11:28; 15:8) applies especially to Abraham, Isaac, and Jacob
(*Sipra Behuq.* pq. 8.269.2.5), although it need not be limited to them (cf. 1 Cor 10:1).

5. Paul nowhere else in Romans applies "covenants" to believers, but their sharing in
the new covenant (explicit in 1 Cor 11:25; 2 Cor 3:6; Gal 3:17; 4:24) is implied in Rom
2:28–29; 7:6.

though Paul more often prefers the divine title "Lord" for him (10:9–13; 1 Cor 8:5–6; Phil 2:9–11 [with Isa 45:23]).[6]

By elsewhere applying most of these benefits to all believers, Paul is not denying the relationship of these benefits to Israel's heritage. Rather, Gentiles who submit to Israel's God-ordained king are grafted into the covenant, whereas Jews who do rebel against him are broken off. It is not the covenant that changed, but some members of Israel (as throughout Israel's history) did not maintain their side of the covenant.[7] In the OT, Gentile adherents to the covenant were a smaller minority, but the obedient remnant of Israel could be either large (as in Joshua's or David's day) or small (as in Moses's or Ahab's day). That so many Gentiles would be welcomed (and without circumcision) might be a "mystery," but it can be made known from Scripture precisely because Gentiles had always been welcome to join the covenant (16:25–26).

God's Choice Not Bound by Ethnicity (9:6–29)

The conjunction of God's promises (9:4–5) with Israel's tragic alienation (9:1–3) raises the issue of theodicy: has God's promise failed (9:6)? Paul responds that God's covenant is secure, but it does not apply automatically to all of Israel's ethnic descendants (9:6).[8] He demonstrates this premise from unexpected yet undisputed historic examples: not all of Abraham's children received the promise (9:7–9), nor did all of Isaac's (9:10–13). (Ishmael was blessed, but not the primary line of descent; Esau received even more limited blessing.)[9] The echoes of the Greek text of 9:7 in 9:29

6. The matter is debated, but the title fits Pauline Christology of Jesus as divine, even though he usually prefers other wording (cf. e.g., comment on Rom 1:7). Those skeptical that it refers to Christ include Byrne, Dunn, Johnson, Käsemann, Stuhlmacher; those favoring a reference to Christ (currently the majority) include Origen; Cranfield; Cullmann 1959: 313; Fahy 1965; Jewett; Moo; Sanday and Headlam; Schlatter; see at length Harris 1992: 143–72.

7. Cf. Hays 1989: 96–97 (Israel remains Israel, rather than there being a "new Israel," but Gentile believers are absorbed into it).

8. Paul could have also cited for this point judgment on the wilderness generation (as in 1 Cor 10:5–10); Deuteronomy's blessings and curses, and so forth.

9. Later rabbis counted both Ishmael and Esau as chaff, but insisted that none of Jacob's sons were (*Sipre Deut.* 312.1.1; 343.5.2; *Tg. Ps.-J.* on Gen 35:22; cf. *Jub.* 15:30). Esau appears particularly negatively in Jewish sources (e.g., Philo *Alleg. Interp.* 3.88; *T. Jud.* 9:2; *Pesiq. Rab Kah.* 3:1), and later sources use him as a cipher for Rome (probably *4 Ezra* 6:7–10; pervasively in third century and later rabbis; cf. Freedman 1995; Hadas-Lebel 1984).

make clear that Paul is using this argument to prepare for his case that only a "remnant" within Israel will be saved. Paul cites both Gen 25:23 and Mal 1:1–2 to support the notion that God's favor for Jacob depended on his gracious calling and choice before Jacob performed works.[10] Thus, mere genetic descent is not what counts, but being divinely chosen (9:8);[11] Paul emphasizes the promise, which he has already associated with those who believe (Rom 4:16).

Because Scripture often associated God's righteousness with his covenant faithfulness to Israel, the failure of some Israelites to believe could appear to some as a sign of God's unrighteousness (9:14, essentially repackaging the objection in 3:3, 5). But the very question is misplaced, Paul shows, for God is right to do as he pleases, and what he pleases will always be what is right. Humanity merits punishment, but God shows mercy and compassion where he wills (9:15),[12] graciously saving some though he is obligated to save none (cf. 3:23). In the context of the passage that Paul cites in 9:15 (Exod 33:19, addressed to Moses), Israel has sinned and God plans to withdraw his presence. Because Moses found favor in God's sight, however, his intercession for Israel (33:13–16; 34:9) proved efficacious—God revealed his character, which included compassion to the undeserving (33:17, 19) and his covenant love that exceeded his wrath (34:6–7).[13] (That the runner would not prevail by his own effort recalls biblical pictures of how judgment or death would overtake all, Eccl 9:11; Jer 46:6; Amos 2:14–15.)

---

10. Both of these passages in context emphasize God's grace in treating Israel as special. In the context in Gen 25 the birth of both children was a gift (v. 21); in Malachi, God shows Israel how special they are, versus Edom that has opposed them. Paul approaches the texts not to emphasize Israel's specialness, however, but to emphasize something about God: he is free to show grace where he desires.

11. Cf. Gal 3:14–29; 4:23–28, where Paul is thinking of the inclusion of Gentiles (Hays 1989: 187–88). For discussion of predestination, see comment on 8:29–30.

12. Cf. similar expressions of God's sovereignty in Tob 4:19; 13:2, 5; much later, *Gk. Apoc. Ezra* 2:17. The conjunction of issues of justice (9:14) and mercy (9:15) may recall the concern in 3:26 (on justice and mercy as competing divine attributes in later rabbis, see e.g., Urbach 1979: 1:448–61).

13. Paul in 9:3 alluded to Moses's intercession in Exod 32:32, because of which God spared Israel (comparing himself with Moses hence presumably his Jewish detractors with Pharaoh); the same context remains in view. Moses pleads for favor in God's sight (33:13, 16—all the while asking it for Israel). God does grant Moses favor (33:17), answering his prayer to go with Israel (33:18); he *does* show mercy in response to Moses's request.

Yet not only does God show mercy sovereignly, but he also hardens sovereignly (Rom 9:17–18). In Exod 9:16[14] God had shown mercy in not destroying Egypt (cf. Exod 9:15) so he could continue to reveal his power in them and make his name known. Paul adapts the wording; God had not only spared Pharaoh, but "raised him up," which could develop the idea beyond preservation (it was common LXX language for awakening), or could refer to God even stirring Pharaoh to his mad course (cf. the LXX verb in Jer 6:22; 50:41; 51:1; Hab 1:6). Paul reads this claim in the larger context of Exodus's theology of God's sovereignty: God also hardens Pharaoh to show his glory.

We should keep in mind that God hardening people is not a pervasive Pauline theme (though it does appear), hence it should be balanced with other aspects of his theology and of Scripture. His very example of God judging a stubborn Pharaoh could also be used, for example, to teach God's concern that Gentiles know of him: God kept hardening Pharaoh's heart so God's judgments would notify Egypt that he was the Lord (Exod 7:5, 17; 14:4, 18), just as he wanted to show Israel (Exod 6:7; 10:2; 16:6, 12). Likewise, Paul believes that God gave the world over to its own moral depravity (Rom 1:24, 26, 28), and could have inferred an analogous lesson from Exodus. It is said that Pharaoh hardened his own heart (Exod 8:15, 32; 9:34; 1 Sam 6:6) as well as that God hardened it (Exod 9:12; 10:1, 20, 27; 11:10; 14:8; predicted in 4:21; 7:3; 14:4; cf. the passive "was hardened" in 7:13, 22; 8:19; 9:7, 35).[15] Apparently God chose this Pharaoh not so that an honorable man would become stubborn but so that God would judge a wicked leader, revealing God's power. Certainly Paul shares the text's interest in the honor of God's name throughout the world (Rom 1:5; 2:24).

But Paul emphasizes the appropriate side of "hardening" theology to prepare for a shocking point: the God who shows mercy as he wills is also the God who can harden as he wills, and he has hardened his own people. As God hardened the Gentile Pharaoh to deliver Israel and reveal his

---

14. God now speaks to Pharaoh (Rom 9:17) as he had to Moses (9:15), perhaps continuing in some sense earlier contrasts between God's servant and a "Gentile" (between Ishmael and Isaac, Esau and Jacob). For "Scripture" personified speaking, or identified with God's voice, see e.g., Matt 19:5; *m. Sot.* 9:6; *t. Sot.* 12:2; *Mek. Shir.* 6; 1QM 11.5–6; probable reading of 4Q158 f1 2.11–13.

15. As noted also in Augustine *Exp. prop. Rom.* 62 (though he later changed; Reasoner 2005: 106).

name among the nations, so God has hardened Israel to bring a chance for salvation among the Gentiles (11:7, 25; cf. 2 Cor 3:14).

Jewish people rightly affirmed God's sovereignty alongside his election of Israel. Yet Paul argues that, with respect to individual *salvation*, God being sovereign precludes him from being bound to choose on the basis of ethnicity. He can save Gentiles as well as Jews, and on the terms he chooses. The interlocutor who thinks this unjust (9:14; cf. 3:3) now objects that for God to be *this* sovereign would abnegate human responsibility (9:19), a moral argument parallel to 3:7. Paul will turn to Jewish responsibility in 9:32, but first he disposes of the propriety of this objection altogether. He again responds from Israel's Scripture, in Isa 45:9 (cf. Isa 29:16): will the pot complain to the potter about how it has been made? The context in Isaiah 45 is Israel's salvation, through God's sovereign purposes in international history (an idea Paul will address in ch. 11); the context in the similar passage in Isaiah 29 is the justness of God's judgment against Israel's intransigence (Isa 29:1–16).[16]

In 9:22–24, however, it is clear that Paul's emphasis on God's sovereignty continues to focus especially on grace. Paul has already indicated the purpose for which God was forming vessels for glory: conformity with his Son's image (8:29). God makes vessels for honor, which is his interest, but endures those that are objects of his wrath for the sake of the others (9:22–23).[17] In the context of the text from Exod 9:16 just cited, God endured the objects destined for wrath and destruction, like Pharaoh, so that he could "make his power known" (9:22) and lavish his glory on his people (9:23), just as he demonstrated his "power" in Pharaoh to make known his name (related to his glory) in 9:17 (quoting Exod 9:16). But as that text had declared that he would make known his power and name "throughout the earth," Paul can infer that God cares about Gentiles as well as Jews (9:24). Just as the new exodus of salvation evokes the pattern

16. The potter's right over the clay in Rom 9:21 might also evoke Jer 18:3–6 (Hays 1989: 65–66); it would not be unusual for Paul to have linked the common images. For creatures of "clay" acknowledging God's sovereignty, see 1QS 11.21–22; 1QH 1.21; 3.23–24; 12.24–25; 13.14–15; 18.11–12, 24–27; Sir 33:12–13; cf. analogous rhetorical questions regarding his sovereignty, Wis 12:12; *L.A.B.* 53:13.

17. Fashioning clay into both vessels for clean uses and those for unclean uses (perhaps chamber pots and the like) recalls Wis 15:7, although it lacks contextual resonances (the context involves making idols; cf. 2 Tim 2:20–21). The world existed so the righteous could exist (*4 Ezra* 6:59; 7:11; 9:13; *2 Bar.* 15:7; 21:24; *Sipre Deut.* 47.3.1–2); the wicked were created for destruction (4Q418 f69 ii.6).

of how God saved Israel in the first exodus (see comment on 8:14–17), so is the pattern in this passage. In 9:22–23 the wrath against the Gentile Pharaoh prefigures the eschatological wrath (cf. 2:5; 5:9), but the mercy (evoking 9:16–18 and especially the text in 9:15) involves salvation, for both Gentiles and ultimately Israel (11:30–32; 15:9).

Paul must show from Scripture that God did not use an ethnic criterion that guaranteed salvation for Jews and damnation for Gentiles. As Paul backs up his claim in 9:24 with Scripture in 9:25–26, he again shocks those familiar with traditional readings of the text by inverting those readings. He quotes Hos 2:23 and then 1:10, both of which contextually reverse the judgment of Hos 1:9.[18] In context, God had rejected his people and annulled the covenant (Hos 1:9, presumably involving the coming exile), but would restore them one day (1:10–11; 2:1, 23), a restoration the ultimate fulfillment of which appeared future in Paul's day. Perhaps Paul uses this text to justify the Jewish remnant in 9:24, but he would probably also seek to justify the more controversial incorporation of Gentiles on which that verse climaxes. How could Paul (who knows the context well enough to cite two key restoration texts from it) apply to Gentiles a text about Israel's restoration?[19] Perhaps he reasons that if God could temporarily reject his people, he might meanwhile welcome members of other peoples (cf. 10:19); such an inference would fit Paul's larger understanding of God's plan, articulated in similar terms (cf. 11:30–32). Certainly Paul will go on to speak of a current remnant (9:27–28) and a future restoration of the Jewish people as a whole to God (11:26–27). Perhaps most importantly, Paul reasons that if Israel, rejected from being God's people, could again become God's people, God could also welcome others who were not his people.

After quoting Hosea, Paul in Rom 9:27–28 quotes Isa 10:22–23. Paul can link this text with the one just cited (Hos 1:10) because both mention Israel being "like the sand of the sea." (Linking texts based on a common key term or phrase was a common Jewish interpretive technique, and Paul goes so far as to blend the two texts, importing "sons of Israel"

18. Paul adapts the wording, inserting *kaleō* ("call," 9:24–26; cf. 8:30; 9:12) from his quotation in Rom 9:7 (Hays 1989: 66).

19. Some early Christian interpreters thought Hosea referred to Gentiles (John Chrysostom *Hom. Rom.* 16; Augustine *Exp. prop. Rom.* 65); others that it had been transferred to Gentiles (Theodoret *Interp. Rom.* on 9:25; Bray 1998: 266–67). Hays 1989: 67, argues that Paul simply inverts the text's plain meaning (as he offers other inversions in Rom 9).

from Hos 1:10 into Isa 10:22 to bridge the connection.)[20] Clearly the text from Isaiah refers to God judging Israel so that only a remnant would be delivered (by depending on God, Isa 10:20). Elaborating further Isaiah's remnant theology in Rom 9:29, Paul cites Isa 1:9, which speaks of Israel having few survivors—and being treated nearly as harshly as wicked Gentiles![21] (In context Isaiah went on to compare them precisely with such wicked Gentiles, in 1:10, and to point out that their religion was empty before him because devoid of justice, 1:11–23.) Paul applies the same principle of God's activity to the present: when Israel was disobedient, only a remnant would be delivered. Often in the OT, Israel as a whole was in apostasy, with only a remnant saved; for Paul, that made sense of Israel as a whole not being saved in his generation (though a future generation of Israel would be, 11:26–27).

Two Approaches to the Law and Righteousness (9:30—10:10)

In 9:30—10:10 Paul presents two approaches to the law and righteousness, but he believes that only one (the way of faith) can genuinely save sinful people of flesh. Based on the foregoing scriptural argument (that God does not save based on membership in ethnic Israel), Paul in 9:30–33 addresses the reason for Israel's failure to be saved. He has argued that Gentiles could be saved and Jews could be unsaved (9:30–31)—one cannot predict salvation based on ethnicity. How did God make Gentiles right? By their dependence on his mercy, i.e., by their faith, rather than by their seeking to become right (9:30). By contrast, Israel, seeking righteousness through the law, could not fulfill the law (9:31) because they approached the law the wrong way, as a standard rather than an invitation to depend on God's kindness (9:32). If Jewish people ever prided themselves in keeping the law, this would be especially true in a context like this one that notes their view of "ungodly" Gentiles (who neither received the law

20. Jews and Gentiles alike commonly adjusted the wording of texts to fit the new contexts where they were being quoted. Actually conflating texts could stem from oral memory or more likely in this case part of Paul's rhetorical strategy; on conflation in antiquity, see Stanley 1992: 290–91, 322, 337, 342, 349. The rhetorical *suntelōn* and *suntemnōn* already appeared in the Greek version of Isaiah.

21. Disobedient Israel is compared with Sodom in the prophets (e.g., Isa 3:9; Jer 23:14; Ezek 16:46–56); early Jewish sources continued to use it as an example of immorality (*Jub.* 36:10; 3 Macc 2:5; *t. Sanh.* 13:8; *Shab.* 7:23; *Sipra Behuq.* par. 2.264.1.3; *Sipre Deut.* 43.3.5).

nor sought to obey it). Paul has already indicated that the *right* way to use the law is to inspire trust in God rather than confidence in one's own keeping of its precepts (3:27, 31; cf. 8:2), and will develop this argument further in 10:5–10.

In 9:32–33 Paul notes that Scripture had already indicated Israel's failure (he also notes this in 10:16): many in Zion would stumble, except those who *trusted* in the rock of their salvation. Paul here conflates two related Isaiah texts: 8:14 (a stumbling stone) and 28:16 ("I lay in Zion a . . . stone . . . and whoever trusts in it will not be put to shame").[22] In the context of Isa 8:14, it is God whom Israel should fear (Isa 8:13); God himself would become their sanctuary, but Israel would stumble over this rock instead of welcoming it (8:14–15). In the next passage, God decrees judgment on Israel (28:1–29), but lays in Zion a precious cornerstone, so that whoever trusted in it would not be ashamed (28:16)—i.e., would be kept through the judgment. For Paul, believers would not be "ashamed" or "disappointed" regarding their eschatological hope of salvation (Rom 5:5; 10:11). The saved remnant would be saved through *faith*.[23] For Paul, this faith in the cornerstone must be christocentric faith.[24]

22. On conflation in antiquity, see Stanley 1992, cited above.

23. Part of Israel's problem may be lack of acceptance of God's sovereignty in terms of recognizing the gift as unmerited (9:15–21), although many of Paul's contemporaries would have contested this diagnosis.

24. The rock in Isa 8:14–15 is divine; Paul applies to Jesus the image of a divine rock in 1 Cor 10:4; see comment in Keener 2005b: 85. Jesus had described himself as a cornerstone (Mark 12:10), using Ps 118:22; some early Christians linked that text with those that Paul cites here (1 Pet 2:6–8; see discussion in Longenecker 1970: 50–53).

ROMANS 10

Two Approaches to the Law and Righteousness
(9:30—10:10), *cont.*

As Paul lamented Israel's failure in 9:1–3, so he emphasizes his desire for their salvation in 10:1. He has already noted their failure to be saved because of their failure to depend on the rock, approaching the law wrongly as a matter of observance rather than trust in God (9:31–33).

When Paul testifies of Israel's "zeal" yet laments that its object is misinformed (10:2), he has experience with this misinformed zeal (Gal 1:14; Phil 3:6). He contends that they seek righteousness by their means rather than God's (10:3); God's own righteousness includes his saving character that would put them right (see comment on 1:17). Their failure to "submit themselves" to God's righteousness (10:3) was to be expected insofar as they were not depending on God's superhuman power; mere flesh cannot submit to God's law from the heart (8:7). They could not achieve righteousness by works to fulfill the law any more than any law code makes its non-transgressors truly righteous before God; only in Christ (5:17, 21) and by the Spirit (8:2–4) are people made righteous.

Thus, Paul argues, Christ is the "end" (*telos*) of the law for righteousness from the standpoint of faith. The Greek term for "end" can involve either "goal" or "termination."[1] "Goal" seems the likelier primary nuance, but the context (which defines the *sense* in which the law ends or climaxes)

---

1. A similar interpretive crux appears in 2 Cor 3:13; in both, Paul might think in terms of eras of salvation history, in which case the Mosaic form of law prepared for the current end-time era (Gal 3:24–25). Origen, Erasmus and Calvin preferred "completion" rather than "termination" (Reasoner 2005: 113, 117). For "end," see e.g., Dunn, Käsemann, Rhyne, Sanday and Headlam, Schreiner, Stuhlmacher, Talbert, Watson; for "goal," e.g., R. D. Anderson, Cranfield, Donaldson, D. Fuller, Haacker, Hays, G. Howard, Jewett, Johnson.

clarifies the sense of the statement in any case. Israel failed to attain the law of righteousness because they pursued it by works rather than by faith (9:31–32); Gentiles conversely attained righteousness by faith (9:30). The problem thus is not the law, but the wrong approach to the law (as Paul will further clarify in 10:5–8). Like faith (3:31), Christ is the goal of the law, what the law points to for those with the perspective of faith. But if the law is approached as a "law of works" (3:27), as in 10:5, recognizing the reality of Christ should finish off that approach; those who "believe" (10:4) will not take this approach.

Paul supports his argument exegetically in 10:5–8. Israel's wrong-headed approach to the law was by works rather than by faith (9:31–32). In 10:5 Paul offers a basic text for this wrong approach of works, and in 10:6–8 he counters with a text for the right approach of faith. (Jewish teachers often defended positions by citing counter-texts to refute what they viewed as a misunderstanding of other texts.)[2] We do in fact know that later Jewish teachers applied texts like those in 10:5 (especially Lev 18:5; also Gal 3:12) to eternal life,[3] even though these passages originally meant just long life in the land,[4] and it is entirely possible and even probable that Paul has heard this prooftext in his debates in the synagogues. Paul does not need to elaborate on why the approach to the law in 10:5 is unworkable, because he has already addressed the failure of law-works due to human sinfulness in 3:10–18 and elsewhere, most recently in 9:31–32 (cf. also 3:21; 4:13; Gal 2:21; 3:21; Phil 3:6, 9).

Paul articulates his own case for righteousness in 10:6–10. Instead of the righteousness based on works of the law, Paul advocates righteousness by depending on God's righteousness (9:30–32; 10:3). Paul adapts the wording of his chief passage ("lest you say") to "Do not say in your heart," a small change but one that manages to incorporate Deut 9:4, which explicitly reminds Israel that God is not giving them the land because of

2. Sometimes they even temporarily came down to the level of their erroneous interlocutors (e.g. Daube 1960: 54). Comparing one's argument with that of an opponent was common (Anderson 2000: 22). "Righteousness-by-faith" speaking (as if human) here is personification and *prosopopoiia*, familiar rhetorical devices.

3. See comment on Rom 1:17; also Gathercole 2002: 100–102 (on CD 3.14–16, 20); Evans 2005: 226. Other texts make the connection between obedience and life (e.g., Neh 9:29; Ezek 20:11–13, 21; 33:12–19), probably echoing Lev 18:5; it might reflect court idiom (Gen 42:18).

4. Cf. Deut 4:1, 26, 40; 5:33; 8:1; 16:20; 30:16, 20.

their righteousness (for, as the context in Deut 9:5–6 reiterates, they were *not* righteous).

The heart of Paul's argument here, however, derives from Deut 30:12–14. In a closely argued midrash, Paul offers an analogy with God's way of salvation in Deuteronomy, expecting structural continuity on the level of principle and how God deals with humanity. Both cases involve an obedient response to God's gracious acts in salvation history, rather than authoring such salvation ourselves.

Deut 30:12–14	Paul's application in Rom 10:6–10
Do not say, "Who will ascend to heaven?"[5] (to bring down Torah, God's gift, 30:12)	Do not say, "Who will ascend to heaven?" (to bring down Christ, God's gift, 10:6)
Do not say, "Who will descend into the deep?" (to experience redemption again, crossing the "sea," 30:13)	Do not say, "Who will descend into the abyss?"[6] (to experience salvation again, raising Christ from the dead, 10:7)
The Word is near you (the Torah, 30:14)	The word is near you (the message of faith we now preach, 10:8)
It is in your mouth and in your heart (30:14; as Torah was to be recited continually [Deut 6:6–7])	It is in your mouth and in your heart: confess with the mouth Jesus is Lord, and believe with the heart that God raised him (10:9–10)

The point in Deuteronomy was that the law was not too difficult for Israel (Deut 30:11), provided it was written in the heart (Deut 5:29; 10:16; 30:6). Paul would agree (Rom 8:2–4), while expecting it to be fulfilled only on a widespread scale in the new covenant (Jer 31:33). The law

5. Jewish traditions viewed Moses as having ascended to heaven to receive the Torah (*Sipre Deut.* 49.2.1; cf. Bar 3:29 with 4:1), though in Scripture he ascended only Sinai.

6. In the most common Greek version of Scripture, one could speak of the depths of the sea as an "abyss" (e.g., Job 28:14; 38:16, 30; Ps 33:7; Sir 24:29; Man 3), even in contrast to heaven, as here (Ps 107:26; perhaps also Gen 7:11; 8:2; Deut 33:13; Ps 135:6; Sir 1:3; 16:18; 24:5). Most relevant for Paul's usage here are texts about God bringing his people through the *abyssos* of the sea in the exodus (the point of Deut 30): Ps 106:9, where God "saved" them (106:8–10) despite their rebellion (106:7); and Isa 51:10, emphasizing God's "righteousness" and "salvation" (Isa 51:8); and others (Ps 77:16; Isa 63:13; Wis 10:19); and possibly a new exodus in Isa 44:27. Shifting terms might allow Paul to play on the image's associations with death (Ezek 31:15). Philo and others felt free to adapt this passage's language (Tobin 2004: 344–45), and a later targum speaks of "abyss" here.

was not far from them, nor did they have to work to bring it near (Deut 30:12–13); it was a gift. By analogy with God's earlier savific activity, Paul insists that righteousness is also a gift now. The word was near Israel, and that was why they could carry it out (Deut 30:14)—provided they welcomed its nearness, written in the heart (cf. Pss 37:31; 40:8; 119:80, 112; Isa 51:7). Just as God prefaced the Ten Commandments with a reminder of redemption (Exod 20:2), so now salvation from sin was by grace through faith, expressed by right-doing. God's way of saving through the newer historical salvation event in Christ is analogous to the way he saved through the law:[7] the divine word (the gospel) also involves heart and mouth, though not just by reciting for memory. The heart trusts what God has done for salvation, and the mouth acknowledges Christ as Lord (embracing all the behavioral consequences of this new master).[8] The way of righteousness in 10:5–10 (climaxing in righteousness and salvation) is thus why Jews had no salvific advantage over Gentiles if both heard the message (9:30–31).

Response of Israel and the Gentiles (10:11–21)

Paul has argued that the law does not give Jewish people an unfair advantage over Gentiles with respect to God's righteousness (9:30—10:10). Now Paul makes explicit from Scripture this equality of opportunity (10:11–13). He will afterward show from Scripture that the "message of faith" (10:8) is in fact widely available, but has not been accepted by Israel, a tragic pattern that Scripture predisposes us to accept (10:14–21).

Recalling the believing heart for righteousness in 10:10, Paul shows from a text that he has recently quoted (in 9:33) that whoever trusts in God will not be shamed (in the day of judgment; 10:11). Following the ancient Jewish exegetical principle of linking texts based on a common key word, Paul shockingly uses "all" as the key word (though "not ashamed"

---

7. The parallel between Christ and law here makes sense in view of the early Christian association of Jesus with wisdom (e.g., 1 Cor 8:6; Col 1:15–17; later, John 1:1–18); wisdom was often associated with Torah (Sir 24:23; 34:8; 39:1; Bar 3:29—4:1; 4 Macc 1:16–17; *Sipre Deut.* 37.1.3; cf. further Epp 1975: 133–36). As Paul presumably knew, Bar 3:29–30 in fact applies this very Deuteronomy passage to wisdom/law.

8. Confession from the heart of Christ as the risen Lord thus contrasts with claiming one's own merit in one's heart, as in Deut 9:4, alluded to in Rom 10:6. The language of "confession" as "Lord" by itself would probably connote deity, a connotation confirmed by 10:13.

and "salvation" are also synonymous in the day of judgment): "Whoever calls on the [divine] Lord's name will be saved" (10:13; Joel 2:32). By "all" or "whoever" (*pas*) in both verses, Paul argues that the same Lord (Jesus, 10:9–10) is over all, both Jew and Gentile, who call on him (10:12). (This is also how he used "no distinction" in 3:22; cf. Col 3:11; Acts 15:9.)

In 10:14–17 Paul recognizes that to call on Jesus presupposed access to the gospel message (the "word of faith," 10:8). Paul develops another rhetorical chain in 10:14–15,[9] concluding with a confirmation in 10:15 from Isa 52:7, which refers to the "good news" of "salvation" and God's reign, when God graciously restores his people.[10]

Thus access to the gospel message is needed for salvation; yet Israel's problem, Paul now argues, is not ignorance, but disobedience (10:16, 18–21). Having quoted Isa 52:7, Paul now skips just a little ahead in the same context (as even synagogue readers were allowed to do). From the beginning of a passage about the suffering servant, Paul reminds his audience that Israel itself did not embrace this good news about their restoration (Isa 53:1). This passage belongs to a section (52:13—53:12) that early Christians regularly applied to Jesus's mission (see comment on Rom 4:24–25). Salvific faith is available through hearing the "report" about Christ (10:17), but Scripture warned that Israel would reject this very report about Christ (10:16). Far from Jewish unbelief posing a credibility problem for Paul's Jewish message, it simply fulfilled what the prophets had predicted.

Paul demonstrates Israel's moral accountability (i.e., they are guilty of rejection, not just less culpable ignorance) in 10:18–21. The interlocutor insists in 10:18–19 that perhaps Israel has never heard (hence should not be held so accountable), repeating the objection in different words so that Paul can respond with two different arguments from Scripture. The first, in 10:18, cites Ps 19:4, which might allude back to the testimony of creation available to even Gentiles in Rom 1:19–20.[11] Or perhaps Paul appeals to the biblical revelation about Christ; the context in Psalm 19 seems to link the message about God pervasive in creation (19:1–6)

9. See Anderson 1999: 237; idem 2000: 57–58; and comment on 5:3–4.

10. The runners' feet probably were mostly exposed (hence would have scrapes and mud from their mission), and other ancient sources comment on the beauty of feet. The idea here, however, is probably a metonymy (cf. *Rhet. Her.* 4.32.43), hence a way of praising the message they bring.

11. Cf. e.g., Ps.-Heraclitus *Ep.* 4; *3 En.* 46:3; and comment at 1:19–20.

with God's word in the Torah (19:7–11).[12] Alternatively, Paul may make a simple analogy about the gospel message becoming pervasive just as creation's testimony is (Rom 15:18–19; cf. Col 1:23).[13]

More intelligible are the texts Paul cites for Israel's disobedience in 10:19–21, each of which Paul applies to God welcoming outsiders in relation to Israel's disobedience. In 10:19 Paul quotes Deut 32:21, where Israel made God jealous with idols, so God will make them jealous by a nation that lacked his law.[14] This concept becomes foundational for Paul's eschatological strategy: he believes that his successful Gentile mission will provoke Israel's jealousy, to motivate them to conversion (11:11, 14). Paul then (in 10:20–21) cites Isa 65:1–2, where a nation not seeking God (like the Gentiles of Rom 9:30) found him, an outcome that he contrasts with Israel who rebelled.[15] In Isaiah 65 the second verse may be parallel to the first, so that even 65:1 may originally refer to Israel rather than Gentiles (cf. Rom 9:25–26). Nevertheless, Isaiah does include indications of Gentile adherents being incorporated into Israel (Isa 56:3–8), even nations welcomed as God's people (Isa 19:24–25). Paul's exegesis in this section invites the objection that perhaps God has rejected Israel, an objection that he hastens to refute in 11:1–32.

12. Johnson 2001: 174, thinks it refers to reading of Scripture with messianic significance in the synagogues, not Christian proclamation (a task Paul still strove to complete, 15:20–24).

13. One could speak hyperbolically of a message spread "throughout the world," not intending that every individual has heard (Pliny *Ep.* 6.10.3). Paul could thus intend "representative preaching" to all regions (Munck 1967: 98; Morris 1988: 393; Sanders 1993: 107).

14. Hays (1989: 83) notes that Paul may thus implicitly echo Israel's lack of faith in Deut 32:20 LXX.

15. By contrast, elsewhere in Romans Paul speaks of Gentiles' *obedience* (1:5; 15:18; 16:25). For Paul's use of Isaiah's restoration theme, see further Wagner 2002: 29–33. Because another part of Isa 65:1 speaks of "calling on the Lord's name," Paul possibly connected it implicitly with Joel 2:32 cited in Rom 10:13, at least in his own mind (cf. Grieb 2002: 104).

ROMANS 11

ISRAEL'S ROLE AND SALVATION (9:1—11:36), *cont.*

A Remnant (11:1–10)

Paul has spent much of Romans establishing that God welcomes Gentile believers as equal members alongside Jewish believers without them having to observe the law in the traditional Jewish way. Here, however, he begins to urge Gentile believers (11:13) more explicitly to respect the Jewish people; he will soon warn them not to despise Jewish customs for which Gentiles in Rome often despised them (ch. 14).

While God's covenant with Israel did not save individual Jewish persons who did not maintain the covenant (ultimately through obeying the prophet-king God had provided),[1] it did guarantee a special favor toward this people in other respects (cf. 3:2; 9:4–5). Moreover, God retained a plan for the Jewish people as a whole. (Indeed, various Gentile observers through history have viewed the survival of the Jewish people as a clear mark of divine providence.)

If Israel has rebelled against their own salvation (10:3, 16–21), has God therefore rejected them (11:1)?[2] Paul is adamant that God has not; his own faith as a Jewish believer is itself a testimony that God has left a remnant (11:1).[3] God foreknew both the present disobedience and the

---

1. Most Jews would have agreed with this premise based on Scripture; yet many also held that Israel as a whole would be saved, minus a minority of apostates (see comment on Rom 11:26).

2. The verb for "casting off" in 11:1–2 applies to Israel in the common Greek translation (e.g., Judg 6:13; Pss 44:9, 23; 60:1, 10; 74:1; 108:11), including with the title of "God's people" as here (1 Sam 12:22; Ps 94:14; on connections with the latter's context, see Hays 1989: 69–70). By exile, he did (temporarily) cast them off (2 Kgs 17:20; 21:14; 23:27; Jer 7:29; Hos 4:6; 9:17).

3. After treating Israel's failure to embrace God's way of righteousness (9:30—10:21), Paul returns to the "remnant" theme raised in 9:27–29 (Tobin 2004: 340; Anderson 1999: 235). For views concerning the biblical "remnant," see e.g., Davies 1980: 77–79;

future when he chose Israel (11:2). Scripture confirmed that there was a remnant even in Elijah's day,[4] one of the worst periods of national apostasy (11:2-4). Likewise, there certainly remained a remnant in Paul's day (11:5).

Paul insists that the remnant is chosen by grace (11:5), not by works (11:6). Paul is building on his earlier argument: the "choice" (*eklogē*) refers back to 9:11 (where Jacob was the remnant; cf. believers in 8:33); the contrast between grace (cf. 3:24; 4:16) and works reflects the earlier contrast between faith (dependence on God) and works (3:27-28; 9:32), as well as the irrelevance of works to chosenness (9:11). He might also evoke his contrast between grace and works in 4:4. Far from merely asserting a claim based on his prior argument, however, Paul quickly cites biblical support.

How do we know that Israelites can serve God only by his generosity and not by their own works? Paul indicates that apart from those God chose, the rest were "hardened" (11:7)—just like Pharaoh the opponent of Moses (9:17-18)! Then Paul cites texts referring not to the remnant, as in 11:2-3, but instead proving that at some strategic times in Israel's history many or most Israelites were hardened (11:8-10). In 11:8, Paul covers both law and prophets by conflating texts with similar warnings: in Isa 29:10 God gave them the "spirit of stupor," closing their eyes (blinding them to the prophetic message); in Deut 29:4 God had not given them eyes to see nor ears to hear, "to this day." Isaiah's context involves judgment, God handing people over to the blindness they have chosen (Isa 29:9-14); Deuteronomy's context involves failure to discern despite God's many miraculous acts of grace (Deut 29:2-8). Paul is probably less concerned with the specific texts he has blended than the typical prophetic theme they represent, revealing the obduracy of God's people (cf. Isa 6:10; 42:18-19; Jer 5:21; Ezek 12:2), though this was a human and not specifically Israelite problem.

In 11:9-10 Paul follows the common Greek version of Ps 69:22-23 (except that he may borrow *thēra*, "trap," from Ps 34:8, which also speaks of a *pagis*, "snare"). Like some other early Christian writers, Paul applies Psalm 69 to Jesus (Rom 15:3; cf. Matt 27:34; John 2:17; 19:28), so he pre-

---

Hasel 1980.

4. 1 Kgs 19:18. Perhaps relevant to Paul's context (Rom 10:2, 19; 11:11, 14), Elijah's own "zeal" (1 Kgs 19:10) was often emphasized (1 Macc 1:58; *Mek. Pisha* 1.9), but some later resented his "disloyal" condemnation of Israel (*Mek. Pisha* 1.94-100).

sumably applies this passage to those who oppose him, inviting judgment on them. Because their eyes are blinded (11:10), Paul could link this text with his previous citation (in 11:8): it was not only Gentiles who were "darkened" (1:21), but those who fancied themselves guides to the blind and lights to those in darkness (2:19)![5] Their "table" becoming a "stumbling block" (11:9) might anticipate the danger of stumbling over food customs in 14:13.

God's Purposes for Jews and Gentiles (11:11–24)

No one can boast; Jew and Gentile alike fulfill roles in God's plan, each supporting the other. Clearly Israel "stumbled" (11:11), as Paul has shown in biblical references to stumbling blocks (11:9; also 9:33)—ancient Jewish sources often used "stumbling" as a figure for apostasy.[6] But Paul does not believe that they have "stumbled" in order that (for the divine purpose that) they should "fall" permanently; rather, God's purpose is to let salvation come to Gentiles, in turn provoking Israel to repentance (11:11). That way, representatives from all peoples, Jewish and Gentile, could have the opportunity for salvation (11:30–33). Possibly Paul is thinking of how God's promises to Israel would establish a new world once Israel fully turned to him (e.g., Hos 14:1–7; Jer 29:12–14);[7] only if that general repentance were delayed could Gentiles have the opportunity to turn in large numbers as well.

Paul believes that the Gentile mission is part of God's eschatological plan to provoke Israel to jealousy, hence repentance (11:11, 14),[8] as he has already argued scripturally (10:19). He believes that his mission to

---

5. Against most translations, though, *dia pantos* in 11:10 should be rendered "continually" (as elsewhere in the NT, and with most current commentators) rather than "forever." It does not exclude Israel's future.

6. E.g., Ezek 14:3–7; Sir 9:5; other sources cited at 14:4. Paul normally uses *skandalizō*, *ptaiō*, and *piptō* interchangeably in this context (cf. 11:22; 14:4), despite 11:11 (where *ptaiō* is used to connect with *paraptōma* in 11:11–12).

7. In early Jewish sources, the timing of the kingdom was sometimes (though not always) held to be contingent on Israel's repentance (*Jub.* 23:26–27; *Sipre Deut.* 43.16.3; see further Talbert 2002: 260–61; discussion of later rabbinic material in Moore 1971: 2:350–51).

8. Speakers could deliberately provoke hearers to jealousy of rivals to spur greater action (*Rhet. Alex.* 36, 1445a.12; Polybius 6.39.8).

Gentiles plays a role in this provocation (11:13–14).[9] Perhaps he alludes to the line of Jewish eschatological expectation in which Gentiles would come to obey Israel's God and king;[10] the Christian success at converting Gentiles would show the rest of Israel that God's eschatological blessing was with Jesus's movement.[11]

Israel's "transgression" (11:11–12) evokes that of the Gentile world in Adam (5:15–20), but as Paul's discussion of Adam featured reversal and restoration, so does his discussion of Israel. In 11:12 Paul raises a point that he will return to in 11:15, after an important parenthetical digression in 11:13–14 (mentioned above). As Christ's death produced reconciliation, so did Israel's loss (5:10; 11:15). But just as Christ's risen life will produce even greater benefits than his death (5:9; 8:32), so also Israel's restoration will produce greater blessings than their failure (11:12).[12] Ultimately it would bring about even the promised time of the resurrection of the righteous (11:15; cf. 8:11), because this would be the consummation of God's plan (cf. Acts 3:19–21). Although Israel may not have cooperated with the plan deliberately, Israel's role in God's plan thus mirrors on a corporate level God's activity for humanity in Christ.[13] The turning of the requisite portion of Israel to Jesus (versus the current smaller remnant) is

9. Paul's apostleship to Gentiles may echo Jeremiah as a prophet to the nations (Jer 1:5; a passage Paul elsewhere echoes concerning his call, Gal 1:15).

10. Prophets envisioned Gentile repentance (e.g., Isa 19:19–25; Zech 2:11), subjugation (Isa 60:12; Zeph 2:11), or destruction (Joel 3:19; Zeph 2:9–15); these diverse strands also appear in early Jewish eschatology (Donaldson 1997b: 52–74). Paul is apparently able to piece together an end-time scenario only in Christological retrospect. This may reverse some conventional expectations of Israel's end-time repentance and restoration leading to an ingathering of Gentiles (Allison 1985: 23–30; Sanders 1985: 93), though Jewish sources lacked consensus as to whether these Gentiles were proselytes or merely righteous (Donaldson 1990).

11. See this argument in Nanos 1996: 249–50. The collection (15:26–27), perhaps evoking the eschatological offering of nations (Isa 60:5–16), may offer Jerusalem one strategic expression of that success (Donaldson 1997b: 252).

12. Paul reinforces the point rhetorically in 11:12 by key nouns ending in *-tōma, -tēma,* and *-ōma,* as well as four nouns beginning with *p* (*paraptōma, ploutos* [twice], and *plērōma*).

13. Cf. also God not "sparing" Jesus (8:32) or Jewish branches (11:21). The parallel is functional and limited: in context, Israel's loss made reconciliation available for Gentiles (the contextual sense of "the world" here), whereas Christ cooperated in his vicarious sacrifice.

described as "fullness" (*plērōma*, 11:12), just as the conversion of the full measure of Gentiles is in 11:25.[14]

One could be confident of God's benevolent plan for Israel's future based on its heritage (11:16). Offering the first fruits consecrated the entire batch of dough as acceptable; while "first fruits" could refer to first converts (1 Cor 16:15), here it probably refers to the patriarchs, as in the next illustration. Just as it was a commonplace that a tree was known by its fruit (cf. 7:4; Matt 7:17–18; 12:33; Luke 6:43–44; Jas 3:12), branches would be as holy as the root, which for a Jewish audience would typically point to the patriarchs.[15] Gentiles could be grafted into the tree (11:17), but Jewish believers fit most naturally (11:18, 24), and Paul expects a large-scale turning of Jewish people to faith in Christ (11:23–27).

In 11:17 Paul affirms that Gentile believers are not just second-class (though saved) adherents, as synagogues considered God-fearing, righteous Gentiles. (Some of Paul's detractors in Jerusalem may have shared this synagogue view; cf. the compromise position in Acts 15:20.) Rather, they are spiritual proselytes, grafted into Israel as full members.[16] Thus, they are spiritual children of Abraham (4:12, 16) and spiritually circumcised (2:28–29). Such a status did not, however, give them the right to look down on Jews who had broken the covenant by rejecting the current prophetic message and ruler God appointed for them (11:18). Like the Qumran sectarians,[17] Paul and apostolic Christianity viewed themselves as truly fulfilling God's end-time purposes, and the rest of Israel as apostate.

But to look down on Jewish people as a whole was to despise the very people into which one had been grafted, people who fit that heritage most naturally if they embraced Christ (11:18, 23–24). Earlier Paul warned against "boasting," envisioning Jewish boasting in possession and fulfillment of the law (2:17, 23; cf. 3:27; 4:2); here, however, Paul recognizes that Gentile Christians could be guilty of the same offense, boasting against

14. "Fullness" here and in 11:25 probably indicates the full measure in contrast to the "remnant" (or perhaps "first fruits"; cf. the "fullness" of the land in Jer 8:16; 47:2; Ezek 12:19; 19:7); cf. the idea in Rev 6:11.

15. E.g., *1 En.* 93:5–8; *Pesiq. Rab Kah.* 15:5; other sources in Moo 1996: 699. That 15:12 employs the same term for "root" is probably coincidental, since the root there involves only David's lineage (and the "branch" of the quotation's context is messianic).

16. Donaldson 1993; idem 1997a: 81–82; idem 1997b: 230–47; also Hays 2005: 5.

17. See e.g., 1QS 8.9–10, 9.6; CD 3.12–19; 1QM 3.13.

Jewish members (11:18).[18] (The Gentile boast in 11:19 might be a sort of predestinarian parallel to the exaggerated Jewish boast in 2:17–20.) The key issue was faith, which was why Gentiles as well as Jews could qualify (11:20, 23). Gentile anti-Judaism was common (including Roman contempt for circumcision and foreign customs in Rome), and Paul may seek to head off its presence among Gentiles in the church (perhaps especially threatening since churches formed without most of their Jewish element between 49 and 54 CE).[19]

God's "kindness" (11:22) recalls his patient mercy bringing some to repentance (2:4), while his "severity" involves cutting off unbelieving branches (hence those unfaithful to the covenant). Essentially, Paul compares believing Gentile branches to vessels of mercy like Moses, and unbelieving Jewish branches to objects of wrath like Pharaoh (9:15–18, 22–23). The issue, however, is faith (faithfulness to the covenant, depending on God) rather than ethnicity, as Paul will make clear in 11:23–24. When he describes Israel as "natural" branches (11:21, 24; cf. 2:27) he is not demeaning such connections, though they matter less than spiritual connections (2:29). God also designed what accords with "nature" (1:26–27; 2:14).[20]

Perhaps thinking of cultural heritage, Paul contends that Jewish believers fit more naturally into the covenant than Gentile believers do (11:23–24). Plant images for Israel (e.g., Jer 24:6; *Jub.* 36:6) or the remnant (e.g., 1QS 8.5) were common,[21] including as an olive tree (Jer 11:16, Hos 14:6).[22] As current commentators note, sources from Paul's day confirm that branches from wild olive trees could be grafted into cultivated trees; in the same way, foreigners to Israel's covenant could become part

18. *Katakauchaomai* means "boast against," but hearers of the letter in Greek would not mistake the connection with *kauchaomai* earlier in the letter. In Pauline theology, "boasting" (possible in Jewish practice, Gal 6:13–14; Phil 3:3) is in no way a particularly Jewish offense (1 Cor 1:29–31; 3:21; 4:7; 2 Cor 11:12). Although Paul employs harsher terms for arrogance and boasting in Rom 1:30, the hearer might also recall these.

19. The temptation was present; as Grieb notes (Grieb 2002: 108), Marcion severed Christian beliefs completely from Judaism in Rome less than a century later.

20. Less flattering is Paul's language of connections according to the "flesh" (2:28; 4:1; 9:3; 11:14; esp. 9:8), but this, too, need not be negative (1:3; 9:5; 15:27).

21. See also Tiller 1997.

22. A synagogue in Rome was apparently called the olive tree (though Leon 1960: 146–47 thinks the reason obscure); on tree symbolism generally, see Goodenough 1953–68: 7:87–134.

of God's covenant, while unfaithful Jews could be severed from it.[23] But Jewish branches with faith could be grafted in more naturally than foreign branches, and Gentile believers who depended on their own ethnicity rather than on God's kindness would also be severed.[24]

Fulfilling the Promise to Israel (11:25–32)

After arguing that Jewish believers fit in the covenant more readily than Gentile believers do, Paul articulates his expectation that the Jewish people as a whole will someday embrace Jesus as their deliverer, consummating his covenant with them (11:25–27). Paul's use of "mystery" (11:25) fits one common Jewish use of the term, for end-time secrets revealed to God's prophets (16:25–26; Dan 2:28–30).[25] This end-time mystery that Paul reveals is that God had allowed Israel's hardness for a time just to allow a massive influx of Gentiles into the covenant, but God would ultimately remove the hardness and restore Israel to faith (11:25–26; cf. 11:11–12).

Once the fullness of the Gentiles has come in, "all Israel" (Israel as a whole) will be saved. Some have argued that "Israel" here refers to the "fullness of the Gentiles," i.e., the completed Gentile church from among all nations. But while Paul, like other early Christian writers, certainly regards all believers as part of Israel's heritage (and has indicated as much in the grafting image in 11:17), he has been consistently contrasting "Israel" with Gentiles in the context (9:27, 31; 10:19, 21; 11:2, 7; and most importantly in 11:25). The context also suggests that God will remove Israel's hardness when the full measure of Gentile believers (probably representatives from among the nations, as in Matt 24:14; Rev 5:9; cf. Rom 15:19) has come in (the likeliest sense of *achri*, "until," in 11:25).

23. See here Baxter and Ziesler 1985; on grafting generally, see e.g., Virgil *Georgics* 2.73–82 (olives); Pliny *Nat.* 15.15.49; 15.17.57; 17.24.101–14; 17.26.118–22; *m. Shevi'it* 2:6; *Sipra Qed.* par. 3.202.1.5.

24. Expressions regarding "nature" were applied in a variety of ways in antiquity; use in the moral sphere (as in 1:26–27; Cicero *Inv.* 2.53.161; Musonius Rufus 17, p. 108.7) is predicated on the larger physical world, but not all physical claims need be intended morally (e.g., Cicero *Tusc.* 1.14.31; Aelian *Nat. an.* 11.26). Nevertheless, that Paul has employed such language earlier in such strong terms adds rhetorical shock value here, forcefully warning Gentiles against arrogance.

25. For *1 En.*, see Nock 1964: 30; Gibbard 1956: 109; Caragounis 1977: 126; for the Qumran scrolls, e.g., Brown 1958–59; idem 1968; Ramirez 1976.

Paul thus shared the expectation of biblical prophets and his contemporaries that his people would ultimately turn to God, inaugurating the eschatological consummation.[26] As commentators regularly point out, Jewish sources can speak of "all Israel," or "Israel as a whole," being saved without assuming that this applies to every individual Jewish person.[27] Nor did expectations of God delivering his people from the nations at the end need to involve Jewish people from earlier generations who had died. Given Paul's insistent emphasis (including arguments from the OT) in chapters 1–10 that salvation is only through faith in Christ, Paul can hardly mean that God would provide Jewish people spiritual salvation through a different means at the end, as some have argued.[28] But does Paul refer here only to deliverance from the oppression of the nations, rather than spiritual salvation? The language in 11:26–27 could be so construed if it were isolated, but not in this context. Aside from Paul's usage of the verb *sōzō* ("save") in every other usage in Romans (5:9–10; 8:24; 10:9, 13), including with respect to Israel or Jewish persons in particular (9:27; 11:14), Paul expects a reversal of Israel's hardening against Christ at this time.

This discussion leaves us with two primary options.[29] First, when Jesus as the deliverer returns, Israel as a whole, on learning of his identity, will believe in him as their king truly appointed by God.[30] The language could certainly be so construed: Paul's citation sounds like Jesus's return would precipitate their forgiveness (11:26–27). Although the Hebrew version of Isa 59:20–21, which Paul here adapts, speaks of the redeemer coming *to* Zion after Israel turns from transgression, Paul's wording (probably based on blending the Greek version of the passage with Ps 14:7)[31] seems to suggest the opposite.

---

26. See discussion above; cf. Acts 3:19–21.

27. *m. Sanh.* 10:1. Many would in fact be excluded (e.g., *t. Sanh.* 13:9–10).

28. For challenges to the popular, though minority, two-covenant view, see Das 2003: 96–106; Donaldson 1997b: 231–34.

29. Among others; and even here I am summarizing only briefly arguments in a discussion that includes far more details and arguments than I have space to address.

30. For a short window of end-time opportunity for repentance, see e.g., *1 En.* 50:2–5. Justin *Dial.* 28 rejects this option for Israel.

31. In Greek, the deliverer will come "because of" Zion, and (as Paul has it) turn away ungodliness from Jacob. From Ps 14:7 Paul has Israel's "salvation" come "out of Zion."

Nevertheless, context again raises a likely problem with this approach. Paul expects the obedience of a number of Gentiles from all nations to the God of Israel to provoke Israel to jealousy, hence to turn to Jesus, bringing about the promised restoration (11:11–15). This observation suggests Paul's expectation of the second option: the completion of the Gentile mission in 11:25 would in turn lead to the Jewish people trusting in Christ, precipitating his return (reading *houtōs* in 11:26 as "in this way," "by this means"). On this reading, perhaps Paul uses Isa 59:20–21 to refer to a corporate deliverance and covenant renewal immediately following the turning (or even simply to confirm God's plan to forgive Israel). In any case, the final line of Paul's quotation in 11:27 is not from Isa 59:21, which says, "This is my covenant with them," but lacks "when I take away their sins." Here Paul may interpretively blend an allusion to the Greek version of some texts using this language in the context of end-time restoration (Isa 27:9 or Ezek 36:26).[32]

In 11:28 Paul contrasts two ways of looking at his people: the current demands of the promised good news (which Israel as a whole has not embraced), and the benefits of their heritage. From the first approach, they remain God's "enemies" (like all humanity not in Christ, 5:10; 8:7) "on account of you" (which contextually means, "so that in God's providence you Gentiles have opportunity to enter God's covenant," 11:11, 19, 25). From the second approach, they remain objects of God's love[33] "on account of the patriarchs" (11:28), one of their ancestral blessings (9:5), as Scripture declared (Deut 4:37; 7:7–8; 10:15; cf. Mal 1:2 in Rom 9:13). While some Jewish teachers later associated God's favor on Israel with the patriarchs' "merits," Paul's interest is not ancestral works (cf. 4:2; 9:11) but simply God's grace. While this favor did not save individual Jewish persons, it guaranteed that God would not abandon his plan for Israel and that he would turn the Jewish people to himself in the planned time (11:25–27). Thus, in 11:29 God, who knows the future (cf. 8:29; 11:2), will not regret his "gifts" and "calling" to the Jewish people as a whole, though Gentile believers (individually) participate in these blessings as well.[34]

32. Paul might also think of another "covenant" passage, the "new covenant" (Jer 31:31–34), when God would forgive Israel's sins (Jer 31:34).

33. Again like humanity (5:8), but with a special privilege.

34. For "gifts," see 1:11; 12:6 (esp. for salvation, 5:15–16; 6:23); "calling" includes not only Jewish people (9:7) but all who believe (1:6–7; 8:28–30; 9:24–26). Perhaps Israel's "gifts" include those in 9:4–5.

Paul concludes this section regarding God's plan for the Jewish people as well as Gentile believers in 11:30–32. That Gentiles and Israel switched places of disobedience may allude back to Hos 1:10 and 2:23 in Rom 9:25–26; "mercy" alludes to 9:15–23; Israel's "disobedience" suggests Isa 65:2 in Rom 10:21 (though cf. more generally 2:8). God locked up all under disobedience so that all might be objects of his mercy (cf. similarly Gal 3:22–23), each in their own time. Jewish disobedience afforded opportunity for Gentiles to join the covenant without God being seen as unfaithful to Israel, and someday, Paul says, Gentile obedience will also provoke Israel's repentance.[35] In this way, God will have saved and formed a covenant people comprised of both Jew and Gentile.

Praising God's Wisdom in History (11:33–36)

Paul has offered briefer doxologies in 1:25 and (near this section's beginning) 9:5, but here his treatment of God's plan in history yields to praising God's great wisdom in designing history in such a way. This doxology offers a rhetorically rousing conclusion to the section. As often in Romans, Paul echoes the language of Scripture (frequently Isaiah) that God's ways are beyond human ways (Isa 55:8). In 11:34 Paul cites (making slightly more concise) the Greek version of Isa 40:13: "Who has known the Lord's mind, and who has become his counselor that one should counsel him?"[36] In 11:35 the closest echo is of God's reproof about divine ways to Job, which can be translated: "Who has given something to me, so that I need to repay them?" (Job 41:11). In context, the Job text involves God's sovereignty over creation; the Isaiah texts involve his sovereignty in history.

Paul has often spoke of God's "riches" (2:4; 9:23; 10:12; cf. 11:12), but the language is particularly appropriate for wisdom and knowledge (cf. Col 2:2–3; Prov 8:10; 16:16; 20:15; Isa 33:6). Other Jewish people also recognized that one could not successfully search the depths of God's mind (Jdt 8:14; cf. 1 Cor 2:10–11); or that God was inscrutable (*anexichniastos*, Job 5:9; 9:10; 34:34). The climax of Paul's recitation of God's sovereignty is that all things are "from," "through," and "to" or "for" him (cf. similarly

---

35. Paul employs here carefully crafted rhetorical antithesis. As many note (e.g., Hunter 1966: 54), Paul's language here involves peoples, not the salvation of all individuals.

36. Others also compare similar biblical questions in Job 15:8; Jer 23:18. Cf. analogous early Jewish language in e.g., Wis 9:13–14; 1QS 11.18–19; *2 Bar.* 75:2–4. For Jewish doxologies, see e.g., Aune 2003: 140–41.

1 Cor 8:6). Philosophers tried to distinguish the use of these terms for various sorts of causes.[37] Paul is saying something like that God authored all things, is the necessary agency through which they occur, and in the end all these things will fulfill his purposes. Rather than yielding to the temptation to doubt why only a minority of his people have responded to the gospel, Paul expresses full confidence that history will unfold according to God's perfect purposes. Thus, God has everything under control, as his servants will recognize fully when it is complete.

Fusing the Horizons: Boasting against Other Branches

By "remnant" Paul meant less than Israel as a whole; he would have been shocked and distressed to discover that in much of subsequent history the remnant represented an even smaller proportion of his people than in his own day. For Paul, the massive Gentile church was intended at least in part to provoke Israel's repentance (11:11–12). Paul's own ministry to Gentiles was to push forward this phase of God's plan that would precede the turning of his own people (11:13–14; cf. Matt 24:14; Luke 21:24; 2 Pet 3:9), yet it was the reverse that occurred. This massive Gentile church soon forgot Paul's warnings against being arrogant against the people of their own spiritual heritage (11:18). Inverting an earlier Jewish church's sense of spiritual superiority over Gentiles, they adopted a displacement theology (the Gentile church replacing Israel), and instead of provoking jealousy in Israel, provoked contempt. Centuries of anti–Semitism in the name of Christianity, all the while claiming to obey Israel's God and king, polarized two "religions" and reduced the "remnant." Paul, who saw himself as converting Gentiles to the true faith of Israel (proselytes without ethnic constraints), would have been horrified at the Gentile church despising its own roots and religious siblings. He would undoubtedly have been pleased, however, that in more recent times barriers have begun to break down, with interfaith dialogue and the growth of the Messianic Jewish movement.

Paul moves from the broad historical perspectives of chapter 11 to interpersonal relationships in chapter 12. Because he was concerned with applying this knowledge, we may also consider how some of his fundamental principles apply in other sorts of settings. In addition to his concern for God's

37. Cf. discussion in Grant 2001: 72 (citing the later Marcus Aurelius *Med.* 4.23); Sterling 1997; Moo 1996: 743; Jewett 2007: 721.

faithfulness expressed in his covenant with Israel, Paul's concern about arrogance against Jewish branches (11:18) also offers relevant advice for any peoples who treat God's favor as a permanent ethnic possession. Historically, Christianity itself shifted from especially north Africa and Anatolia to Europe and east Africa, and later elsewhere. In the past century its center has shifted from the West to the Global South. Paul's concern is relevant even more generally to interactions between believers and nonbelievers: those who were saved by grace dare not look down on others, but should welcome them graciously as they have been welcomed.

ROMANS 12

LIVING THE CHRISTIAN LIFE (12:1—15:13)

As in some other letters (Gal 5-6; Col 3-4), Paul addresses specific, practical questions in the church more directly after laying the theological groundwork that demands such behavior (thus his "therefore" in 12:1). If much of Paul's letter addresses the means of righteousness, 12:1—15:13 exemplifies what righteousness should look like in relationships. In the specific context of Israel (chs. 9-11), the issue of Jewish-Gentile relationships in Christ's body remains a central concern (especially obvious in 14:1—15:13). Teaching about serving one another (12:9-21) and the heart of the law as love for one another (13:8-10) provides the practical principles that connect Paul's emphasis on God's desire to form a people of both Jews and Gentiles (chs. 1-11, esp. 9-11) with the specific tensions the Roman congregations are facing (14:1—15:7).

Consider How to Serve One Another (12:1-8)

Paul follows his praise of God's wisdom (11:33-36) with a summons to his audience to worship, wherein they are living sacrifices. The appeal on the basis of God's "compassion"[1] in 12:1 evokes what Paul has just said about his mercy for Jews and Gentiles alike (11:30-32); both alike should respond with worship (12:1; 15:9-11) as one body (12:4-5). Because of its key function in applying Paul's argument in chapters 9-11, plus the allusions to these verses at the strategic juncture of 15:15-16, I must grant 12:1-3 more space than I allot to many passages.

Paul exhorts believers to present their bodies as living sacrifices (12:1).[2] Paul has already urged believers to "present" their bodies as slaves

---

1. Speakers and authors often swore or urged hearers "by" a deity (cf. *deēsis* in Rowe 1997: 139; e.g., Isaeus *Menecles* 47).

2. On spiritual sacrifices, see e.g., Pss 50:14, 16, 23; 51:16-17, 19; 69:30-31; Hos 6:6;

to God, obedience and righteousness (6:13, 16, 19). He has also warned against self-centered use of the body, without the rule of a mind enabled by the Spirit (1:24; 6:6, 12; 7:24; 8:13). Now he will show that believers can choose in their minds to present their bodies for the service of a greater "body," the body of Christ with whom they have been united (12:4–5).[3] When believers offer themselves as sacrifices, they imitate Jesus, whose death Paul has already presented as a bloody sacrifice (3:25; 5:9; 8:3). Nevertheless, believers offer themselves not only by sometimes being martyred (cf. 8:36), but while alive ("living").[4]

Believers offer up their bodies as a sacrifice described by three adjectives: "living," "holy," and "acceptable" or "pleasing." Old Testament sacrifices, involving inanimate things or slain animals, were not described as living. Paul adapts the OT image of sacrifice in a new direction as believers embrace Christ's death even while living (6:2–11; Gal 2:20; Col 2:20—3:5), in accord with Jesus's own teaching (Mark 8:34; Luke 9:23). Offerings could, however, be described as "holy" to God (e.g., Lev 6:17, 25; 7:1; 10:12), and when Israel served God their offerings were "acceptable" or "pleasing" to him (Ezra 6:10; Ps 20:3; Isa 56:7; Jer 6:20; Mal 3:4). Paul describes this worship (*latreia*; cf. 9:4; 1 Chron 28:13) as "rational" (*logikos*),[5] because it is with the mind that one chooses to present the body to God's service (see 12:2–3).

In 12:2 Paul indicates how the mind is instrumental in offering the body (12:1). The renewed mind here contrasts with the depraved mind

---

Mic 6:6–8; Sir 35:1–3; Wis 3:6; 1QS 3.4, 6–9, 11; 8.3; 9.4–5; 10.6; 4Q403 frg. 1, col. 1.39–40. Some Jews writing for Diaspora audiences accommodated Hellenistic philosophy by rejecting animal sacrifices (*Sib. Or.* 4.29–30; Philo *Good Person* 75). Nevertheless, the image of spiritual sacrifices was not itself inherently incompatible with literal ones (e.g., *Let. Aris.* 170, 172, 234). Some pagan thinkers felt that deities desired less or no sacrifice (Dio Chrysostom *Or.* 13.35; Lucian *Demon.* 11; Maximus of Tyre *Or.* 2.1–2; Porphyry *Marc.* 17.282–84; *Pyth. Sent.* 20); others mocked it altogether (e.g., Lucian *Sacr.*); a number rejected animal sacrifice (Philostratus *Vit. Apoll.* 1.1, 31–32; 4.11; 5.25; 8.7; idem *Ep. Apoll.* 27; Diogenes Laertius 8.1.22; Iamblichus *V.P.* 11.54; 18.85; 24.108; 28.150), though society as a whole continued these practices.

3. Cf. perhaps the divine mind that welcomes Jew and Gentile alike (11:34).

4. Paul himself ministers as a priest, offering the Gentiles (to whom he is sent) as his offering (15:16, also an "acceptable" one, albeit using a different term than in 12:1), but again without blood.

5. While it can mean "spiritual" in the sense of "nonliteral" (perhaps 1 Pet 2:2), the meaning in this context is clearly "rational" (cf. 12:2–3), its normal sense.

(1:28), the mind under the flesh (7:23, 25; 8:5–7).[6] "Renewing" the mind involves recognizing and affirming the "newness" already initiated in Christ (6:4; 7:6), which contrasts with the thinking of this "age" (*aiōn*; not merely "world," as in some translations).[7] One is "transformed" to be ready to be "conformed" to Jesus's image (8:29) by identifying not with this age but with believers' future hope.[8] Those who are in Christ have died with him to sin and will share his resurrection life (6:4–5; 8:11). They must thus view their identity in terms of their eternal destiny rather than how they are viewed by this age (6:11).

The renewed mind of 12:2 (related to the perspective of the Spirit in 8:5–7) enables believers to discern (*dokimazō*) God's will.[9] It does so by helping them to recognize what is, in Paul's words, "good, acceptable, and perfect" in God's sight.[10] That these three adjectives help define God's will, just as three adjectives (one of them the same, "acceptable") defined the sacrifice of 12:1, suggests that Paul is still addressing the same subject: God's will here involves how we devote our bodies to God's service.

Paul quickly becomes more specific about how this renewed mind guides believers' service to God: in 12:3 he elaborates how one should "think." Rather than boasting (cf. also 12:16), believers should recognize that God's gifts are acts of his generosity and not merit (cf. 1 Cor 4:7), and each should recognize his or her role as part of the larger body, in which

6. See also Keener 2008a: 226.

7. Various Jewish writers contrasted the present age with the future one (cf. e.g., *4 Ezra* 7:50, 113; 8:1; *2 Bar.* 15:8; *t. Ber.* 6:21; *Pe'ah* 1:2–3; *Sipre Num.* 115.5.7; *Sipre Deut.* 31.4.1; 307.3.2–3; Ferch 1977).

8. Paul's teaching here is consistent with 2 Cor 3:18, where those who view God's glory in Christ are internally "transformed" into his glorious image (in context, in contrast to Moses, who was transformed externally). Moses also provides the background for the verb in Mark 9:2; Matt 17:2 (see Moses 1996), though cf. also the more general concept of mental transformation (Seneca *Ep. Lucil.* 94.48).

9. Clearly this does not mean they will always know what God will do (1:10; 15:32), but they should often have a sense what *they* should do (cf. perhaps God's purposes in history, 11:34). In 2:18, a Jew who knows the law is supposed to be able to know "God's will" and "test" (*dokimazō*) or discern what is best; in 1:28, Gentiles who refused to "acknowledge" (*dokimazō*) God were delivered to an *adokimos* mind.

10. Good was a standard moral criterion (e.g., Musonius Rufus 1, p. 32.22); Stoics also spoke of cognitively discerning what is good (e.g., Epictetus *Disc.* 2.24.19; Arius Didymus *Epit.* 2.7.5b1, p. 12.13–15) or pleasing (Arius Didymus *Epit.* 5i, p. 32.25–30; cf. Wis 9:10); others spoke of thinking on what is good (cf. Phil 4:8; Iamblichus *Pyth. Life* 5.26).

each member has a role. God has distributed to each a measure of faith (Rom 12:3). This observation refers not to a given *amount* of faith but rather faith for a given *ministry* in the body (12:6–8).

In 12:4–5 members belong not only to Christ (cf. 8:9) but to one another, each making their own distinctive contributions (as gifts) to the body. When Paul speaks of believers as members of Christ's body, hence of one another (12:4–5),[11] he is continuing the line of thought introduced in 12:1–3. Believers' renewed minds discern God's will about how to devote their bodies to God's service by building up Christ's body in the various ways that God has made each one capable (12:6–8). Ancient intellectuals commonly used the image of the body for both the cosmos[12] and the state[13] to indicate a sort of organic unity. Whereas some used the image for the state to reinforce hierarchy, Paul uses it to emphasize the complementarity of all members, while also continuing the image's usual connotation of unity.[14]

As elsewhere (1 Cor 12:12–27; cf. Eph 4:4–13), Paul employs the image of the body's members to emphasize the diversity of ministries with which God has graced different believers (12:6–8). Paul has just spoken of God providing gracious gifts (11:29, regarding Israel); now he speaks of God's "grace" (*charis*) as a sort of empowerment expressed in "grace-giftings" (*charismata*; cf. also 1 Pet 4:10–11). Believers each receive grace for different ministries (12:6),[15] just as Paul's ministry to them involved the grace given him (12:3). Elsewhere we learn that believers might seek from God gifts they believe will edify the body (1 Cor 12:31; 14:1, 12).

11. Intimate unity or friendship with one another is sometimes expressed in terms of identity (Cicero *De or.* 31 110; Diodorus Siculus 17.37.6; Philostratus *Hrk.* 48.22).

12. Mainly Stoics (Seneca *Lucil.* 95.52; Epictetus *Disc.* 1.12.26; Marcus Aurelius *Med.* 7.13).

13. First attributed to Menenius Agrippa (Dionysius of Halicarnassus *Ant. rom.* 6.86.1–5; Livy 2.32.9–12; Plutarch *Cor.* 6.2–4; Dio Cassius 4.17.10–13), but often used subsequently (Sallust *Rep.* 10.6; Cicero *Rep.* 3.25.37; idem *Phil.* 8.5.15; cf. Aristotle *Eth. nic.* 1.7; *T. Naph.* 2:9–10).

14. Ancient writers sometimes used the image of the body apart from or together with its "head," just as Paul also can use these images separately or together (1 Cor 11:3; 12:12; cf. Eph 1:22–23; Col 1:18; 2:19).

15. Greek tradition also recognized that "God" gave different enablements to different individuals (Homer *Il.* 13.730–34; for animals, cf. Phaedrus 3.18.10–15); special human abilities were also attributed to the benevolence of other deities (e.g., Xenophon *Cyn.* 13.18; Aelius Aristides *Defense of Oratory* 397, §135D). On different abilities, see also Aristotle *Pol.* 3.7.2–3, 1282b (though in support of hierarchy).

Paul's central point, however, is that each believer has something to contribute to the proper functioning of Christ's body. From this observation it seems not too much to infer that the body would often fail to function properly when individual members fail to recognize their value and contribute their gift, or when other members try to usurp roles not suited for their particular grace or faith. A large number of scholars argue strenuously that "proportion [*analogia*] of faith" in 12:6 represents a standard for faith, useful for evaluating prophecy. (Paul did use gospel teaching as a standard for evaluating teachers, 6:17; 16:17.) Nevertheless, the Greek word is commonly equivalent to Paul's "measure" of faith in 12:3; Paul is again emphasizing that God apportions faith for different gifts to different believers.

Again as elsewhere (1 Cor 12:8–10, 28, 29–30; 14:26), Paul provides a mostly ad hoc list of gifts (Rom 12:6–8), though he values prophecy particularly highly (Rom 12:6; 1 Cor 12:28; 14:1).[16] Dividing the gifts into "natural" (like giving) and "supernatural" (like prophecy) misses Paul's point, since all reflect God's activity. "Service" is a broad term potentially including ministries like Paul's (Rom 11:13; 15:25, 31; 2 Cor 4:1; 5:18) or even any grace-gift (1 Cor 12:5; cf. Eph 4:12; Col 4:17). Whereas Paul counts "teaching" as a gift just like prophecy, prophecy probably depends more directly on inspiration for its message (in its ultimate form, often first-person declaration from God, as in Rev 2–3). Divine empowerment in teaching probably works more through divinely guided cognitive processes (on which cf. Rom 8:5–7; 12:2–3). Earlier Scripture (Rom 15:4; cf. 1 Tim 4:13) and the message about Jesus (Eph 4:21; Col 1:28; 2:7; 2 Thess 2:15) are probably important bases for teaching, although like other gifts the ministry of teaching was subject to abuse or pride (cf. Rom 2:20–21).

Whatever else "exhortation" (note *parakaleō* and *paraklēsis*, 12:8) might include, it surely includes exhortations like Paul's own in this letter (12:1; 15:30; 16:17). One of its sources could be Scripture (15:4), although prophecy could also serve this function (1 Cor 14:3). Although "giving" (*metadidōmi*) can have a broader sense (cf. the same verb for Paul's *spiritual* giving to them, 1:11), it may at least include money (cf. Eph 4:28). The term often translated "generosity" (*haplotēs*) can mean simply "sincerity," but could apply to monetary benefaction (2 Cor 8:2; 9:11, 13). Those gifted

---

16. On these gifts, see further e.g., Turner 1998; Keener 2003a.

to "lead" or "manage" (*proistēmi*) in house churches received respect for their position (1 Thess 5:12), though even most well-endowed homes did not seat beyond forty persons. Finally, "showing mercy" reflects compassionate help, including alms;[17] Paul elsewhere associates "cheerfulness" with economic charity (2 Cor 9:7). That at least two members of the ad hoc list may be associated with financial help to others might suggest that some Roman believers had resources (cf. also Rom 15:24). Though all believers are called to share financially (12:13), God has gifted some in particular with means and the heart to do it abundantly.

Loving Everyone (12:9–21)

In 12:9–21 Paul offers "paranesis," a series of loosely fitted exhortations, most of them widely paralleled elsewhere in the ancient world.[18] Although by their nature such exhortations are of general significance, Paul still writes with the Roman believers in mind. In 12:9–13 he urges loving and serving fellow believers; in 12:14–21 he addresses relationships with people more generally, preparing for relationships with the state in 13:1–7. Paul frames 12:9–21 with exhortations to choose "good" rather than evil (12:9, 21); he has already shown that what is "good" is the will of God (12:2), and will continue encouraging them to do "good" in 13:3–4.

Because of the limited size of this commentary and the number of individual exhortations, I address only some of these individually. First, in 12:9–10 Paul addresses the character of sincere love (a theme revisited in 13:8–10), which expresses itself in part in honoring others above oneself (a value that ran counter to most conventional Mediterranean values for men.)[19]

In 12:10–12 Paul employs an accepted form of repetition (here, starting each Greek clause with a dative noun) to drive home his emphasis

17. The term involves helping the needy (sick, poor, etc.; *T. Iss.* 5:2; *T. Benj.* 4:4; Cranfield, *Romans*, 2:627). Paul's normal use of the term for God's activity, including in Romans, seems relevant, if at all, at most as a model here.

18. See e.g., Diogenes Laertius 1.70; *Dicta Catonis* passim; Ps.-Phoc. passim; geographically distant, cf. even the structure of Confucius's *Analects*. For link words with the context in Romans, see Talbert 2002: 280.

19. On "brotherly love" (*philadelphia*), see e.g., Plutarch *Frat. amor.*; (dramatically) 4 Macc 13:23–27; Klauck 1990; deSilva 2000: 166–67; for the love in *philostorgia*, e.g., Fronto *Verum Imp.* 2.7.6. For valuing another's honor as one's own, see *m. 'Abot* 2:10; *'Abot R. Nat.* 15, 19 A; 29, §60B.

rhetorically: three clauses in 12:10–11 end with *-oi*, and seven successive clauses in 12:11–13 conclude with plural participles ending in *-ontes* or *-ountes*.[20] Scholars debate whether Paul in 12:11 speaks of being fervent "in spirit" or "in the Spirit" (cf. Acts 18:25). Because "spirit" in Romans usually refers to God's Spirit (sometimes even when linked with dispositions or abstract nouns, 8:2, 15), I think it is more likely God's Spirit here. "Serving" the Lord recalls Paul's earlier emphasis on slavery to God (cf. 6:22; 7:6; 14:18). In 12:12, "rejoicing in hope" and "enduring in affliction" recall especially 5:2–5. Paul has modeled "persevering in prayer" (12:12) in his prayers to see them (1:10), and will seek them to keep praying for him (15:30).

In 12:13, "sharing with the needs of the saints" prepares for Paul's mention of his misson to provide for the needy saints in Jerusalem (15:25–27).[21] The term translated "hospitality," one of the highest of ancient social values, meant providing for strangers, often by taking them in.[22] (As such a practice could be dangerous even in antiquity, Jewish travelers often carried letters of recommendation.) At least one case of such provision may be for Paul when he visits (15:24, 28).

In a culture that emphasized honor and shame, blessing those who cursed you might not come naturally. Although many ancient thinkers valued nonretaliation and avoiding revenge (12:14, 17, 19–21),[23] the wording of 12:14 could reflect Jesus's teachings (Luke 6:28; cf. Matt 5:44).[24] Perhaps Paul's focus on nonretaliation and blessing those who curse addresses a local issue (not impossibly related to the Jewish conflict over messiahship and consequent expulsion from Rome, reported in a

20. Paul also connects 12:13 and 12:14 with the same verb *diōkō*, though using it in two different senses ("pursue" and "persecute").

21. Employing some of the same vocabulary; although *koinōneō* could involve "sharing" more generally, early Christians often employed it in an economic way (also Gal 6:6; Phil 4:15).

22. On ancient hospitality, see most fully Koenig 1985.

23. E.g., Seneca *Dial.* 3.6.5; 4.32.1; Musonius Rufus 10, p. 76.18—78.28; Maximus of Tyre *Or.* 12; Diogenes Laertius 6.1.3; Sir 28:1–4; 1QS 10.17–18; CD 9.3–6; Ps.-Phoc. 77; *Jos. Asen.* 23:9; 29:3; *b. Ber.* 17a; *Shab.* 88b, bar.; Flusser 1988: 485, 506. But some limited this to their own community (cf. *Sipra Qed.* pq. 4.200.3.6; Stendahl 1962) and valued vengeance (e.g., Jdt 9:2; 1 Macc 2:67; *T. Levi* 5:3).

24. For Jesus tradition in Rom 12–14, see e.g., Hunter 1961: 46; Davies 1980: 138; Ladd 1974: 514; Kim 2002: 264–69; Wenham 1984: 15–17. Even so, epistolary genre did not lend itself to many direct citations (Stuhlmacher 1991: 16–19; Gerhardsson 1991), and the textual nature of Scripture afforded simpler quotation material.

garbled way in Suetonius *Claud.* 25.4). The value of sharing others' joys and sorrows was common[25] (though rather than weeping with mourners, philosophers, in contrast to Paul here, often advocated not weeping); the most typical examples were weddings and funerals. Paul probably echoes a Jewish tradition about mourning with those who mourn (Sir 7:34–35), and the practice would certainly encourage unity.[26]

In 12:16 Paul reinforces warnings against wrong thinking that leads to disunity, twice using "think" (*phroneō*) and once *phronimos*; in other words, appropriate perspectives are crucial (cf. 8:5–7). "Thinking the same" (NRSV "live in harmony with one another") recalls the sound thinking that does not exalt oneself (12:2–3). The call to harmony that the phrase entails was a frequent ancient topic (including in the form of "being of one mind"),[27] and is particularly relevant for this ethnically divided congregation (cf. 14:1—15:13, esp. 15:6; 16:17; cf. 1 Cor 1:10–12; Phil 2:1–3). Whatever else Paul's warning against conceit in 12:16 includes, it includes the corporate sense of superiority expressed by either Gentiles looking down on Jews (11:20) or the reverse, presumably as well as boasting in one's own gifts (12:3). "Associating with the lowly" again challenges ancient society's emphasis on honor, but follows the way of Jesus (cf. e.g., Mark 9:35–37; 10:42–45). Not counting oneself "wise" contrasts with those who became fools by this means (Rom 1:22), perhaps including the Greeks' belief in their own ethnic superiority (1:14), and certainly Gentile disdain Jews (11:25, with similar wording).

As noted above, nonretaliation (12:17–20) appears in other ancient sources. Its unanimity in early Christian sources,[28] however, is striking and suggests a common background in Jesus, whose submissive death dependent on God set the example for his early followers. Being considerate toward outsiders' views of what was right (12:17) offers another ele-

---

25. E.g., Tob 7:7–8; Josephus *Ag. Ap.* 2.205; *T. Jos.* 17:7; cf. friendship in Dio Chrysostom *Or.* 1.30–31; Fronto *De nepote amisso* 2.7; Marshall 1987: 46. In another culture, cf. the example of Confucius (*Analects* 7.9; 9.9; 10.16).

26. Perhaps Gentile believers did not mourn when Jewish believers were expelled; but the practice would now build unity whatever the previous local particulars.

27. Cf. e.g., Xenophon *Mem.* 4.4.16; Lysias *Or.* 2.24, §192; Cicero *Phil.* 6.1.2; Dionysius of Halicarnassus *Ant. rom.* 7.53.1; Musonius Rufus 8, p. 64, line 13; Dio Chrysostom *Or.* 39.8; Menander Rhetor 2.3, 384.23–24; most fully Mitchell 1991: 60–79 (see here esp. 76, 79). Cf. traditional Jewish equivalents in Ezra 3:9; *Mek. Bah.* 1.108–10.

28. See discussion in Talbert 2002: 292–93.

ment of getting along with outsiders. It reflects a popular ethic,[29] yet also prepares Paul's audience for his emphasis on respecting stricter opinions among fellow believers, when possible, in 14:13–21.

In contrast to some Judean nationalists, some Pharisees (vindicated by the outcome of the war in 66–70 that began less than a decade later) would have shared Paul's emphasis on living at peace with others (12:18).[30] Paul, like many other thinkers, intends it as a principle for relationships more generally, including regarding issues of division in the Roman church (14:17, 19; 15:13, 33). Here, however, the context's emphasis lies on relations with nonbelievers. His "insofar as you are able" recognizes that believers cannot control how others act toward them; a few years later, in fact, Christians' enemies in Rome had many of them killed.

One reason to avoid avenging oneself was that God would avenge those who left the matter with him (12:19).[31] (A song I learned while serving in some African-American churches summarizes this basic sentiment: "If I hold my peace, let the Lord fight my battles, victory, victory shall be mine!") Paul backs up his claim with a quotation from Deut 32:35, a context he has used heavily in Romans.[32]

In 12:20 Paul quotes Prov 25:21–22 (which goes on to add that the Lord will reward the person who shows kindness to their enemy).[33] Scholars debate whether burning coals on an enemy's head in 12:20 refers to the enemy's conversion or embarrassment (the "positive" approach held by Origen, Augustine, Jerome and others) or to their destruction (the "negative" approach held by John Chrysostom). Many commentators prefer the former approach, and it is possible to construe 12:21 in terms of winning over enemies.[34] Nevertheless, the Egyptian background

---

29. Hesiod *Op.* 760–64; Isocrates *Demon.* 17; *Nic.* 54 (*Or.* 3.38); Polybius 22.10.8; Cornelius Nepos 25 (Atticus), 6.4; Quintilian *Inst.* 2.2.14; Plutarch *Cic.* 29.7; *m. 'Abot* 2:1; 3:10; *t. Ber.* 3:3; *t. 'Abod. Zar.* 6:6.

30. Supporting peace with others, see e.g., *m. 'Abot* 1:12 (attributed to Hillel); *Git.* 5:8–9. Also others, e.g., Marcus Aurelius *Med.* 5.31; Diogenes Laertius 7.1.123.

31. Cf. Josephus *J.W.* 5.377. The divine vengeance in Rom 12 would be eschatological, as at Qumran (1QS 9.23; Flusser 1988: 199; also in *2 En.* 50:4).

32. Haacker (2003: 100) notes especially Deut 32:21 in Rom 10:19; 32:43 in 15:10; 30:12–14 in 10:6–8; and 29:4 in 11:8.

33. An audience in Rome could easily envisage giving drink; most of the city's residents lacked potable water near their residences (Carcopino 1940: 38–39).

34. Some did value turning enemies into friends (cf. Diodorus Siculus 21.21.9; 27.16.1; Dionysius of Halicarnassus *Ant. rom.* 5.30.2; Suetonius *Jul.* 73; Diogenes Laertius

sometimes cited for the former approach is too rare and chronologically distant,[35] and the Lord's "vengeance" of 12:19 probably points toward fiery judgment here for those who do not repent. Other Pauline uses of "fire" refer to the judgment (1 Cor 3:13, 15; 2 Thess 1:8), and burning coals can stand for judgment in his Bible (2 Sam 22:9, 13; Pss 120:4; 140:10).[36] Granted, Paul does contrast 12:19 and 12:20 (signified by the strong "but," *alla*, in 12:20); on either reading, acts of kindness in 12:20 provide an alternative to acts of vengeance in 12:19. But while one could overcome evil with good (12:21) by converting the evil to the good, such an outcome cannot be guaranteed (cf. 12:18; 1 Cor 7:16). One can, however, overcome evil by refusing to come down to its moral level, not retaliating in kind, an approach that fits this context.

8.1.23; Iamblichus *Pyth. Life* 8.40; Prov 16:7; *Let. Aris.* 227; Ps.-Phoc. 142).

35. Whether or not it is useful for the original proverb, this background (and any orally transmitted sense of the proverb) would not be available to Greek readers in Rome. For shaming an enemy with kindness, cf. *ANET*² 422; more useful background (on reapplying the language of burning coals) could be *Gen. Rab.* 50:11 (though *Sipre Deut.* 45.1.2 applies the proverb to conquering the evil impulse by doing good).

36. Paul cited Ps 140:3 with reference to the wicked in Rom 3:13; Ps 140:10 refers to judgment on the wicked. For wrath on heads, see e.g., Ezek 9:10; 22:31; Jdt 9:9. For various positive readings of the verse, see e.g., Käsemann, Michel, Cranfield, Dunn, Byrne, Jewett; for the much less common negative reading adopted here, see Stendahl, Schreiner.

ROMANS 13

LIVING THE CHRISTIAN LIFE (12:1—15:13), *cont.*

Respecting the State (13:1-7)

This passage continues the preceding ethical exhortation about how to behave toward outsiders, and as such makes sense in its context. Yet Paul elaborates it at much greater length than even the exhortations for nonretaliation in 12:14, 17, 19-21. Why? Perhaps we should think of a chiastic approach:

A Exhortations regarding fellow believers (12:9-13)

   B Exhortations regarding outsiders (12:14-21)

   B′ A detailed issue regarding outsiders (13:1-7)

A′ A detailed question regarding fellow believers (14:1—15:7)

Such an approach is possible (though weakened by its asymmetry and failure to account for 13:8-14), but even if it is correct, it begs the question. Why does Paul elaborate on this *particular* issue regarding outsiders?

Ancient writers often addressed the topic of societal relationships, in terms of relationships to the state, parents and elders, wives, children, and household slaves.[1] Where parts of this conventional topic appear in early Christian sources, they often relate to concern how outsiders will view believers (1 Tim 5:14-15; 6:1; Titus 2:5, 8, 10).[2] That is, the authors write at least partly from apologetic concern for the reputation of this

---

1. See concisely Isocrates *Demon.* 16, *Or.* 1; Cicero *Inv.* 2.22.65; Diogenes Laertius 8.1.22-23; further, Lührmann 1980; Malherbe 1986: 89-90, 135, 145-47. For Stoic loyalty to the state, see e.g., Erskine 1990: 181-204; for Judaism, e.g., *m.* ʾ*Abot* 3:2; Tobin 2004: 397-98; Stuhlmacher 1994: 199-200. The frequency of the topic challenges the interpretation that this passage is directed toward submission to synagogue authorities (the argument of Nanos 1996: 289-336, despite many other strong features in his work).

2. See e.g., discussion in Padgett 1987.

small, potentially persecuted minority sect,[3] as John Chrysostom also recognized here.[4] Diaspora Jews followed the same approach of submission to traditional structures, often to undermine Gentile suspicions of their subversiveness.[5] Synagogues, like other associations in Rome, had to remain apolitical or face dissolution;[6] the political relevance of a "messianic" claim may have led to the banning of Jewish believers from Rome a few years earlier (Suetonius *Claud.* 25.4).

Paul clearly is concerned how others in Rome will view the church there (12:17–18; cf. 14:16, 18; 15:2). If we grant an apologetic element in Paul's purpose, the question remains as to why he focuses on relations with the state rather than other societal relationships. The local situation in Rome may help answer that question. Probably less than a decade earlier, the emperor had apparently punished a conflict in the Jewish community over the identity of the Messiah, a conflict that had probably included Jewish believers in Jesus.[7] This could have left Jewish messianists' reputation tenuous, inviting special attention to this issue. (It could also fit the warning not to seek their own revenge; see comment on 12:17–21.) That Nero scapegoated and massacred Christians beginning less than a decade (and perhaps just six years) after Paul wrote this letter suggests that Paul's apologetic concern was a viable one.[8]

Having established God's sovereignty in history in chapters 9–11, Paul now recognizes that God also appoints rulers for his purposes (13:1–2, 4).[9] Paul elsewhere appeals to God's sovereign plan when exhorting believers to remain content (2 Cor 9:8; Phil 4:11) and to remain in one's situation (unless opportunity arises to change the situation, 1 Cor 7:21–24); this bears some resemblance to Stoic submission to fate, ex-

---

3. For 1 Pet 2:13—3:7, see Balch 1981; idem 1988; for the household codes in Eph 5:21—6:9, see Keener 1992: 139-224 (esp. 146-47).

4. John Chrysostom *Hom. Rom.* 23 (on Rom 13:2; Bray 1998: 326).

5. Cf. 4 Macc 5:18; also Josephus (Spilsbury 2003).

6. Stuhlmacher 1994: 191; cf. Bammel 1984: 367-68.

7. Suetonius *Claud.* 25.4. Although Rome boasted of the multiculturalism of its empire, many "patriotically" xenophobic elements remained in the city itself.

8. It is also possible that the conflict had involved some messianists' actual retaliation against synagogue opponents, hence Paul's insistence on nonretaliation (12:17–19), hoping that the state would punish perpetrators and not pure victims. While plausible, however, we lack sufficient information to treat this proposal as more than mere speculation.

9. See also Prov 16:10 (but cf. 16:12); Wis 6:3; *b.* ʿ*Abod. Zar.* 18a, bar.

cept with trust in God's gracious providence.[10] But no one assumed that such language was absolute; Stoics themselves would not compromise their integrity for the state, but submitted to what they believed the state *should* be.[11] Paul speaks here of the moral function of civil government in restraining evil (13:3–5), a function shared with laws in general, which includes their role in punishing errant citizens (13:4).[12] While believers must not avenge themselves (12:19), the state is right to avenge wrong-doing (13:4), at least for the sake of public order (cf. Deut 13:11; 17:13; 19:20; 21:21). Christians must submit to the state not only because of such punishments, however, but because they recognize that God appointed such rulers (13:5). Writing a few years before nationalist Judeans sought liberation from Rome by military means, Paul articulates instead a different prophetic view, that God expects his people to live in the societies where he has placed them (Jer 29:4–7).

Clearly Paul does not believe that Christians must always agree with governments. He would have warned against participation in the "patriotic" emperor cult (cf. 3:29–30), and he recognized Moses's divinely commanded opposition to Pharaoh (cf. 9:15–17). But as a general rule, including in a pagan and unjustly structured society like the Roman Empire, he expected Christians to be model citizens. This does not mean that they should not work for change by evangelizing and seeking justice, but we should keep in mind that Paul's audience did not have all the same recourses for political transformation available in a modern democracy, and they were a small minority movement in any case.

Moral exceptions like abstention from the emperor cult do not absolve Christians from paying taxes or customs (13:6–7). Taxes helped to fund Roman armies, which did evil as well as maintained order, and state cults. Nevertheless, Christians had to support their societies. In a society that emphasized honor and shame, showing honor to leaders was important (believers obeying 12:10 would already have practice relinquishing honor to others). Some noncitizens in Rome may have resented the taxes levied on them. Some have pointed out that the Jews expelled by Claudius would have been taxed as immigrants once they returned to Rome, and

10. Cf. e.g., Seneca *Lucil.* 96.1–2; Marcus Aurelius *Med.* 4.25; 5.27.

11. E.g., for disputes about obeying orders not in the giver's own interests or intentions, see e.g., Musonius Rufus 16, p. 102.28–31 (with parents); Aulus Gellius *Noct. att.* 1.13.

12. Probably also the "condemnation" of 13:2. During the Empire Rome decapitated citizens by the sword (Seneca *Dial.* 3.18.4; *m. Sanh.* 7:3).

many have noted controversy in Rome over particular taxes at about this point in Nero's reign, controversy that would surely have been known in Corinth where Paul wrote.[13]

Fusing the Horizons: Church and State

Paul depicts relations with the state within a particular kind of situation. What happens, however, when a state, far from avenging wrongdoing, is itself the persecutor? Paul wrote early in Nero's reign, before he began persecuting Christians.[14] Nevertheless, as a Jew who had faced Roman rods (2 Cor 11:25) and lived in Judea, Paul was well aware that the empire already oppressed peoples and that injustices often occurred under its auspices. Injustice notwithstanding, he does not side with the Judean nationalist ethos already building when he was writing (cf. Rom 15:31), which would soon climax in open war with Rome.[15]

Many historically used this passage (among others) to support the divine right of kings.[16] But if Paul follows Jesus's teaching on giving to Caesar what is Caesar's (13:6–7; Mark 12:17),[17] he presumably also agreed with his caveat that some things belonged only to God (Mark 12:17). For example, Paul surely would not, out of allegiance to the state, sanction participation in the popular imperial cult (cf. 1 Cor 10:20–21). Further, submission was a temporary expedient; Paul did not expect Rome or other worldly empires to continue

13. See the varying interpretations of Tacitus *Ann.* 13.50–51 in Dunn 1988: 766; Tobin 2004: 399–400; Jewett 2007: 798–99, though it is hard to be certain; even early interpreters differed regarding which taxes Paul intended (Bray 1998: 329). Haacker (2003: 121 n. 19) suggests that Paul says "you" (excluding himself) here because he was a Roman citizen (though Paul says "you" frequently in this context).

14. The early Nero, under Seneca's influence, behaved better (see Griffin 1984: 50–82).

15. Some early Christian writers thought Jewish nationalism Paul's target here (Apollinaris of Laodicea *Pauline Commentary from the Greek Church* on Rom 13:1–7; Bray 1998: 324), though Jews in Rome were probably mostly immune to it.

16. For its treatment through history, see concisely Reasoner 2005: 130–36; Bray 1998: 323–26. Luther's approach may have been unconsciously co-opted by his political patrons, not unlike the co-opting of the religious right and left by political patrons in recent U.S. history.

17. Jewish sources that emphasize allegiance to the state also offer this qualification (Tobin 2004: 397–99; see esp. Josephus *Ant.* 18.266–68; idem *J.W.* 2.197; idem *Ag. Ap.* 2.76–77); philosophic treatises on kingship also qualified royal authority.

for long (cf. Rom 2:5; 8:21–23; 9:22; 11:26–27; 12:19; 13:12).[18] Nor did Paul have reason to envision modern democracies, in which Christians as citizens would in a sense constitute part of the government, and hence need to evaluate and critique government activities. Finally, Paul lacked reason to envision this minority movement ending up in a situation of significant influence over the political process and so being able to address large-scale injustices like slavery (despite Paul's personal concerns, cf. Phlm 16–21). Opposed to ideologies behind the Judean revolt, Paul was likely in practice a pacifist. But what do personal pacifists do in extreme cases, when their influence affects whether genocide may be forcibly stopped? German theologian Dietrich Bonhoeffer, a pacifist, ultimately participated in a plot against Hitler because of the magnitude of evil involved.

While few would support the divine right of kings today, the subservience of the leaders of the German state church to Hitler's Third Reich, based on this passage, raised anew the issue of its application, and Christian cooperation with the apartheid government in South Africa had the same effect. Abolitionists and liberation theologians have long grappled with these issues. Most likely, Paul would have applied 13:1–7 as the norm where possible, living in a respectable manner in society but allowing dissent where necessary and political participation for justice when possible. For example, he would presumably urge Christians in China (given the normal situation there at the time I am writing this) to be model Chinese citizens, yet without imbibing atheism. In cases of wholesale massacres of Christians or their neighbors, such as have happened at various times in northern Nigeria, the Indian state of Orissa, parts of Indonesia, and so forth, conclusions are harder to come by (though these were not sponsored by national governments, a situation closer to, e.g., the Turkish genocide of Armenians in 1915). I am inclined to think that Paul would not endorse armed resistance in such cases, but it is admittedly easy for me to pontificate from a currently safe location. I know of other settings where suppression and the killings of individuals led to armed uprisings, which most often led to more suffering without decisive liberation; but other solutions seemed hard to come by. Once we recognize that Paul's words addressed a particular historical situation, translating the message into new situations becomes more problematic.

Respect for one's government and the expected obligations of citizenship have limits (though as a modern Western reader I am probably overly inclined

18. See Elliott 2008: 56.

to emphasize this qualification). Paul cooperated with the Jerusalem church's identification with their culture (which was also his culture, Acts 21:20–26), but not to the extent of honoring such nationalism above his commitment to the Gentile mission (Acts 22:21–22). When Christians are more loyal to our ethnicity or nation than to Christ's body, when nationalism or racism corrupts our love for fellow believers, we have gone beyond giving Caesar what is Caesar's to giving Caesar what is God's. On many other points, however, Christian ethicists debate the boundaries between those two spheres.

Live God's Way (13:8–14)

The subject of taxes (13:6–7) may raise the issue of obligations to others more generally (13:8), but avoiding financial indebtedness was a common topic in antiquity.[19] While moralists often warned against debts, Paul's far more demanding alternative strikes at the heart of the obligation/reciprocity ethic of ancient Mediterranean culture: love, which gives freely without thought of fulfilling or seeking repayment (13:8–10; cf. 12:9; Gal 5:13–14). In a particular setting where Jewish and Gentile Christians differed over the law (cf. Rom 3:19–31; 7:1–25; 9:30—10:13), recalling them to this basic thrust of the law summoned them to consideration and unity. Other Jewish writers also recognized the importance of the love commandment,[20] but Paul's summary of individual commands may also recall the earlier-specified failure of some who affirm themselves as law keepers (adultery in 2:22; theft in 2:21; immoral desire in 7:7–8) as well as others (murder in 1:29; immoral desire in 1:24; 6:12).[21]

In 13:11–14 Paul concludes his general exhortations with an apparently eschatological moral summons. Although Paul's audience in Rome could not compare 1 Thess 5:2–8 as we can to recognize the eschatological character of this exhortation, it probably reflects more general early Christian usage of eschatological images rather than only a recycled sermon of Paul (cf. Mark 13:33–37; Matt 24:43). The "day," then, is the "day

19. E.g., Publilius Syrus 11; Petronius *Sat.* 57; Plutarch *Ought not Borrow Mor.* 827D–832A; Prov 22:7; 4Q416 f2ii:4–6; Ahiqar 111, saying 29.

20. Much discussed: see e.g., Neudecker 1992; Konradt 1997; Söding 1994–1995; idem 1995; idem 1998; Berthelot 2003 (though cf. de Jonge 2002); Bernard 2003; Flusser 1988: 55–65; see Mark 12:31.

21. Paul's selection of examples from the Decalogue is consistent with its prominence among the commandments as well (e.g., Philo *Decalogue* 154; Yadin 1969).

of the Lord" (1 Thess 5:2), and the day as the time for being awake (Rom 13:11) and sober (13:13) was a commonplace Paul's audience could have understood (cf. 1 Thess 5:5–7). Believers thus need to live in the light of the eschatological reality they have already entered in Christ (Rom 12:2; cf. 2 Cor 5:5). Others used the image of awakening intellectually or morally,[22] and being awake also contrasts with the spirit of stupor in 11:8 (Isa 29:10) and those darkened in 11:10.

Many connect the image of "putting off" and "putting on" with waking from sleep in the morning; whatever was worn during the night, certainly people did clothe themselves in the morning.[23] Although Paul's audience may think in terms of praetorian soldiers stationed just outside Rome, the "armor of light" (Rom 13:12; cf. 1 Thess 5:8; Eph 6:11–17) for him might recall additionally a sectarian Jewish expectation of an end-time battle between the children of light and the children of darkness (1QM 1.1, 11; cf. 1 Thess 5:5). Here, however, the exhortation is not to fight but to stand guard, to watch; ancients regularly condemned guards who would fall asleep or get drunk on duty.

Most importantly, Paul envisions not a literal physical battle but a spiritual one;[24] staying alert here means avoiding the sorts of deeds done in darkness, at night or in secret. Such deeds include drunkenness, sexual immorality, and mistreatment of others (13:13; cf. Gal 5:21; 1 Pet 4:3).[25] Paul has earlier warned of war with the passions (7:23) and condemned the premeditated following of the flesh and its lusts. Now he reiterates the only solution: "putting on" the new person, Christ (13:14; cf. Rom 5:12—8:13). Christ, then, is their "armor of light" (13:12). Paul's meta-

---

22. E.g., Valerius Maximus 7.2.3; Seneca *Ep. Lucil.* 20.13; Tacitus *Hist.* 3.55; Lucian *Hermot.* 71, 83; Maximus of Tyre *Or.* 10.6; Marcus Aurelius *Med.* 6.31; in prophetic or eschatological settings, Isa 51:17; 52:1; Joel 1:5; *1 En.* 82:3; Rev 3:2; cf. the quotation in Eph 5:14. It might also prepare for eschatological resurrection (Dan 12:2).

23. Cf. the conjunction of "awake" and "clothe" in Isa 52:1, which Paul would apply to that eschatological time (cf. Isa 52:7 in Rom 10:15).

24. For figurative armor for rhetorical "battles," see e.g., Horace *Ep.* 1.18.15–16; Seneca the Elder *Controv.* 9, pref. 4; Fronto *Eloq.* 1.16; for moral or philosophic ones, Seneca *Ep. Lucil.* 109.8; 117.7, 25; Ps.-Diogenes *Ep.* 19; Dio Chrysostom *Or.* 16.6; 49.10; cf. Malherbe 1989: 101–5; 2 Cor 10:3–5. It is prayer in Wis 18:21.

25. Sexual immorality was sometimes available at drinking parties (e.g., Valerius Maximus 4.3. ext. 3a; Quintus Curtius 5.7.2; Alciphron *Courtesans* 13, frg. 6), though the warning here is doubtless broader, given "jealousy."

phor should have been intelligible, as the image of "putting on" God's strength appears in other Jewish sources.[26]

To speak of "putting on" the Lord Jesus Christ, however, reflects Paul's (and early Christians') distinctive Christology. Paul can apply the language to the past act of baptism, as in Gal 3:27, or to a command to *be* what they *are* in Christ, as here (cf. Eph 4:24; Col 3:10, 12; on the indicative and the imperative, see comment on 6:11).

26. The Spirit in Judg 6:34 LXX; 1 Chron 12:19; 2 Chron 24:20; *L.A.B.* 27:9–10; Luke 24:49; *b. Meg.* 14b; cf. immortality in 1 Cor 15:53–54; eschatological garments of life in *1 En.* 62:15–16; Israel's glory at restoration in Isa 52:1; 61:10; *Ps. Sol.* 11:7; natural metaphors in 4 Macc 6:2; *b. 'Abot* 6:1, bar. Cf. Eph 4:22, 25; Col 3:8; Jas 1:21; 1 Pet 2:1.

ROMANS 14

LIVING THE CHRISTIAN LIFE (12:1—15:13), *cont.*

Serve the Lord vs. Foods and Days (14:1–12)

Although the subject changes here from 13:11–14, it continues Paul's practical exhortations about relationships. Instead of generalities, however, Paul now addresses at extended length (14:1—15:7) a more specific tension among believers in Rome. Paul has preached before against causing stumbling over foods (1 Cor 8–10, addressing food offered to idols), but now adjusts that theme to the specific tensions in the Roman church.[1]

Very detailed reconstructions regarding the views of diverse house churches (sometimes divided into four or five distinct camps) extract too much from our limited evidence, but the *general* situation is clear from Romans as a whole: Jewish and Gentile believers need mutual respect (see introduction). Aside from concern with Jewish success at converting Roman women, Roman literature cites three issues for which Roman Gentiles particularly looked down on Jews: circumcision, food customs, and holy days (see e.g., Juvenal *Sat.* 14.96–106). Paul has already addressed circumcision in 2:25–29 and 4:9–12, but has reserved the other two issues for his current exhortation. Because a major practical issue might be reserved for the end of an argument, and because this section focuses mostly on foods (holy days take up only 14:5–6), looking down on one another's food customs was probably a major problem among believers in Rome.

Paul's key exhortation is "accept one another." Apart from Phlm 17, Paul's extant letters employ this verb (*proslambanō*) only three times: at the beginning (14:1, 3) and end (15:7) of this section. The context of 15:7 indicates that Jews and Gentiles accepting one another (as Christ has accepted them) is a key issue (15:8–12).

1. For comparisons with 1 Cor 8–10 see Talbert 2002: 311–12.

Excursus: Ancient Mediterranean Food Customs

Besides Jews, some other peoples in the East also avoided pork, including Phoenicians (Herodian *History* 5.6.6), perhaps some Syrians (Lucian *Syr. d.* 54), and Egyptian priests.[2] Some other cults,[3] peoples,[4] or sects (especially the vegetarian Pythagoreans)[5] also had special food customs. Some of these groups influenced other persons not belonging to their group.

Most Jewish people maintained their ancestral food customs. Because of severe persecution for this practice in the Maccabean period, Jewish food customs had become a significant distinctive of Jewish ethnicity.[6] Gentiles knew that Jews avoided pork and widely mocked them for it;[7] Juvenal, for example, complained that Jews saw no difference between eating pork and cannibalism (*Sat.* 14.98–99). Most Diaspora Jews observed food laws;[8] other peoples would hardly have ridiculed Jews for this practice otherwise. What God ordained to separate Israel from the world (Lev 11:44–45) had proved effective, but Paul saw the emphasis now on mission rather than cultural separation (though he insisted on maintaining purity in sexual and theological areas).

---

2. Herodotus *Hist.* 2.47; Sextus Empiricus *Pyr.* 3.223; Plutarch *Isis* 5, *Mor.* 352F, 353F; Josephus *Ag. Ap.* 2.141; Lewis 1983: 131; *ANET2* 10. Earlier, Hittites treated pigs as unclean (*ANET2* 209; Moyer 1983: 29; idem 1969: 106).

3. E.g., Athenaeus *Deipn.* 10.422D; *PGM* 4.52–55; Apuleius *Metam.* 11.21; Plutarch *Isis* 2, *Mor.* 351F.

4. E.g., Britons (Caesar *Bell. gall.* 5.12); Romans (Plutarch *Quaest. rom.* 21, *Mor.* 268E); Libyans (Sextus Empiricus *Pyr.* 3.223); Egyptians (Plutarch *Isis* 7, *Mor.* 353C); Syrians (Diodorus Siculus 2.4.3; Artemidorus Daldianus *Onir.* 1.8); Indians (Herodotus *Hist.* 3.100); and others.

5. Diodorus Siculus 10.6.1; Plutarch *De esu* 1.1, *Mor.* 993A; Lucian *Vit. auct.* 6; idem *Gall.* 4–5, 18; Philostratus *Vit. Apoll.* 1.1, 8, 21; 6.10–11; 8.5, 7; *Ep. Apoll.* 8, 43, 84; Iamblichus *V.P.* 3.13 (avoiding also wine); 16.68–69; 24.106–9; 30.186; Diogenes Laertius 8.1.12–13, 19, 24. Some others also taught vegetarianism (Edwards and Reasoner 2000: 1015; Ovid *Metam.* 15.72–73, 75–110, 453–78; Orphics in Linforth 1941: 263; Guthrie 1966: 16–17, 197, 201), at least as a preference (Musonius Rufus 18A, p. 112.19–23).

6. See e.g., Holmén 2001: 224–25; Dunn 1988: 800.

7. E.g., Epictetus *Disc.* 1.22.4; Plutarch *Quaest. conv.* 4.4.4, *Mor.* 669C; Juvenal *Sat.* 6.160; cf. Josephus *Ant.* 2.137; Leary 1993; Leon 1960: 39.

8. So Josephus *Ag. Ap.* 2.282; see also evidence in Trebilco 1991: 18 (though conservative Judeans were often suspicious, *t. 'Abod. Zar.* 4:6).

Scholars sometimes demur from a Jewish focus in Romans 14 because Jews were not restricted to "vegetables" (14:2) or avoiding wine (14:21). But this may be simply Paul's hyperbole, given factors supporting a Jewish focus. It is soon clear that Paul is addressing the issue of Jews and Gentiles accepting one another (15:7–12); issues of law predominate in Romans, and "clean" and "unclean" foods do refer to Jewish *kashrut* (14:14).[9] Nevertheless, whether or not the vegetarianism is hyperbole, it is grounded in reality: when other kosher food was unavailable for whatever reason, Jews might resort to figs and nuts (Josephus *Life* 13–14), food in the wild (2 Macc 5:27), or vegetables more generally (Josephus *Ant.* 10.190).[10] It is doubtful that the problem is the lack of kosher butchers, which would have undoubtedly existed in Rome (even if much of the Jewish community had been expelled, enough members would have now returned to demand some such accommodations).[11] Most people in antiquity probably could not afford meat very often, except in connection with pagan cults;[12] abstaining from such cults (as Paul would expect all believers to do, 1 Cor 10:19–21) could also curtail available meat (see discussions of 1 Cor 8–10).

Some Jewish people debated among themselves whether there was a higher moral significance to the laws, and what that significance was.[13] Philo kept the food laws literally but found in them allegorical significance that led to higher moral behavior,[14] and he was not the first Alexandrian

9. Most commentators do recognize Jewish *kashrut* here; see especially Barclay 2001: 289–93; earlier, see some ancient commentators like Ambrosiaster and Theodoret (in Bray 1998: 337–38). Jewett (2007: 837) regards "vegetables" as the strong's stereotype.

10. Some scholars note that one might avoid Gentile wine from which libations had been poured (*m. ʿAbod. Zar.* 2:3–4; 3:8—5:11; probably Dan 1:12; Jdt 12:1–2), though some could also avoid wine as a (voluntary, not expected) partial fast to God (Dan 10:3; *T. Reu.* 1:10; *T. Jos.* 3:5; some cite also *T. Jud.* 15:4, but cf. 14:6; 16:3–5).

11. Cf. the later Roman butcher in Williams 2002. Rome accommodated Jewish customs even in their various enclaves (Winter 2001: 288–93).

12. So most scholars, though the case is debated (see the concerns of Meggitt 1994; information in Frost 1999).

13. Cf. e.g., *Sipre Deut.* 75.2.1. Cf. the private view attributed to Paul's contemporary Yohanan ben Zakkai (but reported much later) in Daube 1956: 142; Flusser 1988: 38 (surprisingly similar to Mark 7:14–23).

14. See *Spec. Laws* 4.100–118; Rhodes 2003; Sanders 1990: 273. Philo had a problem with extreme allegorizers (*Migration* 89–93; Hay, "Extremism"). Pigs were thought unable to control sexual appetites (Xenophon *Mem.* 1.2.30).

Jew to think in these terms.[15] Paul does not clearly allegorize food laws here; he seems to treat them as a matter of the old form of the law applicable only to Israel (and in Lev 11, they were intended distinctively for Israel).

For Paul, foods themselves are religiously neutral; that is, one may keep food customs because of upbringing, cultural preference or ethnic attachment, but one who keeps them out of the belief that it is religiously profitable is "weak in faith" (14:1). (Paul might even formulate this designation as a contrast with the ancestral archetype of faith who was "not weak in faith," 4:19.) This contrasts with one who genuinely believes and hence may eat anything (14:2); nothing is really intrinsically "clean" or "unclean" (14:14).

Nevertheless, Paul's agenda in this chapter is not to denigrate the keeping of these food customs, but to keep those who viewed themselves as "strong" from looking down on the "weak." Paul does not want stumbling blocks placed before those who continue to keep kosher by others eating non-kosher food in front of them (14:13–21).[16] Although Paul spent much of the letter establishing from Jewish Scripture that God welcomed Gentiles into the covenant, he is now emphasizing his central issue for the Gentile majority among Roman believers, namely, that they should not look down on Jews (11:18–21) or on those who keep the laws (ch. 14). Paul warns against abstainers disdaining eaters (14:3, 10), and against eaters "judging" abstainers (14:3, 4, 10, 13); he frequently used "judge" (*krinō* and cognates) earlier in the letter, probably including for Jews judging Gentiles (2:1, 3). It is true that some may "fall" (14:4), like the Jewish branches in 11:22 (falling is identical with "stumbling," falling away from the faith, 14:13, 21; cf. 9:32–33; 11:9, 11),[17] but God is able

15. See *Let. Aris.* 128–29, 147 (cf. 223); cf. *T. Ash.* 2:9–10. Some think that *Let. Aris.* reflects Pythagorean influence (Berthelot 2001). Some also allegorized regulations concerning Isis's priests (which included food rules; see Plutarch *Isis* 4, *Mor.* 352DE).

16. On some plausible views, this might have occurred sometimes at common meals (e.g., Lung-Kwong 1998: 140; Das 2003: 68). Some envision common meetings (in Corinth) in 16:23; perhaps some house congregations were mixed. But certainty seems difficult, as Jews did not concern themselves with what Gentiles or God fearers ate, though claims of "spiritual" proselytism (cf. 11:17) might raise different expectations. If the meals were potlucks (and individuals rather than hosts seem addressed here), no one could force Jewish attenders to eat non-kosher food.

17. For the seriousness of "stumbling," see e.g., Ezek 14:3–7; Sir 9:5; 25:21; 34:7, 17; 35:15; 39:24; 1QS 2.12; 3.24; 1QpHab 11.7–8; 4Q174 f1 2i:8–9; *T. Reu.* 4:7.

to make one "stand" (14:4), i.e., stand firm in the faith (cf. Rom 11:20; 1 Cor 10:12), and it is no one else's place to judge God's slaves (Rom 14:4; for God's slaves cf. e.g., 1:1; 6:22). (Although Paul uses "falling" language here, perhaps based on his more general preaching on this topic reflected in 1 Cor 8:9, 13, "judging" others is also central here.)

In 14:5–6 Paul briefly introduces, as if by way of a supporting illustration, the keeping of different days. Perhaps Paul expected his audience in Rome to agree with him regarding days, and hence he could use this as part of his argument. Paul himself did not have high regard for merely exchanging Gentile sacred days for Jewish ones (Gal 4:9–10). Nevertheless, it would seem surprising if the Sabbath were less of a controversy than food customs, even if everyone believed that the law of Moses was no longer in effect. While God-fearing Gentiles who were not full proselytes might not be expected to keep the Sabbath,[18] the Sabbath, in contrast to the food laws, was illustrated in creation before the birth of Israel (Gen 2:2–3; Exod 20:11). Although Jesus countered a strict approach to the Sabbath, it is not clear that he did away with it,[19] and early believers in Jesus continued to designate the seventh day by that term (Acts 1:12), albeit especially regarding conventional Jewish gatherings (e.g., Acts 13:44; 16:13).

How do we reconcile this brief passage with the larger witness of the OT on which Paul normally depended (cf. e.g., Exod 31:14–15; 35:2; Jer 17:21–27; Ezek 20:12–24; 22:26; 44:24; 46:1–12), including regarding faithful Gentiles (Isa 56:3–8)? Perhaps Paul simply did not expect Gentiles to keep festivals celebrating specifically Jewish deliverances (e.g., Passover, Purim), in contrast to the more universal Sabbath. This is a possibility, but early Christians in general apparently remained familiar with these other festivals as well (1 Cor 5:7; Acts 20:6, 16), and the Sabbath was the largest issue of contention between Jews and Gentiles regarding holy days. Others have suggested that Paul refers not to the Sabbath or even festivals but to fast days (which some strict Judean pietists observed even twice a week); this proposal fits the context of foods. If he refers to the Sabbath, perhaps Paul was simply pragmatic: unless they belonged to the ethnic enclave of Israel, Gentile slaves and workers normally could not observe the Sabbath fully, and Paul did not require this ideal of those who could

18. The later practice of using a Gentile as an agent on the Sabbath, however, was problematic (CD 11.2; *m. Shab.* 16:8; *t. Shab.* 13:9; cf. Exod 20:10; Deut 5:14).

19. See e.g., Vermes 1993: 13; Keener 1999: 350, 353–54; idem 2003b: 643–46.

not observe it. Perhaps for Paul the spirit of setting aside time for rest and worship was the point behind the day, hence took precedence over literal observance especially when, as just noted, literal observance was impossible (cf. circumcision in 2:25–29, though this, like food customs, was particular to Israel). For Paul, in any case, the issue is a secondary one and not a basis for dividing believers, and this is his primary point.[20]

Romans also had festivals[21] and regarded particular days as inauspicious.[22] But while the Roman world took off regular market days every eight or nine days, they lacked a weekly Sabbath.[23] The Sabbath was central to Jewish practice throughout the ancient world.[24] Gentiles were widely aware of the Jewish Sabbath,[25] and some Gentiles attracted to Judaism apparently avoided pork and honored the Sabbath in symbolic ways, such as lighting lamps.[26] Judaism was rife with debates about festival days, though normally these conflicts involved simply the correct date for observance (especially stemming from differences between the solar and lunar calendars). Perhaps within two generations of Paul's writing some of Jesus's followers were clashing with traditional Jews over fast days (*Did.* 8.1).

Whether regarding special worship days or food customs, the issue is motivation: one should observe or not observe such customs "to the Lord" (14:6).[27] For Paul, this issue simply reflects the larger principle of doing everything for the Lord. That principle, rather than an outward regulation, is the real criterion for true religion (14:7–9). The "Lord" for whom believers are to live and die (14:7–8) is Jesus, who died and rose

20. Cf. prophets who regarded Sabbath observance as meaningless without justice (Isa 1:13; cf. Amos 8:5; Hos 2:11).

21. Ovid *Fast.*; Dupont 1992: 195–218; Stambaugh 1988: 221–24 (for other holidays, 225–40); Shelton 1998: 378–84; Cole 1992; Harmon 2004.

22. E.g., Aulus Gellius *Noct. att.* 5.17; Ovid *Fast.* 1.8, 45–48; Plutarch *Alc.* 34.1; idem *Cam.* 19.1; idem *Alex.* 14.4; Dionysius *Epid.* 3.266–67; Iamblichus *V.P.* 28.152; cf. also *b. Pesah.* 112b; *Shab.* 129b.

23. See e.g., Dionysius of Halicarnassus *Ant. rom.* 7.58.3; Sherk 1988: 252–53, §198.

24. E.g., Josephus *Life* 279; *t. Shab.* 1:13; see further Abrahams 1967: 1:129–35; Safrai 1974–76: 804–7; Sanders 1992: 208–11; idem 1990: 7–8.

25. See e.g., Suetonius *Tib.* 32.2; Tacitus *Hist.* 5.4; Dio Cassius 65.7.2; Whittaker 1984: 63–71.

26. Barclay 2001: 295–98.

27. "Thanks to God," connected here with eating, probably evokes the blessing over the food (*Jub.* 22:6; Josephus *J.W.* 2.131; *Sib. Or.* 4.25–26; *m. Ber.* 3; cf. *Apos. Con.* 7.26.4; Safrai 1974–76: 802; Slater 1969).

as Lord (14:9). (Cf. the emphasis on sharing his death and new life in 6:2–11; on Jesus as risen Lord cf. also 10:9–10.)[28]

Because all would stand before God's judgment seat (14:10), judging others now was both pointless and dangerous, usurping a divine prerogative and inviting stricter judgment (2:1–3).[29] (Residents of Rome were familiar with a *bēma* or judgment seat, corresponding to the *rostrum* in the Roman forum.) Verifying the need for "all" (Jew and Gentile) to stand before God (14:10, 12), Paul cites Isa 45:23: "every" knee and tongue would acknowledge God at the judgment (Rom 14:11).[30] (The context in Isaiah, 45:21–24, emphasizes that God is the only savior and source of righteousness, even for the Gentiles.)[31]

Do Not Risk Siblings Stumbling (14:13–23)

Rather than "judging" others, Paul admonishes (playing on senses of "judge," cf. 14:10), one should "judge" not to provoke a fellow believer to fall away from faith (14:13). Food is a secondary matter not worth risking anyone's salvation over (14:13, 15). For Paul, foods are neutral, neither clean nor unclean (14:14; Paul is speaking ritually, according to Lev 11, not equating all food hygienically or nutritionally).[32] The issue is how one views the food (14:14), because one must eat "to the Lord" (14:6; cf. 1 Cor 10:31). To risk grieving or even "destroying"[33] another believer over food is to fail to walk in love (14:15), hence to violate the true heart of the

28. For "whether we live or die," cf. 2 Macc 6:26.

29. On judgment before God's throne (on the analogy with royal thrones), cf. e.g., *1 En.* 47:3; 90:20; *4 Ezra* 7:33; by the elect one, *1 En.* 55:4; 61:8; 62:3; 69:27–29 (all from the Similitudes, of uncertain date).

30. That Paul can apply this text directly to Jesus elsewhere (Phil 2:11), as well as the image of the "judgment seat" (2 Cor 5:10), shows just how closely he connected the Father and Son.

31. Because God swears by himself in Isa 45:23, Paul summarizes with the common OT "As I live" (e.g., Deut 32:40, a context cited in 15:10; esp. prominent in Ezek; in Isaiah, see 49:18), equivalent to other swearers' "As YHWH lives."

32. Many find here a reference to the tradition in Mark 7:15 (e.g., Jeremias 1964: 14; Dunn 1998: 685; Kim 2002: 264–65); this may well be the case, but we should note that the application to foods is ambiguous without Mark's explanation (Mark 7:19).

33. A common Pauline term that can suggest eternal destruction (2:12; 1 Cor 1:18–19; 2 Cor 2:15; 4:3); the closest parallel here, suggesting that Paul preached such material more than once, is 1 Cor 8:11. This fits the sense of "stumble" in 14:13; cf. John Chrysostom *Hom. Rom.* 26.

law (13:8–10). What the eater may intend as good (affirming freedom in Christ) may be viewed by others as evil (as disobeying Scripture, 14:16);[34] although Paul may have thought some postmodern approaches today extreme, he exhibits a tremendous pastoral sensitivity to different persons' motivations and perspectives.[35] Now Paul applies to Christians who do not observe the law the very critique against strict Jews they may have earlier applauded: in view of God's judgment (14:10–12; cf. 2:3–5), they must not judge (14:13; cf. 2:1), nor dare they let what they mean for good cause ill speaking (*blasphēmeō*, 14:16; cf. 2:24).

In contrast to what does not matter very much, namely foods, Paul comes in 14:17 (as he had in 14:6–8) to what really does matter: the true righteousness he has been discussing throughout the letter (beginning in 1:17). It is only life empowered by God's Spirit, not by the flesh, that can please God (8:2–13, especially 8:8). This life, rather than external rules, fulfills the hearts of the law (8:2–4). As in Galatians, this principle means that merely external rules involving the flesh cannot produce righteousness; but the genuine purpose of God's inspired law will never oppose the life yielded to God's Spirit (Gal 5:18–23). For Paul, peace seems especially relational (Rom 14:19); joy at least often occurs in the context of relationships (Rom 15:32; cf. 2 Cor 1:24; 2:3; 7:4, 13; 1 Thess 2:19–20).[36] In 14:17, Paul understands God's future reign (proclaimed by Jesus) as being initially actualized in believers' present lives through the Spirit.[37]

34. Others also warned against what others could construe as evil (see note on 12:17).

35. Scholars often compare his approach to Stoic *adiaphora*, matters that are neither intrinsically right nor wrong though they may tend toward or become either (Cicero *Fin.* 3.15.50; Seneca *Ep. Lucil.* 82.10–14; Lucian *Vit. auct.* 21; Arius Didymus 2.7.7, p. 42.13–15; 2.7.7b, p. 44.14–33; 2.7.7g, p. 50.18–20; cf. Deming 2003: 384–88); cf. even Epicurus in Diogenes Laertius 10.120. On motivation as a mitigating factor, see also Philodemus *On Criticism* col. 9B.

36. Paul's understanding of joy (as of the kingdom) reflects a biblical and Jewish context (see e.g., Halpern-Amaru 2005) more than a Stoic approach to emotion (on which, see the essays in Sihvola and Engberg-Pedersen 1998; also Musonius Rufus 17, p. 108.7; Dio Chrysostom *Or.* 25.1; Arius Didymus *Epit.* 2.7.5g, p. 32.4; 2.7.5k, p. 34.1; 2.7.6d, p. 40.1; 2.7.11g, p. 70.33–36; Engberg-Pedersen 2000: 73; idem 2003: 612), though there may be some overlap on positive emotions.

37. See especially Cho 2005: 11, 52–109; cf. Hamilton 1957: 21–22; on the kingdom in Paul, cf. also Donfried 2002: 233–52, esp. (regarding his use of Jesus's message) 247–48, 250–51.

Just as the spirit of the law will never contradict a life genuinely following God's Spirit (Gal 5:18, 23), it is by Spirit-filled character (Rom 14:17) rather than debates about foods that one serves Christ properly (Rom 14:18; cf. Heb 13:9). Paul describes this service as "pleasing" to God (as in 12:1–2) and tested and approved by people, a conventional combination for describing what is honorable to everyone (2 Cor 8:21).[38] Since God's way is peace (Rom 14:17), believers (divided in Rome, as we have noted) should seek[39] "peace" (cf. Rom 12:18; 1 Thess 5:13), hence reconciliation and unity, and beyond that to "build one another up" (14:19). "Building up"[40] contrasts with "tearing one another down" over foods (14:20).

In light of the priorities specified in 14:19–20, foods are clean,[41] hence neutral, but they become agents of evil if used in such a way as to provoke another's apostasy. Better to avoid not only unclean food, but even (perhaps hypothetically in this case) all meat and wine, or anything that could destroy a fellow believer (Rom 14:21; cf. 1 Cor 10:31–33). By faith one can know that food is clean, so that one is not condemned unless through causing another to stumble (14:22). But the one who cannot eat with confidence that God has approved the food will disobey what they genuinely believe is God's will, hence fall into sin (14:23).[42] For Paul, then, sin is not only a matter of behaviors, but of motives. A weak conscience with weak faith would be healthier if it were strong, but such maturation must come by persuasion regarding what is God's will, not by

38. Prov 3:4 LXX; Polybius 22.10.8; 27.8.4; Chariton *Chaer.* 1.10.3; *t. Šeqal.* 2:2; *Sipre Deut.* 79.1.1.

39. Possibly "pursue" here evokes 9:30–31, again implying faith as the right way to pursue righteousness. "Pursuing peace" also evokes Ps 34:14, as in 1 Pet 3:11. Both the allusion and the context support reading the subjunctive "let us" rather than the indicative "we do" here (mishearing a vowel was a common scribal error, as we noted at 5:1).

40. A frequent Pauline metaphor regarding God's people (15:20; 1 Cor 3:9; 8:1, 10; 10:23; 14:3–26; 2 Cor 10:8; 12:19; 13:10; 1 Thess 5:11), borrowed from the OT (Jer 1:10; 24:6; 31:28; 42:10).

41. A Stoic could speak of some foods as "pure" in the sense that they were not heavy, weighing down the soul (Musonius Rufus 18A, p. 112.27–28), but the idea in 14:20 is the Jewish idea of ritual purity, since speaking of *koinos* in 14:14 makes sense only on Jewish terms.

42. Some other Jewish teachers addressed the concern of doubtful issues that, while not necessarily sinful in themselves, could allow a negligent person to slide into sin (e.g., *'Abot R. Nat.* 30A; *'Abot R. Nat.* 32, §72B; cf. the rabbinic "fence around the Torah" in *m. 'Abot* 1:1; Moore 1971: vol. 1, 259).

simply changing behavior without regard for motives. By appealing to the larger principle that "anything not 'from faith' is sin," Paul also returns to his emphasis on faith as a relationship with God in contrast to mere regulations (for the specific Greek expression for "from faith" here, see 1:17; 3:26, 30; 4:16; 5:1; 9:30, 32; 10:6). Because Paul is concerned about those weak in faith (14:1), the doubters (14:23), he advises the "strong" not only to avoid terminally tripping them up in their faith (14:13) but to actively support them (15:1).

ROMANS 15

LIVING THE CHRISTIAN LIFE (12:1—15:13), *cont.*

Jewish and Gentile Believers Must Welcome One Another
(15:1–13)

Paul concludes his exhortation from 14:1–23 by calling believers not just to tolerate but also to serve one another's interests (to "please" one another, 15:1–3).[1] Just as those who are physically strong would be expected to help[2] weaker family members, Paul reminds those apt to criticize the "weak" that they should be helping them instead (15:1). Echoing the context, the "weak" refer to those weak in faith hence abstaining from particular foods lest they injure their relationship with God (14:1–2).[3] Paul ranks himself among the "strong" here, and will soon offer himself as an example of serving the poor saints in Jerusalem (15:25–27). "Build up" in 15:2 evokes 14:19–20, where believers should build up (by the fruit of the Spirit) rather than tear down one another over foods.

"Pleasing" others rather than oneself (15:1–3) refers not to entertaining every whim, but to being considerate of what might cause them

---

1. Some early manuscripts omit Rom 15–16, probably due to Marcionite influence; yet Paul does not complete the thought of 14:1–23 until 15:7 at the earliest.

2. "Bearing burdens" (cf. Gal 6:2, 5) might possibly remind this exhortation's largely Gentile hearers that Israel "bore" them (Rom 11:18). For the ideal of the stronger protecting the weaker, see e.g., 1 Thess 5:14; Mitchell 1991: 127; Stoics in Cicero *Fin.* 3.20.66; Seneca *Ep. Lucil.* 90.5; for the greater protecting and ruling the lesser, Dio Chrysostom *Or.* 3.62; for the "weak" as those dependent on rules, Seneca *Ep. Lucil.* 94.50. For the terms regarding social strength, see Dio Chrysostom *Or.* 38.31; Mitchell 1991: 126–27; for philosophers' self-view, see Arius Didymus *Epit.* 2.7.11g, p. 72.18.

3. Paul employed this designation with regard to abstainers from idol food in 1 Cor 8:7–12. His language in that passage seems to have been borrowed from the "strong"; he certainly did not approve of eating food offered to idols (see Keener 2005b: 73, 87–88; Garland 2003a; idem 2003b: 365–66, 395). "Strong" is presumably the group's self-designation here as well.

to stumble. Although Paul regarded circumcision as too much to ask of Gentiles, for Gentiles to accommodate Jewish food tastes in mixed company was a minimal sacrifice for the objective of unity in Christ's body.[4] Christ offered the example of this readiness to forgo pleasing himself; in 15:3 Paul cites Ps 69:9 from a psalm of a righteous sufferer, applied *par excellence* to Jesus (cf. John 2:17 for a different part of the same verse; Matt 27:34 for Ps 69:21). Here Jesus suffers on behalf of God, offering a model of laying down one's desires to serve others.

Explaining why he has cited Ps 69:9 for hortatory purposes, Paul notes that Scripture was written to teach believers (15:4). He believed that the events actually happened partly for later generations to learn from (1 Cor 10:6, 11), but here emphasizes more precisely that they were *written* for this purpose. He does not treat them as symbols of later realities, but indicates that one may learn by analogy from examples. The Scriptures were meant to sustain hope through "endurance" (NRSV "steadfastness") and "encouragement" (Rom 15:4).[5] Paul has earlier emphasized "endurance" (2:7; 12:12) and its role in serving hope (5:3–4; 8:25); the term for "encouragement" here includes also "exhortation" (as in 12:8). God gives endurance and encouragement (15:5) through Scripture (15:4), and Paul prays that God will give them the same mind toward one another (15:5; cf. comment on this exhortation in 12:16).[6] That is, Paul's exhortations from Scripture throughout this letter have been to help them endure the tensions and to come into unity.

As Jesus is the example for not seeking one's own interests (15:3), he is also the example for seeking this unity: they should have the same mind "according to [the standard of] Christ Jesus" (15:5; cf. Phil 2:1–11, esp. 2:2–5; see comment on 12:16). Believers may with united voice glorify the Father (15:6) just as Jesus prayed to the Father in 15:3 (and establishes Gentiles' praise in 15:9–12). Believers should again follow Jesus's example by accepting one another as he accepted all of them (15:7). This expectation climaxes the section's opening exhortation to accept one another (14:1) because of God's acceptance (14:3). That Christ accepted believers

4. Paul disapproved "pleasing" people at the expense of disobeying God (Gal 1:10; 1 Thess 2:4); but he was ready to "please" people strategically for their spiritual welfare (1 Cor 10:33).

5. On comfort through Scripture, see e.g., 2 Macc 15:9; on hope, e.g., *T. Jud.* 26:1.

6. Addressed grammatically to them but implicitly to God, this is a blessing or "wish-prayer" (see Wiles 1974: 25–29, 71).

to the Father's "glory" (15:7) fits the exhortation to "glorify" God together (15:6), a model relevant for Gentile believers (15:9).

Lest we suppose that Paul envisions the need for unity in the Roman church in a purely abstract or theoretical way, Paul appeals to Christ's example as one who served both Israel (15:8) and the Gentiles (15:9). In 15:8 he returns to his emphasis on God's faithfulness to his promises to the ancestors (9:4; 11:26-27; cf. God being "true" in 3:4), though Gentile believers have also been grafted into these (4:13-16; cf. Gal 3:14-29). (Although Paul will offer other biblical support first, citing Christ as a "servant" for Gentiles as well as for Israel may also prefigure his citation about the suffering servant in 15:21, and recall 10:15-16.) In 15:9 he begins his final major collection of citations, a rhetorical climax and his most compelling exegetical case for Gentile inclusion, reserved for the finale of his letter's body.[7] Jewish interpreters often linked biblical texts based on a common key term or concept, and Paul here links four texts about Gentiles, implying their faith. Many texts revealed God's interest in Gentiles praising him, sometimes along with his people (15:9-10) and under the same king of Israel in whom even Gentiles would hope (15:12).

Paul thus summons believers to common, cross-cultural worship of the one God (15:6-12; cf. 3:30). In glorifying God, Gentile believers (15:9) along with Jewish ones (15:6) would follow the faithful steps of their ancestor Abraham (4:20). Gentiles glorify God for his mercy (15:9) as Paul did in 11:33-36—Paul has already shown how Gentiles receive "mercy" (9:15-24) as part of God's plan that includes Israel as well (11:30-32). In 15:9 Paul cites Ps 18:49, which illustrates that God would be glorified among the nations.[8] In 15:10 he cites Deut 32:43, a context familiar from 10:19 and 12:19; that Gentiles rejoice "with his people" (in the Greek ver-

---

7. Verse 4 shows the emphasis Paul places on biblical support. For clinching finales, see e.g., Isaeus *Hagnias* 50; Cicero *Quinct.* 25.78-80. For the sake of the most biblically literate, he apparently samples the major parts of the canon (writings, law, and prophets; Jewett 2007: 893) to show how pervasive the interest is in Scripture. LXX Isaiah in particular exhibited an ethnically universalist agenda (Roetzel 2003: 52).

8. He might also cite it as a Davidic psalm. It might also be understood as the Messiah's prayer (as in Rom 15:3), given the LXX mention of "Christ" in the next verse (cf. also Johnson 2001: 219). See for this Hays 2005: 102 (who notes on 107 that Paul's repertoire of psalms applied to Christ's prayers share the superscription *eis to telos*, "for the end," which early Christians may have viewed as eschatologically significant).

sion) fits Paul's theme.[9] In 15:11 he cites Ps 117:1.[10] Paul's final citation of Isa 11:10 (in Rom 15:12) is particularly compelling; no one disputed that this root of Jesse (the restored stump of David's line) was messianic (Isa 11:1–11; cf. Rom 1:3).[11] This messiah would bring salvation and the knowledge of God to all nations (Isa 11:9–10; though he would remove the wicked, 11:4), and would likewise precipitate the restoration of the scattered Jewish people (Isa 11:11–16). Paul follows the common Greek translation, in which the Gentiles will hope on him, which Paul undoubtedly understands salvifically (cf. Rom 5:2–5; 1 Cor 15:19).

Paul concludes these texts with a prayer for them: as he has spoken of Scripture providing hope (15:4) and Gentiles hoping in Christ ("will hope" being the final term in 15:12), he now invokes the God of hope (15:13). Earlier in the letter he has established that the way of faith allows Gentiles to be accepted alongside Jews. Now he speaks of joy and peace in this way of believing (15:13). As Paul has already argued, it is not laws but the Spirit that brings "joy and peace" (14:17), here available through trust (like righteousness elsewhere in Romans, cf. 5:1); the Spirit also ultimately sustains hope (5:5; Gal 5:5). "Peace" is partly relational (with one another, 12:18; 14:19).

CLOSING OF ROMANS (15:14—16:27)

As in some other letters, Paul concludes with important closing business (Rom 15:14–33; cf. 1 Cor 16:1–18) before turning to final greetings (Rom 16:1–16, 21–23), exhortations (16:17–20), and praise (16:25–27).

Paul's Missionary Program (15:14–33)

Having completed the body of his argument, Paul now turns to something more like a normal letter closing.[12] Whenever their subject did not

9. Paul's "again" for providing another citation is not unusual style (Musonius Rufus 5, p. 50.14–15.

10. The reason for praise in Ps 117:1 appears in v. 2: God's "mercy" (relevant to Rom 15:9) and "truth" (relevant to 15:8). Hays (1989: 71–72) notes that "mercy" also appears in Ps 18:50, after the verse cited in Rom 15:10.

11. Starting with this passage, "root" or "shoot" sometimes became a messianic title, like "branch" in Isa 11:1.

12. See the comparisons with Paul's other letter conclusions in Moo 1996: 884. The section recalls themes from 1:8–15 (with e.g., Kennedy 1984: 154; Lung-Kwong 1998:

demand otherwise, speakers and writers liked to build rapport with their audience, assuring them of confidence in them.[13] Paul thus assures the believers in Rome that he does not assume that they *need* all his exhortations; he is simply reminding them of values that he trusts they already know and share (15:14–15).[14] They were "full" of goodness and had been "filled" with knowledge (both in contrast to the wicked of 1:29). They thus would be able to admonish one another on their own (Rom 15:14; cf. 1 Thess 5:14; contrast 1 Cor 4:14).[15]

If Paul has written "boldly," it is not because he thinks ill of them but because God has given him special grace to impart to them in this way (15:15; cf. 1:11–12).[16] He had earlier spoken through "the grace given to me" in calling them to humble cooperation (12:3), "grace given" representing a ministry gifting from God (12:6). God has graced Paul in a special way as a minister to Gentiles (1:13; 11:13), hence his ministry to them, both by this letter now and eventually in person (15:24, 28–29).

In particular, God has called him to offer the good news as a priest (*hierourgeō*), so he might offer the Gentiles as a "pleasing offering" to God, consecrated by the Holy Spirit (15:16). By reminding Gentiles to remain in unity with their Jewish siblings, hence their sacred "root" (11:16), Paul seeks to fulfill his (figuratively) priestly office.[17] His words recall his earlier

---

159; Talbert 2002: 327; Harvey 1998: 138; Jewett 2007: 902). For the "apostolic parousia" structure here, see Funk 1967: 251–53; this fits letters' interest in announcing the writer's coming.

13. See Olson 1985; Stowers 1986: 128–30; in antiquity, John Chrysostom *Hom. Rom.* 29; Ambrosiaster. Such expressions of confidence were also common before requests (cf. 15:24–28; see Olson 1985: 286).

14. See e.g., epistolary "reminders" in Cicero *Fam.* 13.75.1; Pliny *Ep.* 8.24.1, 10; in other exhortation, e.g., Isocrates *Demon.* 21; Cicero *Font.* 13.28; idem *Amic.* 22.85; Epictetus *Disc.* 4.4.29; 4.13.23; different sources in Aune 1987: 191.

15. A role usually assigned to teachers and elders (e.g., Iamblichus *Pyth. Life* 22.101; 33.231), but among Epicureans shared by all (Jewett 2007: 904–5; cf. Malherbe 1986: 48). Notably, Paul assigns the role to all members, not to the "strong" (Jewett 2007: 905). For "letters of admonition," see Stowers 1986: 125–32. "All knowledge" is conventional hyperbole (e.g., *Let. Aris.* 139, 239) in contrast to the ideal Stoic (which involves idealization; e.g., Arius Didymus *Epit.* 2.7.11m, p. 94.5).

16. Admitting that he has spoken "boldly" may reflect the rhetorical technique of *parrēsia* (cf. Anderson 2000: 94).

17. We should not read into this depiction later sacerdotal functions borrowed from Gentile civic religion, though Paul probably applies the image to gospel ministry (cf. 1 Cor 9:13) in a manner somewhat different from the "priesthood of believers" more generally (Rom 12:1; also the evocation of Exod 19:6 in 1 Pet 2:9; Rev 1:6; 5:10).

summons to the believers to offer themselves as living sacrifices "pleasing" to God (12:1) by engaging in humble cooperation (12:3). Drawing on an image from the law, Paul is careful to attribute the consecration (using the verb *hagiazō*) to the same source as all new life (8:2–13), the Holy (*hagios*) Spirit (cf. the connection between the "Holy" Spirit and holiness, or separation to God, also in 1 Thess 4:7–8.) Believers become consecrated to God at conversion in Christ (1 Cor 1:2; 6:11), hence are called "saints" (*hagioi*, holy or consecrated ones; Rom 1:7; 8:27; 16:2, 15), but as in 6:11 Paul wants to help them "be" what they "are" (cf. 2 Cor 7:1; 1 Thess 3:13).

While Paul has disavowed all boasting in works (2:23; 3:27; 4:2),[18] he is ready to boast in what Christ has worked[19] through him (Rom 15:17–19; cf. 1 Cor 1:31; 2 Cor 10:17). Paul is explaining the importance of the "grace given to him" to share with them (15:15), hence why they should heed him. The goal of his ministry (presenting Gentiles as an offering to God, 15:16) is Gentiles' obedience in word and deed[20] (15:18), precisely what Paul wishes to accomplish among them (1:5; 16:26). Christ has been achieving this obedience through Paul by means of the power of the Spirit (15:19), the same "power" active in believers' lives and ultimately in their resurrection (cf. Rom 1:4; 15:13; 1 Cor 2:4; 1 Thess 1:5).[21] This power of the Spirit (cf. Acts 10:38) was also expressed in "signs and wonders" (as in 2 Cor 12:12; cf. Acts 2:22, 43; 14:3; 15:12). If Paul's hearers had not caught earlier prophetic allusions in his comparisons with Moses (Rom 9:3) or Elijah (Rom 11:2), the mention of "signs and wonders" should have evoked the exodus and ministry of Moses (Exod 7:3; 11:9–10; Deut 4:34; 6:22; 7:19; 11:3; 26:8; 34:11; Jer 32:20–21; Wis 10:15–16; Bar 2:11). Paul not only theologized about a new exodus (Rom 8:14–17), he was an agent demonstrating its current reality (cf. the comparison with Moses

18. Though Paul spoke "daringly" (*tolmēros*, 15:15) about Christ, he would not "dare" (*tolmaō*) to boast of himself (15:18). On the impropriety of boasting, see e.g., Plutarch *De laude*; Forbes 1986.

19. In 7:8, 13, 15, 17, 18, 20, sin "worked" (*katergazomai*) in the person under law, beyond the person's volition; here Paul credits Christ for the good work in him (cf. Christ working through him in Col 1:29, albeit with a different verb).

20. "Word and deed" appears throughout ancient sources as a way of summarizing all behavior or demonstrating behavioral consistency with verbal claims.

21. On the connection of "power" and the Spirit in Paul, see also Gräbe 1992; elsewhere, e.g., *Ps. Sol.* 17:37 (for the Messiah); *L.A.B.* 27:10; but especially Mic 3:8; Zech 4:6.

in 2 Cor 3:7–18). Miraculously, Paul had preached from Jerusalem[22] as far as Illyricum (Rom 15:19), just as he planned to evangelize in Spain (15:24, 28). Illyricum was on the eastern coast of the Adriatic, across from Italy. The province was technically north of Macedonia, but he may mean Illyris Graeca in western Macedonia,[23] or simply that he went "up to" (the border of) Illyricum.[24] (His belief that the full measure of Gentiles will precede Israel's deliverance, articulated in 11:25–26, undoubtedly motivated his Gentile mission, including finally Spain,[25] which was often said to be at the ends of the earth.)[26]

Why then has Paul not come to them in person? It is obvious that he does not underestimate their strategic importance; people in antiquity simply would not write letters of this length without a significant purpose. But while Paul is eager to bring good news to believers in Rome, his primary mission is to bring the good news to unevangelized regions (15:20–22),[27] hence only now that he had completed this ministry is he ready to come to them (15:23). Paul was a foundation layer (1 Cor 3:10), and did not want to squander his ministry time simply building on a foundation already laid (Rom 15:20; cf. 2 Cor 10:13–16).[28] Paul did

22. The ideal starting point in Acts 1:8; cf. Paul's ministry there in Acts 9:28–29. Paul was converted and did some ministry near Damascus (Acts 9:19–22; Gal 1:17; 2 Cor 11:32), but counts his mission from Jerusalem. His language here indicates clearly a circuitous route (e.g., Moo 1996: 895), but some think that it also suggests that he had "circled" around in an arch, which could make sense on the Jewish tradition that Jerusalem was the world's center (Schreiner 1998: 769; Jewett 2007: 913; cf. Ezek 5:5; 38:12; *Jub.* 8:12, 19; *Sib. Or.* 5.249–50; more sources in Scott 1994: 526; Keener 2003b: 729–30). Paul's systematic approach to reaching all peoples was distinctive (Bowers 1980: 318–19).

23. Hengel and Schwemer 1997: 261; cf. Bruce 1977: 316.

24. Either way, he presumably ministered near it during his recent visit to Macedonia (2 Cor 2:13).

25. See Aus 1979; cf. Munck 1967: 98.

26. Strabo *Geog.* 1.1.5, 8; Seneca *Nat.* 1.pref. 13; Silius Italicus 1.270; 15.638; Pliny *Ep.* 2.3.8. Other "ends of the earth" included Nubia, Scythia, and the land of the eastern dawn.

27. Riesner 1998: 248, compares "have not heard my name" in the Greek version of Isa 66:19, a passage also mentioning a divine "sign."

28. He apparently knew of others missionizing other regions to the south and east (Latourette 1970: 82; on first-century mission see esp. Schnabel 2004). The "foundation" image coheres well with "building" the church (cf. 14:19; 15:2; here, Derrett 1997); Qumran sectarians employed some analogous images. The image was, of course, a common one in cities (cf. White 1996: 1:27).

not need to reach every individual; he believed that once an indigenous church was founded, it could reach its own culture.[29]

Paul in 15:21 provides a biblical argument for this agenda from Isa 52:15, a context he knows well (Isa 52:7 in Rom 10:15; Isa 53:1 in Rom 10:16).[30] The immediate context involves God's suffering servant (Isa 52:13—53:12), and Paul chooses the one verse of the passage that specifically refers to Gentiles coming to know (52:15), a verse that coheres with his interpretation of Isa 65:1 in Rom 10:20 (where God is found by some who did not seek him). The Gentile response in 52:15 contrasted with Israel's negative response to the servant in 53:1–3—which Paul quoted in Rom 10:16.

Paul now explains both his plans to visit them (15:23–24, 28–29) and the one remaining mission that will delay him a bit longer before he can come (15:25–27). Paul's mission to the unevangelized will take him to Spain (15:24, 28), allowing him to visit Rome en route (15:23–24, 28–29). (We should keep in mind that ancient travel took time, and it would also incur great expense, especially given Paul's standard practice of bringing fellow workers.) Spain was part of the Latin west, closely connected with Rome,[31] so Paul would undoubtedly start in the Roman colonies in Spain, where Latin was spoken.[32] Whereas he had normally started in synagogues where available (e.g., 2 Cor 11:24; Acts 13:5), in Spain he might have to break further new ground, because so far we have little evidence for a significant number of Jews in Spain during this period.[33]

His connection of his visit to the Roman believers with the Spanish mission functions partly as a polite form of request; to be "sent on his way" (15:24) implies not only provision while in Rome but also at least his ship fare to Spain. Nevertheless, such hospitality was a treasured value

---

29. Cf. Bornkamm 1971: 54.

30. Perhaps Paul also presupposes Isa 52:1 in Rom 13:11–12, though the language is too vague to suggest a deliberate allusion the ideal audience should have grasped.

31. On trade connections, see e.g., Charlesworth 1970: 150–67.

32. Cf. Ramsay 1910: 276; Garnsey and Saller 1987: 186. Paul's Roman citizenship (Acts 16:37) would not guarantee any proficiency in Latin, but he would have had opportunity for further exposure in Corinth.

33. See Bowers 1975. For recent archaeological work on Roman Spain, see Keay 2003; on Roman Spain, see Pliny *Nat.* 3.1.6—3.3.30; articles in Cancik and Schneider 2002–: vol. 6, 388–400. On Paul's Spanish mission, see further Jewett 2007: 74–79; that he reached Spain is fairly likely (*1 Clem.* 5.7; cf. later *Muratorian Canon* 38–39), but most traditions of the actual visit are later (Meinardus 1978).

in Paul's day and the believers would likely have counted it a special privilege to partner with an important apostle in this way—they might well do more than he requests here.[34] Paul's expectation of financial support at least for his voyage to Spain does not demand more of believers in Rome than the mission demands elsewhere (cf. the significant offerings in 15:25–27). That he frames the mission to Jerusalem with his Roman and Spanish plans (15:24, 28) suggests that whereas the eastern church has covered the Jerusalem offering (though Roman Gentiles, too, should have been obligated, 15:27), the Roman believers can sponsor a different, groundbreaking ministry of the apostle.

Eager as Paul is to visit the western Mediterranean, he must first return to Jerusalem (15:25) where his mission began (15:19). He does not expect this final mission in the east (15:25–27) to delay him long unless he meets trouble there, but is concerned that trouble is a possibility (15:30–32).[35] Paul's mission of laying foundations for the unevangelized (15:20) coheres with his mission of keeping the new Diaspora churches in spiritual unity with the Jerusalem church despite all their differences.[36] It also provides a model for the unity of the culturally different Jewish and Gentile believers in Rome.[37] If Paul, apostle to the Gentiles (11:13; 15:18–29), serves needs in Jerusalem, then Gentile believers more generally should look out for their Jewish siblings in Christ (cf. 11:18; probably relevant to law-observers in 15:1). Moreover, and in the immediate context, if the eastern churches have supported Paul's Jerusalem mission, the believers in Rome should support his Spanish mission, which is in their direct sphere of cultural influence (15:24, 28). Paul's report also implies that the eastern churches trust him financially (a reputation for integrity that Paul was careful to maintain, 1 Cor 16:3–4; 2 Cor 8:19–21).

34. On eagerness to entertain respected guests, cf. e.g., Euripides *Alc.* 1039–41; Cicero *Att.* 12.36; Plutarch *Cic.* 32.1.

35. We know from Acts 21:27—26:32, and infer from his subsequent letters and execution in Rome, that unfortunately trouble occurred.

36. Many connect the collection with Paul's ethnic universalism (see e.g., Park 2003: 65–67) and continuing respect for the Jerusalem church (Hill 1992: 173–78, against F. C. Baur).

37. Incidentally, it united Diaspora churches in a common mission (Harrison 2003: 308). Though Paul names provinces, people thought primarily in terms of cities (Judge 1960: 20); Christians' later trans-geographic network, perhaps growing from Judaism's "trans-nationalism" (cf. Meeks and Wilken 1978: 27), was highly distinctive (Wilken 1998: 43) and may have disturbed some Roman authorities.

The collection for the poor believers[38] in Jerusalem was in fact a major concern in this phase of Paul's ministry (1 Cor 16:1–4; 2 Cor 8—9; cf. Gal 2:10). While most passages concerning the collection stress concern for the recipients' needs and God's glory, this passage illumines another aspect of his motivation: Gentile or mixed Diaspora churches showing their appreciation for the Jerusalem church. Ancient Mediterranean culture emphasized the obligation of reciprocity (cf. note on 1:12), which involved repayment, but not in kind (e.g., one repaid economic benefactors with honor, not money; cf. Paul's adaptation of the principle in 2 Cor 9:11–15). Thus Paul speaks of Gentiles' spiritual "debt" to those in whose spiritual blessings (such as are listed in Rom 9:4–5, many elements of which Paul elsewhere attributes to all believers) they now share.[39] Some have compared the collection to the annual temple tax from the Diaspora to Jerusalem (a comparison that explains the mechanics better than the motivation).[40] Some have also compared the Jewish expectation of Gentiles bringing tribute to Jerusalem in the end time (Isa 45:14; 60:6–10; 66:20), which might be how the Jerusalem church could have viewed the offering.[41] Such a significant symbol of unity might help reduce the slanders that Paul's mission was not producing true converts to Israel's faith (cf. Acts 21:21; Gal 5:11–12). Indeed, Paul's "ministry" to Jerusalem (Rom 15:31) was linked to his "ministry" to Gentiles (11:13); very possibly he hoped to provoke his people to jealousy, hence hopefully contribute to their turning and the consummation of God's plan (11:14–15).[42] No other

38. Like Qumran sectarians, the Jerusalem church could call itself "the saints"; but Paul calls the believers in Rome "saints" also (1:7). Again on the analogy of Qumran (e.g., 1QM 11.9, 13; 13.14; 14.7; 1QpHab 12.3, 6, 10), some have viewed "the poor" as a label for the Jerusalem church (cf. Fitzmyer 1966: 244; Hengel 1974: 34), but the parallels seem inadequate (Keck 1966) and Paul's language here does not identify the poor as coextensive with all Jerusalem's saints. On the poor in early Judaism, see e.g., Hoyt 1974: 13–61; as a character type in the LXX, see Roth 1997: 112–32.

39. Contrast Paul's "debt" to Gentiles (Rom 1:14; see comment there) based on his call (1:1).

40. See especially Nickle 1966: 75–93 (noting also differences). For motivation, see early Jewish and Christian concern for the poor in Watson 2006.

41. In an economic context, *leitourgeō* could connote economic levies on wealthy individuals (Bell 1966: 301–2; Llewelyn and Kearsley 1994: 93–105), but in the context of *leitourgos* in 15:16 (where it is linked with *hierourgeō*) it might bear priestly connotations (see also Llewelyn and Kearsley 1994: 105–11).

42. With e.g., Donaldson 1997b: 252. Against some, however, this should not be understood in terms of unrealistic utopian expectation; Paul hoped to be able to save

similarly-sized Jewish groups could boast an analogous proportion of Gentile converts that might be construed as the beginning of the eschatological harvest of Gentiles.

Paul employs a variety of terms like "service" and "sharing,"[43] viewing this economic help as ministry. Despite Paul's earlier concern (2 Cor 8:11; 9:3–4), Corinth (leading the province of Achaia) has joined the Macedonian churches (including Philippi and Thessalonica) in supporting Paul's collection. Paul must figuratively "fix his seal" on the collection (Rom 15:28); business texts used such language for securing containers to prevent loss (as commentators often note), but also for attesting or certifying something's content.[44]

In 15:30 Paul solicits prayers (as in 2 Cor 1:11; Phil 1:19; 1 Thess 5:25; 2 Thess 3:1; Phlm 22), in this case for protection in Judea and that the Jerusalem church will welcome the offering (Rom 15:31). Some doubt that the church accepted his offering, but that suspicion seems misplaced. Rejecting a gift was culturally tantamount to declaring enmity,[45] and the leaders of the Jerusalem church had initially requested such help (Gal 2:10). Luke probably makes little of the collection in Acts (24:17) simply because it was not relevant in his day. Paul's concern of hostility in Jerusalem, however, seems to have materialized. The mention of the "disobedient" in Judea recalls Paul's understanding that Scripture predicted this disobedience (Rom 10:21) and that it remained part of God's plan for all humanity (11:30–32).

Only success and safety in Jerusalem would guarantee Paul's ability to proceed with the following mission in the west, when Paul could find "rest" among them (15:32; for such hospitality, cf. 1 Cor 16:18; 2 Cor 7:13; Phlm 7). As it turned out, from Luke's subsequent perspective, God spared Paul's life and got him to Rome despite and ultimately even by means of hostility in Jerusalem (Acts 21–28). Paul elsewhere invokes the "God of

---

"some" (11:14), and anticipated opposition (15:30–32). Rather than expecting his collection to consummate history, he hoped to visit Rome afterward (15:24). His mission played a part in Israel's salvation, but not the entire role.

43. For an even wider array of terms, see 2 Cor 8–9 (e.g., 9:1); Dahl 1977: 37–38. Such diverse terminology fits epigraphic conventions (Harrison 2003: 300).

44. E.g., 1 Cor 9:2; Aelius Aristides *Defense of Oratory* 340, §112D (figuratively); cf. Deissmann 1923: 238–39.

45. Marshall 1987: 13–21. At the least it displayed contempt (Pliny *Ep.* 8.6.9).

peace" (Rom 15:33; 1 Thess 5:23), but the phrase seems particularly apropos when addressing divided congregations (Rom 16:20; Phil 4:9).[46]

---

46. Noted also by Theodoret of Cyr; Pelagius; and Ambrosiaster (Bray 1998: 367–68). The expression was not common (*T. Dan* 5:2; though cf. the similar formulation "God of righteousness" in *T. Jud.* 22:2).

ROMANS 16

CLOSING OF ROMANS (15:14—16:27), *cont.*

Commending the Bearer (16:1–2)

Although for a time scholars suspected that Romans 16 was the fragment of a letter to Ephesus appended to Romans, most now agree that it is an integral part of Romans. Paul knows so many of the people because people often traveled to and from Rome, and expelled Jewish believers Paul had met earlier (like Prisca and Aquila) have now returned there.[1]

In Rome as elsewhere in the urban Mediterranean world, respected persons wrote letters of recommendation to their peers to request favors for others.[2] Paul elsewhere writes recommendations, but this is his most explicit (employing the same verb as when mentioning recommendation letters in 2 Cor 3:1). Why does he preface his more extensive greetings with this recommendation of a church leader from Cenchrea, Corinth's Aegean port town? Phoebe was carrying the letter to the Romans, and letters sometimes identified special bearers.[3] Phoebe's status is important, because as the letter's bearer who knew Paul's intention directly, she might read it (hence "perform" it orally, and by gestures communicate his emphases and ironies) in the congregations in Rome;[4] certainly she would

---

1. Gamble 1977 has persuaded most subsequent scholars (cf. also arguments in Fitzmyer 1993: 55–67; Lung-Kwong 1998: 24–35). On frequent migration to Rome, see e.g., Ramsay 1904: 376; Leon 1960: 238–40; Stambaugh 1988: 90–92; Dresken-Weiland 2003.

2. See e.g., Cicero *Fam.* 13; Kim 1972; more briefly, Stowers 1986: 153–65.

3. E.g., Dio Chrysostom *Ep.* 1. Mail service existed only for the government; other letters went with couriers or (more often) travelers (e.g., Cicero *Fam.* 1.7.1; 2.1.1; 3.1.2; 5.5.1; Pliny *Ep.* 2.12.7; Fronto *Ad Amic.* 2.2; Nicholson 1994; Richards 2004: 177–82).

4. Although a minority, female readers were known (e.g., Schmidt 2005), though she might delegate the reading proper to a scribe (Jewett 2007: 23). On public readings, see Shiell 2004: 102–36.

be called on to explain elements if questions arose.[5] They should welcome her, reciprocating her own hospitality to others (16:2).[6]

What does the passage reveal about her status?[7] First, she is a *diakonos* of the Cenchrea church (16:1). Paul can employ this term quite generally (cf. a possibly related gift in 12:7). The title encompasses the ministry of Jesus (15:8), Paul (Rom 15:25; 2 Cor 3:6; 6:4; 11:23; Col 1:23–25), and his companions (Col 1:7). When employed for an office, it seems distinct from overseers (Phil 1:1; cf. 1 Tim 3:1–13), but Paul does not define it, nor is the "office" sense his usual usage. It thus seems safest to claim merely that she was a minister of some sort without defining the character of her ministry more specifically. If the office of *diakonos* was related to those in charge of the synagogue building, this role might relate to her function as patron of a house congregation, but we lack sufficient information to be certain.[8]

Second, she has been a *prostatis* to many. Most scholars concur that this term designates her as a "patron."[9] We know of many women patrons, though they were a minority;[10] the most common independent, property-owning women might be widows, but others could also fill this role. In any case, she likely hosts the house congregation in Cenchrea,[11] giving her some influence there, and probably had a home of ample size. Given the mercantile character of Cenchrea, she may be traveling to Rome on busi-

---

5. As with other bearers (Xenophon *Cyr.* 4.5.34). Travelers often supplemented letters with oral information (e.g., Cicero *Fam.* 1.6.1; 3.1.1; 9.2.1; 12.30.3; cf. Danker 1989: 109).

6. See Winter 2001: 202.

7. Although Corinth was a Roman colony, the citizens of which were Romans, Phoebe's name is Greek; if she were a Roman citizen, Paul might have used one of her Roman names, as he uses his own.

8. The office of "deacon" is clearer in later texts (e.g., 1 *Clem.* 42.4–5; *Did.* 15.1; Ign. *Eph.* 2.1; Ign. *Mag.* 2.1; 6.1; 13.1; cf. possibly the feminine *ministra* in Pliny *Ep.* 10.96.8).

9. E.g., White 2003: 467. *Prostatis* could evoke the spiritual gift of leading (*proistēmi*) in 12:8, as it derives from that verb (cf. the cognate *prostatēs*, including in the LXX); but most often it designates simply patron. Patrons and hosts were not necessarily leaders (Lampe 2003b: 497; though cf. Lane 1998: 210), though in the plural leadership of the small house churches hosts (who would tend to have more means and education) probably often proved influential. For women patrons of house churches, see Osiek and MacDonald 2006: 194–220; many pagans found this heavy involvement of women objectionable (MacDonald 2003: 184; Cook 2002: 113–14, 166–67).

10. E.g., Hemelrijk 2004 (for cities); Winter 2001: 199–201; benefactresses in Forbis 1990; among synagogue patrons, White 1996–97: 1:81.

11. On Cenchrea, see e.g., Rothaus 2000: 64–83; Scranton, Shaw, and Ibrahim 1978.

ness; trade ties between Rome and Corinth were strong, and business-women did travel. Given Paul's praise of her business skills, some suggest that he also hoped that she could raise support for his Spanish mission in Rome.

Greetings to Roman Believers (16:3–16)

Paul sends greetings to believers (probably mostly or wholly leaders) whom he knows or knows about in Rome, in some cases "recommending" them as well. Adding greetings to individuals at the end of letters was common[12] (though usually not so many). Building rapport with one's audience was important, but given the risks of inadvertently omitting anyone, Paul seems especially interested in building rapport here, probably because he plans to visit and has not been there previously. Western readers may think of greetings as mere formality, but they held a deeper social meaning in Paul's culture. Paul's personal interest in believers in Rome (as elsewhere) illustrates concretely the character of love he has been urging (12:3–5, 10; 13:8–10; 14:1—15:7; cf. 1:11–12; 15:23–24).

The constant travelers between Rome and Corinth (where Paul writes) and the various Jewish believers from Rome who had recently resided in Corinth and elsewhere during Claudius's ban (Acts 18:2) help explain Paul's knowledge of so many leaders in the church in Rome. While we can identify some persons as Jewish, we cannot certainly infer ethnicity from names; many Diaspora Jews used typical Gentile names (even named for pagan deities, such as Hermes).[13] That Greek names are more common than Latin ones in Paul's list suggests that, as we would expect, the churches have made the greatest inroads among eastern provincials living in Rome, as well as among slaves.[14]

12. E.g., *P. Oxy.* 114.16–18; 1296.9–19; Cicero *Att.* 6.3, end; Fronto *Verum Imp.* 2.6, end; Weima 1994: 39–42.

13. A name in 16:14; for Jews, see *CPJ* 3:9, §453; 3:175–76; *CIJ* 1:23, §26; 1:75, §108; 1:255, §324.

14. A Latin name does not guarantee Roman citizenship, but Roman citizens here would probably be addressed by Roman names. Half of Rome's Jewish population had Latin names, whereas only six of the twenty-six persons Paul greets do (and some of these predominate among slaves and freedpersons, like "Julia"); fourteen have common slave names. Up to one-third of Paul's associates have Latin names, vastly higher than average in the Greek east (Judge 1982: 13), but a high percentage of these are from Corinth.

Not all names require equal comment for this short volume. Particularly significant and different from some churches in the east is the dominance of women explicitly involved in some forms of ministry (16:1–7, 12).[15] This is not surprising, since women exercised much more freedom in Rome (and in a Roman colony in Macedonia, Phil 4:2–3) than in much of the Greek east. Although Paul greets over twice as many men as women, he commends more women than men for ministry, perhaps partly because even in Rome their ministries still faced more challenges than men, hence invited more affirmation.[16]

Paul begins with Prisca and Aquila (16:3–5), his close coworkers in Corinth and Ephesus (1 Cor 16:19; Acts 18:1–2, 18, 26) who have now returned to Rome. It was unusual for a wife to be named first, as Prisca (a Latin name that had a more familiar form, Priscilla) usually is by Paul and Luke; this sequence signified either higher social status (as normally in antiquity)[17] or higher status in the church (as possibly relevant in the churches).[18] Paul calls them his "fellow workers," a title that, along with *diakonos* (16:1), is among Paul's most common designation for his colleagues in ministry (Rom 16:9, 16, 21; 2 Cor 8:23; Phil 2:25; 4:3; Col 4:11; 1 Thess 3:2; Phlm 1, 24).

"Risking necks" was an idiom for risking lives (employing the image of beheading, 16:4).[19] Somehow they may have protected Paul, whether in Corinth or (more often proposed) Ephesus, so that those touched by his Gentile mission owe gratitude to them. That the church meets in their "house" (16:5) may simply mean that it meets in their dwelling; the vast majority of dwellings in Rome itself were tenement apartments, the larger homes being nearer the ground floor.[20] (Upper floor apartments might

15. Often noted, e.g., Scholer 1980; Venetz 2002; Pizzuto-Pomaco 2003. Note even many of the patristic opinions in Bray 1998: 368–72.

16. All the more noteworthy in that men probably outnumbered women in Rome (Stambaugh 1988: 89).

17. See Flory 1984; cf. Euripides *El.* 931–33; MacMullen 1980: 210.

18. Though husband-and-wife teams are well-known in business, *possibly* Aquila now supervised more of the business and Prisca more of the house church ministry.

19. Cf. Xenophon *Anab.* 7.4.7–10; Terence *Andr.* 676–77; Seneca *Nat.* 4. pref. 15; cf. Deissmann 1978: 117–18. One being beheaded would "lay down" the neck (Seneca the Elder *Suas.* 6.17; Seneca the Younger *Nat.* 2.59.7; Epictetus *Disc.* 1.1.18–25; cf. *Tg. Neof.* 1 on Gen 22:10).

20. On Roman housing, see e.g., Juvenal *Sat.* 3.190–211; Packer 1967; Clarke 1991; Stambaugh 1988: 172–78; Wallace-Hadrill 2003: 7–10. Carcopino (1940: 23–24) calcu-

include barely enough room to sleep. Rome's structures were notoriously unstable and flammable, worse near the top; much of this housing perished in the fire of 64 CE a few years later.)

Even if this family did use a house (as they may have in Ephesus; 1 Cor 16:19), it is noteworthy that this label is not applied to the other congregations implied in this chapter. Possibly guests could also be accommodated in the long hall connecting apartments on upper floors, if neighbors proved amenable. Because ground floor rooms were often businesses with small mezzanine apartments for sleeping above the work area, some have suggested that the church may have met in such a place (cf. Acts 18:3).

As "firstfruits" of the Roman province of Asia, Epaenetus (a Greek name, 16:5) was probably converted through Paul's early Ephesian ministry (Acts 18:19—19:41). Romans had a name like "Mary" (literally *Maria*, 16:5), but it is also a frequent variant (including in every other usage in the NT) of "Miriam," by far the most common name of Jewish women (especially in Palestine). Like Persis in 16:12, Mary "labored much" (16:6); the context and "for you" suggest spiritual labor, as in Paul's own ministry (1 Cor 15:10; Gal 4:11; Phil 2:16; Col 1:29) and that of others (1 Cor 16:16; 1 Thess 5:12).

Andronicus and Junia seem to be a husband-wife apostolic team (16:7; brother-sister is less likely, and anything else would have been scandalous). "Junia" is plainly a woman's name, as ancient commentators commonly recognized (and often found surprising).[21] It is grammatically possible to read "of note among the apostles" as being honored by other apostles,[22] but Paul nowhere else appeals to the opinion of "the apostles" as a group, so most scholars prefer the other possible grammatical reading, namely, that Paul calls them "noteworthy apostles." The larger question is what Paul means by calling them apostles. Whereas Luke usually reserves the title for the Twelve, Paul applies the title much more widely (begin-

---

lates that Rome had "only one private house for every 26 blocks of apartment houses."

21. E.g., John Chrysostom *Hom. Rom.* 31.2. The supposed contraction of the male "Junianus" here is nowhere attested in antiquity and is unlikely, since such contractions do not occur with *Roman* names (as this one is); see e.g., Cervin 1994; cf. Schulz 1987. The attempt to make Junia male (found even in some translations) seems a case of theological special pleading.

22. Burer and Wallace 2001; but cf. the detailed response by Bauckham 2002: 172–80.

ning with his own ministry; see 1 Cor 15:5–7; Gal 1:19; 1 Thess 2:7 [with 1:1]). Detractors to Junia being an apostle note that Paul speaks twice of apostles (commissioned agents) of churches; yet these are always specified as such (2 Cor 8:23; Phil 2:25). One cannot insist that Paul speaks here merely of "agents of churches" as opposed to his normal sense of "apostles," since he offers no such specification here, unless one argues on the basis that women could not be apostles (which would constitute a circular argument here, assuming what it is designed to prove). The other uses in Romans apply to himself (1:1; 11:13). We should keep in mind, however, that Paul's broader usage for an agent commissioned by Christ does not specify, as people sometimes assume, "members of the Twelve" or "writers of Scripture."[23] It does seem to imply special authorization and is normally accompanied by suffering (1 Cor 4:9) and signs and wonders (2 Cor 12:12).

Although Paul could employ "fellow prisoners" figuratively,[24] he later employs the language for those who were with him at least somehow in his captivity (Col 4:10; Phlm 23); given Paul's "many imprisonments" (2 Cor 11:23), we cannot be sure where (in view of 1 Cor 15:32, perhaps Ephesus?). That they were "in Christ" before Paul, however, suggests that they belonged to the Jerusalem church. Their Greek (Andronicus) and Latin (Junia) names suggest that they hailed from Diaspora families in Jerusalem, possibly in Junia's case descended from freed slaves of Roman citizens (as Paul likely was; thus they may have attended the same "synagogue of freedpersons" mentioned by Luke in Acts 6:9).[25] But while it might therefore be tempting to envision Junia as Paul's "relative" in a closer sense, Paul uses the term "kin" (*suggenēs*) here for all fellow Jews (Rom 9:3; 16:11, 21).

"Ampliatus" and "Urbanus" (16:8–9) were common slave names; if Paul met them in the east, they are probably freedmen.[26] Given the movement's birth in Rome's Jewish community, many think that the "household

23. Given the culture, we also cannot be certain as to the sphere of ministry; perhaps Andronicus and Junia each focused on ministry to their own gender (but cf. Acts 16:13–15; 18:26).

24. Cf. perhaps Phlm 23; figurative captivity in e.g., Pliny *Ep.* 2.8.2.

25. Alternatively, Bauckham (2002: 165–94) suggests that Junia was a Roman citizen follower from Jesus's Galilean ministry, namely Joanna, who likely remarried after Chuza's death (Luke 8:3). On Junia as an apostle, see also e.g., Bruce 1990: 262; Epp 2005.

26. Urbanus's Latin name probably suggests that he had been named by a Roman citizen; on manumission he probably achieved citizenship.

of Aristobulus" (16:10) refers to slaves and freedpersons of the Herodian prince Aristobulus, who lived in Rome, though he himself may have died by this point. (A "household" included slaves and freedpersons.) A Jew named "Herodion" (16:11) may have also been a slave or freedperson from the Herodian family. (Slaves in prominent households were often well-educated, and could wield significant power.) Some scholars think that the "household of Narcissus" (16:11) refers to those attached to the powerful and wealthy imperial freedman Narcissus. The period and location do fit, though in the vast city of Rome it is not surprising that there were other freedpersons and slaveholders with this name.

The matching names "Tryphaena" and "Tryphosa" (16:12) suggest twin sisters. "Persis" (16:12) was a common name for slaves imported from Persia, so she may have been a slave or freedwoman. Because Paul knew Rufus's mother (16:13),[27] it is plausible that this is the Rufus known soon afterward to Mark's possibly Roman audience, the son of Simon of Cyrene (Mark 15:21). Since Diaspora Jewish believers were scattered from Jerusalem, and many Cyrenian ones settled in Antioch (Acts 8:4; 11:20), Paul could have known the family there.[28] The multiple names in the two congregations in 16:14, 15 suggest multiple leaders and perhaps sizeable congregations; Paul may have less personal acquaintance with these individuals (not even informed as to the name of Nereus's sister).

Kissing (16:16) was employed for greeting relatives or close friends in antiquity. Though typically on the mouth, such light kisses were normally readily distinguishable from the erotic ones emphasized in modern Western culture.[29] (The "holy" kiss specifies its limits; still, later abuses led to more explicit restrictions in the churches.) Paul here might practice the rare but attested custom of secondary kissing, something like "Give so-and-so a kiss for me."[30] Whether Paul simply advises believers to kiss each other, or to convey his kiss greetings, his admonition would help cement

27. For viewing another's mother as one's own, see e.g., 1 Tim 5:2; Pseudo-Callisthenes *Alex.* 2.20; Horsley 1987: §9, p. 34.

28. Alternatively, a Jerusalem tomb inscription might identify them (e.g., Lane 1974: 563), but the names are too common to be sure.

29. E.g., Ovid *Metam.* 2. 356–57, 430–31; 10.362, 525; Arrian *Alex.* 4.11.3; Plutarch *Quaest. rom.* 6, *Mor.* 265B; for further details, see Keener 2000c.

30. A letter's reader might convey the writer's kiss to another on behalf of the writer (Fronto *Ad M. Caes.* 1.8.7; 5.33 [48]; 5.42 [57]).

unity. He sends greetings from the churches of the east (16:16) and will offer more specific greetings in 16:21–23.

Beware Selfish Teachers (16:17–20)

Paul offers a final, closing exhortation.[31] While it is framed in general terms, its warning against those who cause division (*dichostasia*, "factious hostility"; 16:17) is relevant to the problems among believers in Rome (see particularly 14:1—15:7), especially since these schismatics also cause "stumbling" (16:17; cf. 14:4, 13, 21). Paul also earlier held as a standard the teaching they had received (including the gospel, 6:17); this message offered the criterion for evaluating other teachings.

That such contentious persons who hurt others' faith were "slaves not of Christ but of their own bellies" (16:18) recalls Paul's earlier teaching about being slaves of God rather than sin (6:6, 16–22; 7:6; 12:11; 14:18) and comments on passions and desires (1:24, 26; 6:12; 7:5, 7–8; 13:14). It might also hint at those reluctant to forgo foods for the sake of others' faith (14:21), but need not be construed so narrowly; moralists regularly mentioned "bellies" (originally as a metonymy for gluttony) for self-indulgence (also in 1 Cor 6:13; Phil 3:19).[32] Because Paul has not mentioned "opponents" elsewhere in this letter (despite 3:8), he might warn about a potential external threat (cf. Phil 3:2), or he might envision the possibility of some current leaders being corrupted (cf. Acts 20:29–30). Though sensitive to build rapport, Paul disclaimed flattery (1 Thess 2:5); his rhyming "fine" and "blessing" speech (*chrēstologia*, *eulogia*) warns against those who would merely encourage and pander to hearers' desires (cf. 2 Tim 4:3; 2 Pet 2:1–3, 10–14). Especially if it is connected with the following context (16:20), Paul's mention of deception in 16:18 might echo the killing role of sin exploiting the law in 7:11 (which some see as an echo of how the devil destroyed Adam; cf. Gen 3:13).

31. A minority of scholars treat the paragraph as an interpolation, because it interrupts greetings; but textual evidence is against this proposal, and Paul's letters are full of digressions. Paul may break up the greetings sections deliberately with this reminder; closing exhortations (e.g., Fronto *Ad M. Caes.* 3.16.2) and summaries were common toward a work's conclusion. Some material could follow a closing summary (e.g., Isaeus *Cleon.* 48 with 49–51).

32. E.g., 3 Macc 7:11; Philo *Spec. Laws* 1.148, 192, 281; 4.91; further sources in Keener 1999: 342; hence "slave of the belly" in Maximus of Tyre *Or.* 25.6; Achilles Tatius *Leuc. Clit.* 2.23.1; Philostratus *Vit. Apoll.* 1.7 (cf. also Sallust *Bell. Cat.* 2.8).

Paul, whose mission is to bring Gentiles to obey Israel's God (1:5; 15:18; 16:25), encourages them that their obedience is widely known (16:19; for the fame of the capital's church, cf. 1:8; for Paul's encouragement in the midst of exhortation, cf. 15:14–15). Nevertheless, he wants them to be "wise" in good matters (contrast 1:22) and "innocent" or unskilled in what is evil (16:19).[33] He is not suggesting that they should be naïve regarding evildoers, a potential interpretation that he has already expressly disavowed at the end of 16:18. In view of 16:20, it is possible that Paul has in mind the disastrous consequences of the first humans partaking from the tree that provided experiential knowledge of the difference between good and evil (cf. Rom 5:12–21; Gen 3:5).

When Paul speaks of God crushing Satan under their feet (16:20), he probably thinks of Gen 3:15 in light of a line of Jewish tradition that identified Satan or the devil with the serpent in that passage (cf. Rev 12:9).[34] Because they belong to the new Adam (5:12–21), perhaps understood as the woman's promised seed of Gen 3:15, their victory is certain, even if not yet consummated.[35]

Greetings from Corinth (16:21–23)

Having sent greetings to individuals in Rome, Paul now includes greetings from others to the church in Rome, also a common custom in letters.[36] Timothy is one of Paul's chief companions (e.g., 1 Cor 4:17; 16:10; Phil 2:19–22; 1 Thess 3:2), who will soon leave with Paul for Jerusalem (Acts 20:4). Likewise, Jason[37] and Sosipater (a variant form of Sopater) are with Paul in Corinth as Macedonian delegates for the collection that all of them will soon accompany to Jerusalem (Acts 17:5–9; 20:4; cf. Rom

33. This may echo the saying behind Matt 10:16, which was probably in Q (cf. the abbreviated version in Luke 10:3).

34. Because snakes often bit feet (Aeschylus *Suppl.* 896–97; Sophocles *Phil.* 632; Ovid *Metam.* 11.775–76), stepping on one was a dangerous maneuver (Virgil *Aen.* 2.379–81; Diodorus Siculus 20.42.2; *Sib. Or.* 1.59–64).

35. Some find messianic hints even in the common Greek version of Gen 3:15 (Martin 1965; Collins 1997; Alexander 1997), but this seems unclear. In any case, the Targum so applied it (McNamara 1972: 121).

36. See e.g., Cicero *Att.* 5.9; Fronto *Ad M. Caes.* 3.12; 4.10; especially Weima 1994: 42–45.

37. Many Jews bore this Greek name, as here (see e.g., *CPJ* 3:179; *CIJ* 1:25, §32; 2:15, §749).

15:26; 2 Cor 9:4; 1 Cor 16:3). The author of Acts, traditionally identified as "Luke," may have accompanied Paul from Philippi (Acts 20:5–6);
whether this is the "Lucius" of the present verse (who might then have
gone on ahead to Philippi) is difficult to say.[38]

Tertius (whose Latin name suggests a third-born male) in 16:22 was
the scribe who penned the letter at Paul's dictation. Scribes were sometimes professionals and sometimes educated slaves of the wealthy; the
poor needed their help, and the rich could afford it.[39] That he adds his
own greeting suggests that he belonged to the Christian community, presumably in Corinth (from which Paul is writing).

Scholars debate how Gaius was "host" to the entire church in Corinth
(16:23), which now met in multiple homes. Some think he had a wealthy
villa where all the house churches could assemble together periodically;
others believe that he was the original church's sponsor (before multiple
assemblies grew), his full Roman name being Gaius Titius Justus (Acts
18:7). Perhaps he simply had shown hospitality to many and Paul offers
hyperbolic praise. In any case, he is a patron and person of means, presumably part of Corinth's citizen class (who were Roman citizens). As
"Tertius" (16:22) identifies a third-born male, "Quartus" (16:23) identifies a fourth-born.

Most intriguing is Erastus, city treasurer or manager (16:23).
Because the Greek phrase describing his work here is more general than
a corresponding Latin one would be, scholars debate his exact role. An
inscription from this era mentions one Erastus (presumably from the
city's same political class) as Corinth's aedile. While some scholars believe that a different Erastus is in view, others (including the editor of the
Corinthian inscriptions) identify them.[40] Although a "manager" (*oikono-
mos*) was usually of lower status than an aedile (because the former was
a much more common office), it was also one of the Greek terms used

38. Traditional identifications of "Luke" are with the Gentile physician in Col 4:14
(cf. Col 4:11), whereas those named in Rom 16:21 are Jewish (as a Jewish name, e.g.,
CIJ 1:111, §155). The matter is discussed in greater detail in various commentaries on
Romans and Acts, including my forthcoming commentary on Acts with Hendrickson.

39. For others' help for the illiterate, e.g., P. Oxy. 269.17–18; 1636.45–46; P. Lond.
1164.h.30; for the wealthy, e.g., Cicero *Att.* 14.21; Fronto *Eloq.* 2; idem *Ad Amic.* 2.3; *Ad
M. Caes.* 5.26; for degrees of literary freedom, cf. Richards 2004: 64–83.

40. Cf. e.g., various views in Koester 2005: 339–40; Winter 1994: 180–96; Gill 1989;
Meggitt 1996.

to translate the Latin title *aedile*.[41] Alternatively, *aedile* may have been a subsequent office that Erastus held. Candidates for the office of aedile had to be wealthy, since they offered pledges of the funds they would provide the city if elected.[42] Since Paul grants no Christian title, *possibly* Erastus was simply a patron for the Christian community rather than a member (like the Asiarchs in Acts 19:31).[43] The Erastus of Acts 19:22 is clearly a believer, but a Corinthian political figure probably would not be free to travel with Paul (though cf. 2 Tim 4:20).

Praising God's Wisdom (16:25–27)

Paul has been concluding his letter in stages (greetings to Rome, a closing exhortation, greetings from Corinth), and now offers a final praise to God (cf. 1:25; 9:5; esp. 11:33–36). Some manuscripts relocate this closing doxology to after 14:23 or elsewhere (or include it in both locations), and a few omit it (though most early manuscripts have it here, and the widest geographic range also supports its inclusion).[44] The passage provides such a fitting conclusion for Romans, however, it seems likelier designed by Paul than by a typical scribe.[45] As 15:14–33 repeats many themes of 1:8–15, so 16:25–27 recalls earlier material, especially 1:2–5 (the most important echo being the "obedience of faith").[46] As 11:33–36 praised God for his wisdom in designing history (11:1–32), so here Paul again praises the "only wise God," the designer of history.

41. Winter 1994: 185–87; Erastus was not a common name in Corinth (cf. Winter 1994: 180, 191–92). A city manager could even be a public slave, though often a temporary one merely for the duration of the activity.

42. Winter 1994: 182–83. Erastus apparently promised to pave a street (Winter 1994: 184).

43. See Keener 2006.

44. Some manuscripts of Romans ended with 14:23, probably (as we noted earlier) due to Marcion's predilections; if Marcion omitted most of chs. 15–16 but retained the closing words, this might explain the tradition of this location preserved in some MSS. See textual discussion in Metzger 1975: 533–36, 540.

45. With many, e.g., Marshall 1999: 183; Stuhlmacher 1994: 256; Grieb 2002: 146. Jewett (2007: 998), himself viewing it as inauthentic, opines that scholars are fairly evenly divided on the question. As Schlatter (1995: 278) observes, the letter probably did not end with the greeting to Quartus.

46. Conclusions often summarized elements of a work (e.g., *Rhet. Alex.* 36, 1443b.15–16; Aeschines *Tim.* 196; Cicero *Fin.* 5.32.95–96; Dionysius of Halicarnassus *Thuc.* 55; idem *Dem.* 32; Musonius Rufus 3, p. 42.23–29).

Rom 16:25–27	Earlier points in Romans
God is powerful to "establish" you according to my gospel (16:25)	I yearn to share some grace-gift by God's Spirit so you may be "established" (1:11)
"my gospel" (16:25)	God will judge people according to "my gospel" (2:16); Paul serves the gospel (1:1, 9, 16; 15:16, 19–20; cf. 10:15–16) and wants to share it with them (1:15)
"Preaching" of Jesus Christ (16:25)	Preaching (10:8, 14–15)
"Revelation" (*apokalupsis*) of the gospel mystery (16:25)	God's righteousness "revealed" in the gospel (1:17)
"Mystery" of Gentile inclusion (16:25)	"Mystery" of how Gentiles are included (11:25)
God's mystery is now "revealed" (*phaneroō*) from the Scriptures of the prophets (16:26)	God's righteousness is now "revealed" from the law and prophets (3:21); Paul's good news was already promised in the prophets (1:1–2); cf. *apokaluptō* in 1:17
The objective is the "obedience of faith" among all nations (16:26)	The objective is the "obedience of faith" among all nations (1:5; 15:18; cf. moral righteousness in chs. 6–8)
To the only wise God be glory forever (16:27)	To God be glory forever (11:36), for his incomparable wisdom (11:33)

Paul's frequent concern for God's honor and name in this letter[47] climaxes in a final praise to God[48] for the wise way he has arranged history so that Gentiles as well as Jews may come to obey Israel's God through faith in Jesus the Messiah. In this doxology, on some points more obviously than in 1:16–17, Paul ties together some of the main themes that bind this renowned letter together.

47. See especially this emphasis in Schreiner 1998: passim.

48. "Glory to God" was an appropriate praise, including at a work's ending (4 Macc 18:23; Jude 25). On God alone as wise, see e.g., Sir 1:8. Although readers' marks of agreement could be interpolated into texts (Maximus of Tyre *Or.* 16.3; 27.1), "amen" was a natural close to praises (3 Macc 7:33) and some books (Tob 14:15; *3 Bar.* 17:4; *2 En.* 68:7).

Bibliography

Abrahams, I. 1967. *Studies in Pharisaism and the Gospels.* 1st series. Prolegomenon by Morton S. Enslin. Library of Biblical Studies. New York: KTAV. Originally published Cambridge: Cambridge University Press, 1917.

Alexander, T. D. 1997. "Further Observations on the Term 'Seed' in Genesis." *TynBul* 48: 363–67.

Allen, Leslie C. 1964. "The OT in Romans I–VIII." *VE* 3: 6-41.

Allison, Dale C. 1985. "Romans 11:11–15: A Suggestion." *PRSt* 12: 23–30.

Anderson, R. Dean, Jr. 1999. *Ancient Rhetorical Theory and Paul.* Rev. ed. CBET 18. Leuven: Peeters.

———. 2000. *Glossary of Greek Rhetorical Terms Connected to Methods of Argumentation, Figures and Tropes from Anaximenes to Quintilian.* CBET 24. Leuven: Peeters.

Aune, David Edward. 1987. *The New Testament in Its Literary Environment.* LEC 8. Philadelphia: Westminster.

———. 2001. "Anthropological Duality in the Eschatology of 2 Cor 4:16—5:10." In *Paul beyond the Judaism/Hellenism Divide,* edited by Troels Engberg-Pedersen, 215–40. Louisville: Westminster John Knox.

———. 2003. *The Westminster Dictionary of New Testament and Early Christian Literature and Rhetoric.* Louisville: Westminster John Knox.

Aus, R. D. 1979. "Paul's Travel Plans to Spain and the 'Full Number of the Gentiles' of Rom. xi.25." *NovT* 21: 232–62.

Avemarie, Friedrich. 1996. *Tora und Leben: Untersuchungen zur Heilsbedeutung der Tora in der frühen rabbinischen Literatur.* TSAJ 55. Tübingen: Mohr.

Balch, David L. 1981. *Let Wives Be Submissive: The Domestic Code in 1 Peter.* SBLMS 26. Chico, CA: Scholars.

———. 1988. "Household Codes." In *Greco-Roman Literature and the New Testament: Selected Forms and Genres,* edited by David Edward Aune, 25–50. SBLSBS 21. Atlanta: Scholars.

Bamberger, Bernard J. 1968. *Proselytism in the Talmudic Period.* 2nd ed. New York: KTAV.

Bammel, Ernst. 1984. "Romans 13." In *Jesus and the Politics of His Day,* edited by Ernst Bammel and C. F. D. Moule, 365–83. Cambridge: Cambridge University Press.

Barclay, J. M. G. 1995. "Paul among Diaspora Jews: Anomaly or Apostate?" *JSNT* 60: 89–120.

———. 2001. "'Do We Undermine the Law?': A Study of Romans 14.1—15.6." In *Paul and the Mosaic Law,* edited by James D. G. Dunn, 287–308. The Third Durham-Tübingen Research Symposium on Earliest Christianity and Judaism (Durham, 1994). Grand Rapids: Eerdmans. Without English translations of the essays, originally published Tübingen: Mohr, 1996.

Barrett, C. K. 1956. *A Commentary on the Epistle to the Romans.* New York: Harper.

Barrow, R. H. 1968. *Slavery in the Roman Empire*. New York: Barnes & Noble. Originally published London: Methuen & Co.: 1928.

Barth, Karl. 1933. *The Epistle to the Romans*. Translated from the 6th ed. by Edwyn C. Hoskyns. London: Oxford University Press.

Barth, Markus. 1974. *Ephesians*. 2 vols. AB 34, 34A. Garden City, NY: Doubleday.

Bassler, Jouette M. 1982. *Divine Impartiality: Paul and a Theological Axiom*. SBLDS 59. Chico, CA: Scholars.

Bauckham, Richard. 2002. *Gospel Women: Studies of the Named Women in the Gospels*. Grand Rapids: Eerdmans.

Baxter, A. G., and J. A. Ziesler. 1985. "Paul and Arboriculture: Romans 11.17–24." *JSNT* 24: 25–32.

Beale, G. K. 1999. *The Book of Revelation: A Commentary on the Greek Text*. NIGTC. Grand Rapids: Eerdmans.

Beasley-Murray, Paul. 1980. "Romans 1:3f: An Early Confession of Faith in the Lordship of Jesus." *TynBul* 31: 147–54.

Bell, H. Idris. 1966. "Egypt under the Early Principate." In *The Augustan Empire: 44 B.C.–A.D. 70*, edited by S. A. Cook, F. E. Adcock, and M. P. Charlesworth, 284–315. Vol. 10 of *The Cambridge Ancient History*. 1st ed. Cambridge: Cambridge University Press.

Bernard, J. 2003. "L'amour de Dieu et du prochain dans le judaïsme tannaïtique." *MScRel* 60: 41–52.

Berthelot, Katell. 2001. "L'interprétation symbolique des lois alimentaires dans la Lettre d'Aristée: une influence pythagoricienne." *JJS* 52: 253–68.

———. 2003. "Les parénèses de la Charité dans les *Testaments des douze patriarches*." *MScRel* 60: 23–39.

Betz, Hans Dieter. 2000. "The Concept of the 'Inner Human Being' (ὁ ἔσω ἄνθρωπος) in the Anthropology of Paul." *NTS* 46: 315–41.

Bird, Michael F. 2007. *The Saving Righteousness of God: Studies in Paul, Justification and the New Perspective*. Eugene, OR: Wipf & Stock.

———. 2008. "Reassessing a Rhetorical Approach to Paul's Letters." *ExpTim* 119: 374–79.

Boers, Hendrikus. 1994. *The Justification of the Gentiles: Paul's Letters to the Galatians and Romans*. Peabody, MA: Hendrickson.

Bonsirven, Joseph. 1964. *Palestinian Judaism in the Time of Jesus Christ*. Translated by William Wolf. New York: Holt, Rinehart & Winston.

Bornkamm, Günther. 1971. *Paul*. Translated by D. M. G. Stalker. New York: Harper & Row.

Bowers, W. Paul. 1975. "Jewish Communities in Spain in the Time of Paul the Apostle." *JTS* 26: 395–402.

———. 1980. "Paul and Religious Propaganda in the First Century." *NovT* 22: 316–23.

Bradley, Keith R. 1987. *Slaves and Masters in the Roman Empire: A Study in Social Control*. New York: Oxford University Press.

Bray, Gerald Lewis, editor. 1998. *Romans*. Ancient Christian Commentary on Scripture, New Testament 6. Downers Grove, IL: InterVarsity.

Brown, Raymond E. 1958–59. "The Semitic Background of the New Testament *Mysterion* (II)." *Bib* 39: 426–48; 40: 70–87.

———. 1968. *The Semitic Background of the Term "Mystery" in the New Testament*. Facet Books, Biblical Series 21. Philadelphia: Fortress.

Bruce, F. F. 1977. *Paul, Apostle of the Heart Set Free*. Grand Rapids: Eerdmans.

————. 1990. *A Mind for What Matters: Collected Essays of F. F. Bruce*. Grand Rapids: Eerdmans.

Buchanan, George Wesley. 1970. *The Consequences of the Covenant*. NovTSup 20. Leiden: Brill.

Buckland, W. W. 1908. *The Roman Law of Slavery: The Condition of the Slave in Private Law from Augustus to Justinian*. Cambridge: Cambridge University Press.

Burer, Michael H., and Daniel B. Wallace. 2001. "Was Junia Really an Apostle? A Reexamination of Rom 16.7." *NTS* 47: 76–91.

Byrne, Brendan. 1996. *Romans*. SP 6. Collegeville, MN: Liturgical.

————. 1997. "Christ's Pre-Existence in Pauline Soteriology." *TS* 58: 308–30.

Cairus, Aecio E. 2004. "Works-Righteousness in the Biblical Narrative of Josephus." *ExpTim* 115: 257–59.

Campbell, D. A. 1992. "The Meaning of Πίστις and Νόμος in Paul: A Linguistic and Structural Perspective." *JBL* 111: 91–103.

Cancik, Hubert, and Helmuth Schneider, editors. 2002–. *Brill's New Pauly: Encyclopaedia of the Ancient World: Antiquity*. 13 vols. Leiden: Brill.

Caragounis, Chrys C. 1977. *The Ephesian Mysterion: Meaning and Content*. ConBNT 8. Lund: Gleerup.

Carcopino, Jérôme. 1940. *Daily Life in Ancient Rome: The People and the City at the Height of the Empire*. Edited by Henry T. Rowell, translated by E. O. Lorimer. New Haven: Yale University Press.

Carson, D. A., Peter T. O'Brien, and Mark A. Seifrid. 2001–4. *Justification and Variegated Nomism*. 2 vols. WUNT , 2nd ser., 140, 181. Grand Rapids: Baker Academic.

Cervin, Richard S. 1994. "A Note Regarding the Name 'Junia(s)' in Romans 16.7." *NTS* 40: 464–70.

Charlesworth, M. P. 1970. *Trade-Routes and Commerce of the Roman Empire*. 2nd rev. ed. New York: Cooper Square.

Cho, Youngmo. 2005. *Spirit and Kingdom in the Writings of Luke and Paul: An Attempt to Reconcile these Concepts*. Foreword by R. P. Menzies. Paternoster Biblical Monographs. Waynesboro, GA: Paternoster.

Clarke, Andrew D. 1994. "Rome and Italy." In *The Book of Acts in Its Graeco-Roman Setting*, edited by David W. J. Gill and Conrad Gempf, 455–81. The Book of Acts in Its First Century Setting 2. Grand Rapids: Eerdmans.

Clarke, John R. 1991. *The Houses of Roman Italy, 100 B.C.–A.D. 250: Ritual, Space, and Decoration*. Berkeley: University of California Press.

Cohen, Boaz. 1966. *Jewish and Roman Law: A Comparative Study*. 2 vols. New York: Jewish Theological Seminary of America.

Cole, Susan Guettel. 1992. "Festivals, Greco-Roman." In *ABD* 2:793–74.

Collins, J. 1997. "A Syntactical Note (Genesis 3:15): Is the Woman's Seed Singular or Plural?" *TynBul* 48: 139–48.

Cook, John Granger. 2002. *The Interpretation of the New Testament in Greco-Roman Paganism*. Peabody, MA: Hendrickson. Originally published Tübingen: Mohr/ Siebeck, 2000.

Cranfield, C. E. B. 1975. *A Critical and Exegetical Commentary on the Epistle to the Romans*. 2 vols. ICC. Edinburgh: T. & T. Clark.

Cullmann, Oscar. 1956. *The Early Church*. Edited by A. J. B. Higgins, translated by A. J. B. Higgins and S. Godman. London: SCM.

———. 1959. *The Christology of the New Testament*. Translated by Shirley C. Guthrie and Charles A. M. Hall. Philadelphia: Westminster.

Dahl, Nils Alstrup. 1977. *Studies in Paul: Theology for the Early Christian Mission*. Minneapolis: Augsburg.

Danker, Frederick W. 1989. *II Corinthians*. ACNT. Minneapolis: Augsburg.

Das, A. Andrew. 2003. *Paul and the Jews*. Library of Pauline Studies. Peabody: Hendrickson.

———. 2007. *Solving the Romans Debate*. Minneapolis: Fortress.

Daube, David. 1956. *The New Testament and Rabbinic Judaism*. Peabody, MA: Hendrickson, n.d. Originally published London: Athlone.

———. 1960. "Three Notes Having to Do with Johanan ben Zaccai." *JTS* 11: 53–62.

———. 1969. *Studies in Biblical Law*. New York: KTAV.

Davids, Peter H. 1982. *The Epistle of James: A Commentary on the Greek Text*. NIGTC. Grand Rapids: Eerdmans.

Davies, W. D. 1973. "Reflections on the Spirit in the Mekilta: A Suggestion." *JANESCU* 5: 95–105.

———. 1980. *Paul and Rabbinic Judaism: Some Rabbinic Elements in Pauline Theology*. 4th ed. Philadelphia: Fortress.

Deissmann, Gustav Adolf. 1923. *Bible Studies: Contributions Chiefly from Papyri and Inscriptions to the history of the Language, the Literature, and the Religion of Hellenistic Judaism and Primitive Christianity*. Translated by Alexander Grieve. Edinburgh: T. & T. Clark. Reprint, Winona Lake, IN: Alpha, 1979.

———. 1978. *Light from the Ancient East*. Grand Rapids: Baker. Originally published London: Hodder & Stoughton, 1910.

De Jonge, Marinus. 2002. "The Two Great Commandments in the Testaments of the Twelve Patriarchs." *NovT* 44: 371–92.

Deming, Will. 2003. "Paul and Indifferent Things." In *Paul in the Greco-Roman World: A Handbook*, edited by J. Paul Sampley, 384–403. Harrisburg, PA: Trinity.

Derrett, J. D. M. 1997. "Paul as Master-builder." *EvQ* 69: 129–37.

DeSilva, David A. 2000. *Honor, Patronage, Kinship & Purity: Unlocking New Testament Culture*. Downers Grove, IL: InterVarsity.

Donaldson, Terence L. 1990. "Proselytes or 'Righteous Gentiles'? The Status of Gentiles in Eschatological Pilgrimage Patterns of Thought." *JSP* 7: 3–27.

———. 1993. "'Riches for the Gentiles' (Rom 11:12): Israel's Rejection and Paul's Gentile Mission." *JBL* 112: 81–98.

———. 1997a. "Israelite, Convert, Apostle to the Gentiles: The Origin of Paul's Gentile Mission." In *The Road from Damascus: The Impact of Paul's Conversion on His Life, Thought, and Ministry*, edited by Richard N. Longenecker, 62–84. McMaster New Testament Studies. Grand Rapids: Eerdmans.

———. 1997b. *Paul and the Gentiles: Remapping the Apostle's Convictional World*. Minneapolis: Fortress.

Donfried, Karl P. 1991. *The Romans Debate*. Rev. ed. Peabody, MA: Hendrickson.

———. *Paul, Thessalonica, and Early Christianity*. Grand Rapids: Eerdmans.

Donfried, Karl P., and Peter Richardson, editors. 1998. *Judaism and Christianity in First-Century Rome*. Grand Rapids: Eerdmans.

Dover, K. J. 1978. *Greek Homosexuality*. Cambridge: Harvard University Press.

Dresken-Weiland, J. 2003. "Fremde in der Bevölkerung des kaiserzeitlichen Rom." *RQ* 98: 18–34.

Dunn, James D. G. 1970. *Baptism in the Holy Spirit: A Re-examination of the New Testament Teaching on the Gift of the Spirit in Relation to Pentecostalism Today*. SBT, 2nd ser., 15. London: SCM.

————. 1975. *Jesus and the Spirit: A Study of the Religious and Charismatic Experience of Jesus and the First Christians as Reflected in the New Testament*. NTL. London: SCM.

————. 1988. *Romans*. 2 vols. WBC 38A, B. Dallas: Word.

————. 1992. "Yet Once More—'The Works of the Law': A Response." *JSNT* 46: 99–117.

————. 1998. *The Theology of Paul the Apostle*. Grand Rapids: Eerdmans.

————. 1999. "Spirit Speech: Reflections on Romans 8:12–27." In *Romans and the People of God: Essays in Honor of Gordon D. Fee on the Occasion of His 65th Birthday*, edited by Sven K. Soderlund and N. T. Wright, 82–91. Grand Rapids: Eerdmans.

Dupont, Florence. 1992. *Daily Life in Ancient Rome*. Translated by Christopher Woodall. Oxford: Blackwell.

Edwards, Ruth B., and Mark Reasoner, rev. by Stanley E. Porter. 2000. "Rome: Overview." In *DNTB*, 1010–1018. Downers Grove, IL: InterVarsity.

Eichrodt, Walther. 1983. "Faith in Providence and Theodicy in the OT (1934)." In *Theodicy in the Old Testament*, edited by James L. Crenshaw. Issues in Religion and Theology 4. Philadelphia: Fortress.

Elliott, Neil. 1990. *The Rhetoric of Romans: Argumentative Constraint and Strategy and Paul's Dialogue with Judaism*. JSNTSup 45. Sheffield: JSOT Press.

————. 2008. *The Arrogance of Nations: Reading Romans in the Shadow of Empire*. Paul in Critical Contexts. Minneapolis: Fortress.

Engberg-Pedersen, Troels. 2000. *Paul and the Stoics*. Edinburgh: T. & T. Clark.

————. 2003. "Paul, Virtues, and Vices." In *Paul in the Greco-Roman World: A Handbook*, edited by J. Paul Sampley, 608–33. Harrisburg, PA: Trinity.

Epp, Eldon Jay. 1975. "Wisdom, Torah, Word: The Johannine Prologue and the Purpose of the Fourth Gospel." In *Current Issues in Biblical and Patristic Interpretation: Studies in Honor of Merrill C. Tenney Presented by His Former Students*, edited by Gerald F. Hawthorne, 128–46. Grand Rapids: Eerdmans.

————. 2005. *Junia: The First Woman Apostle*. Minneapolis: Fortress.

Erskine, Andrew. 1990. *The Hellenistic Stoa: Political Thought and Action*. Ithaca, NY: Cornell University Press.

Eskola, Timo. 1998. *Theodicy and Predestination in Pauline Soteriology*. WUNT, 2nd ser., 100. Tübingen: Mohr/Siebeck.

————. 2002. "Paul et le Judaïsme du Second Temple. La sotériologie de Paul avant et après E. P. Sanders." *RSR* 90: 377–98.

Evans, Craig A. 2005. "Paul and 'Works of Law' Language in Late Antiquity." In *Paul and His Opponents*, edited by Stanley E. Porter, 201–26. Pauline Studies 2. Leiden: Brill.

Evans, Craig A., and Stanley E. Porter, editors. 2000. *Dictionary of New Testament Background*. Downers Grove, IL: InterVarsity. [*DNTB*]

Fahy, T. 1965. "A Note on Romans 9:1–18." *ITQ* 32: 261–62.

Fee, Gordon D. 1994a. "Christology and Pneumatology in Romans 8:9–11—and Elsewhere: Some Reflections on Paul as a Trinitarian." In *Jesus of Nazareth: Lord and Christ. Essays on the Historical Jesus and New Testament Christology*, edited by Joel B. Green and Max Turner, 312–31. Grand Rapids: Eerdmans.

————. 1994b. *God's Empowering Presence: The Holy Spirit in the Letters of Paul*. Peabody, MA: Hendrickson.

Ferch, A. J. 1977. "The Two Aeons and the Messiah in Pseudo-Philo, 4 Ezra, and 2 Baruch." *AUSS* 15: 135–51.

Fitzgerald, John T. 1988. *Cracks in an Earthen Vessel: An Examination of the Catalogues of Hardships in the Corinthian Correspondence*. SBLDS 99. Atlanta: Scholars.

———. 2000. "Affliction Lists." In *DNTB*, 16–18.

———. 2001. "Paul and Paradigm Shifts: Reconciliation and Its Linkage Group." In *Paul beyond the Judaism/Hellenism Divide*, edited by Troels Engberg-Pedersen, 241–62. Louisville: Westminster John Knox.

———. 2003. "Paul and Friendship." In *Paul in the Greco-Roman World: A Handbook*, edited by J. Paul Sampley, 319–43. Harrisburg, PA: Trinity.

Fitzmyer, Joseph A. 1966. "Jewish Christianity in Acts in Light of the Qumran Scrolls." In *Studies in Luke-Acts: Essays Presented in Honor of Paul Schubert*, edited by Leander E. Keck and J. Louis Martyn, 233–57. Nashville: Abingdon.

———. 1993. *Romans: A New Translation with Introduction and Commentary*. AB 33. New York: Doubleday.

Flory, M. B. 1984. "Where Women Precede Men: Factors Influencing the Order of Names in Roman Epitaphs." *CJ* 79: 216–24.

Flusser, David. 1988. *Judaism and the Origins of Christianity*. Jerusalem: Magnes Press, Hebrew University.

Forbes, Christopher. 1986. "Comparison, Self-Praise and Irony: Paul's Boasting and the Conventions of Hellenistic Rhetoric." *NTS* 32: 1–30.

Forbis, E. P. 1990. "Women's Public Image in Italian Honorary Inscriptions." *AJP* 111: 493–512.

Freedman, H. 1995. "Jacob and Esau: Their Struggle in the Second Century." *JBQ* 23: 107–15.

Frost, F. 1999. "Sausage and Meat Preservation in Antiquity." *GRBS* 40: 241–52.

Funk, Robert W. 1967. "The Apostolic *Parousia*: Form and Significance." In *Christian History and Interpretation: Studies Presented to John Knox*, edited by W. R. Farmer, C. F. D. Moule, and R. R. Niebuhr, 249–68. Cambridge: Cambridge University.

Gaca, Kathy L., and L. L. Welborn, editors. 2005. *Early Patristic Readings of Romans*. Romans through History and Culture Series. New York: T. & T. Clark.

Gager, John G. 1983. *The Origins of Anti-Semitism: Attitudes toward Judaism in Pagan and Christian Antiquity*. New York: Oxford University Press.

Gagnon, Robert A. J. 2001. *The Bible and Homosexual Practice: Texts and Hermeneutics*. Nashville: Abingdon.

Gamble, Harry, Jr. 1977. *The Textual History of the Letter to the Romans: A Study in Textual and Literary Criticism*. SD 42. Grand Rapids: Eerdmans.

Garland, David E. 2003a. "The Dispute over Food Sacrificed to Idols (1 Cor 8:1—11:1)." *PRSt* 30: 173–97.

———. 2003b. *1 Corinthians*. BECNT. Grand Rapids: Baker.

Garnsey, Peter, and Richard Saller. 1987. *The Roman Empire: Economy, Society and Culture*. Berkeley: University of California Press.

Gathercole, Simon J. 2002. *Where Is Boasting? Early Jewish Soteriology and Paul's Response in Romans 1–5*. Grand Rapids: Eerdmans.

Gaventa, Beverly Roberts. "The Cosmic Power of Sin in Paul's Letter to the Romans: Toward a Widescreen Edition." *Int* 58 (3, 2004): 229–40.

Gemünden, P. von. 1997. "La femme passionnelle et l'homme rationnel? Un chapitre de psychologie historique." *Bib* 78: 457–80.

Gerhardsson, Birger. 1991. "The Path of the Gospel Tradition." In *The Gospel and the Gospels*, edited by Peter Stuhlmacher, 75–96. Grand Rapids: Eerdmans.

Gibbard, S. M. 1956. "The Christian Mystery." In *Studies in Ephesians*, edited by F. L. Cross, 97–120. London: A. R. Mowbray.

Gill, Christopher. 1998. "Did Galen Understand Platonic and Stoic Thinking on Emotions?" In *The Emotions in Hellenistic Philosophy*, edited by Juha Sihvola and Troels Engberg-Pedersen, 113–48. Texts and Studies in the History of Philosophy 46. Dordrecht: Kluwer.

Gill, D. W. J. 1989. "Erastus the Aedile." *TynBul* 40: 293–301.

Goodenough, Erwin R. 1953–68. *Jewish Symbols in the Greco-Roman Period*. 13 vols. Bollingen Series 37. Vols. 1–12, New York: Pantheon Books. Vol. 13, Princeton: Princeton University Press.

Gosling, F. A. 2001. "Where Is the God of Justice? An examination of C. H. Dodd's Understanding of *hilaskesthai* and Its Derivatives." *ZAW* 113: 404–14.

Gräbe, P. J. 1992. "Δύναμις (in the Sense of Power) as a Pneumatological Concept in the Main Pauline Letters." *BZ* 36: 226–35.

Grant, Robert M. 2001. *Paul in the Roman World: The Conflict at Corinth*. Louisville: Westminster John Knox.

Greenberg, D. F. 1988. *The Construction of Homosexuality*. Chicago: University of Chicago Press.

Greenman, Jeffrey P., and Timothy Larsen. 2005. *Reading Romans through the Centuries: From the Early Church to Karl Barth*. Grand Rapids: Brazos.

Grieb, A. Katherine. 2002. *The Story of Romans: A Narrative Defense of God's Righteousness*. Louisville, London: Westminster John Knox.

Griffin, Miriam T. 1984. *Nero: The End of a Dynasty*. New Haven: Yale University Press.

Gundry, Robert H. 1976. *Sōma in Biblical Theology: With Emphasis on Pauline Anthropology*. SNTSMS 29. Cambridge: Cambridge University Press.

Guthrie, W. K. C. 1966. *Orpheus and Greek Religion: A Study of the Orphic Movement*. Rev. ed. New York: Norton.

Haacker, Klaus. 2003. *The Theology of Paul's Letter to the Romans*. Cambridge: Cambridge University Press.

Hadas-Lebel, Mireille. 1984. "Jacob et Esaü ou Israël et Rome dans le Talmud et le Midrash." *RHR* 201: 369–92.

Hagner, Donald A. 1993. "Paul and Judaism. The Jewish Matrix of Early Christianity: Issues in the Current Debate." *BBR* 3: 111–30.

Halpern-Amaru, Betsy. 2005. "Joy as Piety in the 'Book of Jubilees.'" *JJS* 56: 185–205.

Hamilton, Neill Q. 1957. *The Holy Spirit and Eschatology in Paul*. SJT Occasional Papers 6. Edinburgh: Oliver & Boyd.

Harmon, Daniel P. 2004. "Feriae." In *Brill's New Pauly: Encyclopaedia of the Ancient World: Antiquity*, edited by Hubert Cancik and Helmuth Schneider, 5:385–86. Leiden: Brill.

Harris, Murray J. 1992. *Jesus as God: The New Testament Use of Theos in Reference to Jesus*. Grand Rapids: Baker.

Harrison, James R. 2003. *Paul's Language of Grace in Its Graeco-Roman Context*. WUNT, 2nd ser., 172. Tübingen: Mohr/Siebeck.

Harrisville, Roy A. 2006. "Before πίστις Χριστοῦ: The Objective Genitive as Good Greek." *NovT* 48: 353–58.

Hartmann, Elke. 2005. "Homosexuality." In *Brill's New Pauly: Encyclopaedia of the Ancient World: Antiquity*, edited by Hubert Cancik and Helmuth Schneider, 6:468–472. Leiden: Brill.

Harvey, John D. 1998. *Listening to the Text: Oral Patterning in Paul's Letters*. Foreword by Richard N. Longenecker. ETS Studies 1. Grand Rapids: Baker.

Hasel, Gerhard F. 1980. *The Remnant: The History and Theology of the Remnant Idea from Genesis to Isaiah*. 3rd ed. Berrien Springs, MI: Andrews University Press.

Hay, David M. 1997. "Putting Extremism in Context: The Case of Philo, *De Migratione* 89–93." *SPhilo* 9: 126–42.

Hays, Richard B. 1980. "Psalm 143 and the Logic of Romans 3." *JBL* 99:107–15.

———. 1989. *Echoes of Scripture in the Letters of Paul*. New Haven: Yale University Press.

———. 2005. *The Conversion of the Imagination: Paul as Interpreter of Israel's Scripture*. Grand Rapids: Eerdmans.

Heath, Malcolm. 1997. "Invention." In *Handbook of Classical Rhetoric in the Hellenistic Period 330 B.C.–A.D. 400*, edited by Stanley E. Porter, 89–119. Leiden: Brill.

Hemelrijk, E. A. 2004. "City Patronesses in the Roman Empire." *Historia* 53: 209–45.

Hengel, Martin. 1974. *Property and Riches in the Early Church: Aspects of a Social History of Early Christianity*. Translated by John Bowden. Philadelphia: Fortress.

Hengel, Martin, and Anna Maria Schwemer. 1997. *Paul between Damascus and Antioch: The Unknown Years*. Translated by John Bowden. London: Louisville: Westminster John Knox.

Herman, Gabriel. 2003. "Gift, Greece." In *OCD*, 637.

Hester, James D. 1968. *Paul's Concept of Inheritance*. Scottish Journal of Theology Occasional Papers 14. Edinburgh: Oliver & Boyd.

Hezser, Catherine. 2003. "The Impact of Household Slaves on the Jewish Family in Roman Palestine." *JSJ* 34, no. 4: 375–424.

———. 2005. *Jewish Slavery in Antiquity*. Oxford: Oxford University Press.

Highet, Gilbert. 2003. "Reciprocity (Greece)." In *OCD*, 1295.

Hill, Craig C. 1992. *Hellenists and Hebrews: Reappraising Division within the Earliest Church*. Minneapolis: Fortress.

Hock, Ronald F. 2003. "Paul and Greco-Roman Education." In *Paul in the Greco-Roman World: A Handbook*, edited by J. Paul Sampley, 198–227. Harrisburg, PA: Trinity.

Höcker, Christoph. 2008. "Prostitution. II. Classical Antiquity." In *Brill's New Pauly: Encyclopaedia of the Ancient World: Antiquity*, edited by Hubert Cancik and Helmuth Schneider, 12:58–61. Leiden: Brill.

Holmén, Tom. 2001. *Jesus and Jewish Covenant Thinking*. Biblical Interpretation Series 55. Leiden: Brill.

Horsley, G. H. R. 1987. *New Documents Illustrating Early Christianity: A Review of the Greek Inscriptions and Papyri Published in 1979*. Vol. 4. North Ryde, N.S.W.: Macquarie University.

Horsley, Richard A. 1978. "The Law of Nature in Philo and Cicero." *HTR* 71:35–59.

Hoyt, Thomas, Jr. 1974. "The Poor in Luke-Acts." Ph.D. diss., Duke University.

Hübner, Hans. 1984. *Law in Paul's Thought*. Edited by John Riches, translated by James C. G. Greig. Studies of the New Testament and Its World. Edinburgh: T. & T. Clark.

Hultgren, S. 2003. "The Origin of Paul's Doctrine of the Two Adams in 1 Corinthians 15.45–49." *JSNT* 25: 343–70.

Hunter, Archibald M. 1955. *The Epistle to the Romans: Introduction and Commentary*. TBC. London: SCM.

——. 1961. *Paul and His Predecessors*. Rev. ed. Philadelphia: Westminster.

——. 1966. *The Gospel According to St. Paul*. Philadelphia: Westminster.

Hurtado, Larry W. 2003. "Paul's Christology." In *The Cambridge Companion to St Paul*, edited by James D. G. Dunn, 185–98. Cambridge: Cambridge University Press.

Jeffers, James S. 1998. "Jewish and Christian Families in First-Century Rome." In *Judaism and Christianity in First-Century Rome*, edited by Karl P. Donfried and Peter Richardson, 128–50. Grand Rapids: Eerdmans.

Jeremias, Joachim. 1964. *Unknown Sayings of Jesus*. Translated by Reginald H. Fuller. 2nd ed. London: SPCK.

Jewett, Robert. 2007. *Romans: A Commentary*. Assisted by Roy D. Kotansky, edited by Eldon Jay Epp. Hermeneia. Minneapolis: Fortress.

Johnson, Luke Timothy. 2001. *Reading Romans: A Literary and Theological Commentary*. Reading the New Testament. Macon, GA: Smyth & Helwys.

Johnston, Robert Morris. 1977. "Parabolic Interpretations Attributed to Tannaim." Ph.D. diss., Hartford Seminary Foundation.

Judge, E. A. 1960. *The Social Pattern of the Christian Groups in the First Century: Some Prolegomena to the Study of New Testament Ideas of Social Obligation*. London: Tyndale.

——. 1982. *Rank and Status in the World of the Caesars and St Paul*. The Broadhead Memorial Lecture 1981. University of Canterbury Publications 29. Christchurch, NZ: University of Canterbury.

Käsemann, Ernst. 1980. *Commentary on Romans*. Translated and edited by Geoffrey W. Bromiley. Grand Rapids: Eerdmans.

Keay, S. 2003. "Recent Archaeological Work in Roman Iberia (1990–2002)." *JRS* 93: 146–211.

Keck, Leander E. 1966. "The Poor among the Saints in Jewish Christianity and Qumran." *ZNW* 57: 54–78.

Keener, Craig S. 1992. *Paul, Women & Wives: Marriage and Women's Ministry in the Letters of Paul*. Peabody, MA: Hendrickson. Reprinted 2004 with new preface.

——. 1997. *The Spirit in the Gospels and Acts: Divine Purity and Power*. Peabody, MA: Hendrickson.

——. 1999. *A Commentary on the Gospel of Matthew*. Grand Rapids: Eerdmans.

——. 2000a. "Friendship." In *DNTB*, 380–88.

——. 2000b. "Head Coverings." In *DNTB*, 442–47.

——. 2000c. "Kiss, Kissing." In *DNTB*, 628–29.

——. 2000d. "Marriage." In *DNTB*, 680–93.

——. 2003a. "Gifts (Spiritual)." In *The Westminster Theological Wordbook of the Bible*, edited by Donald E. Gowan, 154–61. Louisville: Westminster John Knox.

——. 2003b. *The Gospel of John: A Commentary*. 2 vols. Peabody, MA: Hendrickson.

——. 2003c. "Some New Testament Invitations to Ethnic Reconciliation." *EvQ* 75: 195–213.

——. 2005a. "'Brood of Vipers' (Mt. 3.7; 12.34; 23.33)." *JSNT* 28: 3–11.

——. 2005b. *1–2 Corinthians*. New Cambridge Bible Commentary. Cambridge: Cambridge University Press.

——. 2006. "Paul's 'Friends' the Asiarchs (Acts 19.31)." *JGRChJ* 3: 134–41.

——. 2008a. "'Fleshly' versus Spirit Perspectives in Romans 8:5–8." In *Paul: Jew, Greek and Roman*, edited by Stanley Porter, 211–29. Pauline Studies 5. Leiden: Brill.

———. 2008b. "Some Rhetorical Techniques in Acts 24:2–21." In *Paul's World*, edited by Stanley E. Porter, 221–51. PAST 4. Leiden: Brill.

Keesmaat, Sylvia C. 1999. *Paul and His Story: (Re)Interpreting the Exodus Tradition.* JSNTSup 181. Sheffield: Sheffield Academic.

Kennedy, George A. 1984. *New Testament Interpretation through Rhetorical Criticism.* Studies in Religion. Chapel Hill: University of North Carolina.

Kim, Chan-Hie. 1972. *Form and Structure of the Familiar Greek Letter of Recommendation.* SBLDS 4. Missoula, MT: SBL.

Kim, Jintae. 2001–5. "The Concept of Atonement in Early Rabbinic Thought and the New Testament Writings." *JGRChJ* 2: 117–45.

Kim, Seyoon. 2002. *Paul and the New Perspective: Second Thoughts on the Origin of Paul's Gospel.* Grand Rapids: Eerdmans.

Klauck, Hans-Josef. 1990. "Brotherly Love in Plutarch and in 4 Maccabees." In *Greeks, Romans, and Christians: Essays in Honor of Abraham J. Malherbe*, edited by David L. Balch, Everett Ferguson, and Wayne A. Meeks, 144–56. Minneapolis: Fortress.

Knox, Wilfred L. 1925. *St. Paul and the Church of Jerusalem.* Cambridge: Cambridge University Press.

———. 1939. *St. Paul and the Church of the Gentiles.* Cambridge: Cambridge University Press.

Koenig, John. 1985. *New Testament Hospitality: Partnership with Strangers as Promise and Mission.* OBT 17. Philadelphia: Fortress.

Koester, Helmut. 2005. "The Silence of the Apostle." In *Urban Religion in Roman Corinth: Interdisciplinary Approaches*, edited by Daniel N. Schowalter and Steven J. Friesen, 339–49. HTS 53. Cambridge: Harvard University Press.

Konradt, M. 1997. "Menschen- oder Bruderliebe? Beobachtungen zum Liebesgebot in den Testamenten der Zwölf Patriarchen." *ZNW* 88: 296–310.

Kraftchick, Steven J. 2001. "Πάθη in Paul: The Emotional Logic of 'Original Argument.'" In *Paul and Pathos*, edited by Thomas H. Olbricht and Jerry L. Sumney, 39–68. SBLSymS 16. Atlanta: SBL.

Krieger, K.-S. 2002. "Das 3. und 4. Makkabäerbuch." *BK* 57: 87–88.

Ladd, George Eldon. 1974. *A Theology of the New Testament.* Grand Rapids: Eerdmans.

Lampe, G. W. H. 1951. *The Seal of the Spirit: A Study in the Doctrine of Baptism and Confirmation in the New Testament and the Fathers.* New York: Longmans, Green.

Lampe, Peter. 2003a. *From Paul to Valentinus: Christians at Rome in the First Two Centuries.* Edited by Marshall D. Johnson, translated by Michael Steinhauser. Minneapolis: Fortress.

———. 2003b. "Paul, Patrons, and Clients." In *Paul in the Greco-Roman World: A Handbook*, edited by J. Paul Sampley, 488–523. Harrisburg, PA: Trinity.

Lane, William L. 1974. *The Gospel According to Mark.* NICNT. Grand Rapids: Eerdmans.

———. 1998. "Social Perspectives of Roman Christianity during the Formative Years from Nero to Nerva: Romans, Hebrews, 1 Clement." In *Judaism and Christianity in First-Century Rome*, edited by Karl P. Donfried and Peter Richardson, 196–244. Grand Rapids: Eerdmans.

Latourette, Kenneth Scott. 1970. *A History of the Expansion of Christianity.* Vol. 1, *The First Five Centuries.* Grand Rapids: Zondervan; New York: Harper & Row.

Leary, T. J. 1993. "Of Paul and Pork and Proselytes." *NovT* 35: 292–93.

Leon, Harry J. 1960. *The Jews of Ancient Rome.* Morris Loeb Series. Philadelphia: Jewish Publication Society of America.

Lewis, Naphtali. 1983. *Life in Egypt under Roman Rule*. Oxford: Clarendon.

Linforth, Ivan M. 1941. *The Arts of Orpheus*. Philosophy of Plato and Aristotle. Berkeley: University of California Press.

Llewelyn, S. R., with R. A. Kearsley. 1994. *New Documents Illustrating Early Christianity: A Review of the Greek Inscriptions and Papyri Published in 1982–83*. Vol. 7 North Ryde, N.S.W.: Macquarie University.

Longenecker, Richard N. 1970. *The Christology of Early Jewish Christianity*. SBT, 2nd ser., 17. London: SCM. Reprint, Grand Rapids: Baker, 1981.

———. 1975. *Biblical Exegesis in the Apostolic Period*. Grand Rapids: Eerdmans.

———. 1976. *Paul, Apostle of Liberty*. Grand Rapids: Baker. Original copyright © 1964 by R. N. Longenecker.

Lopez, Davina C. 2008. *Apostle to the Conquered: Reimagining Paul's Mission*. Paul in Critical Contexts. Minneapolis: Fortress.

Lüdemann, Gerd. 1989. *Early Christianity According to the Traditions in Acts: A Commentary*. Minneapolis: Fortress.

Lührmann, Dieter. 1980. "Neutestamentliche Haustafeln und antike Ökonomie." *NTS* 27: 83–97.

Lung-Kwong, Lo. 1998. *Paul's Purpose in Writing Romans: The Upbuilding of a Jewish and Gentile Christian Community in Rome*. Jian Dao Dissertation Series 6; Bible and Literature 4. Hong Kong: Alliance Bible Seminary.

MacDonald, Margaret Y. 2003. "Was Celsus Right? The Role of Women in the Expansion of Early Christianity." In *Early Christian Families in Context: An Interdisciplinary Dialogue*, edited by David L. Balch and Carolyn Osiek, 157–84. Grand Rapids: Eerdmans.

MacGregor, G. H. C. 1954. "Principalities and Powers: The Cosmic Background of Paul's Thought." *NTS* 1: 17–28.

MacMullen, Ramsay. 1980. "Women in Public in the Roman Empire." *Historia* 29: 209–18.

Malherbe, Abraham J. 1977. "Ancient Epistolary Theorists." *Ohio Journal of Religious Studies* 5.2: 3–77.

———. 1986. *Moral Exhortation: A Greco-Roman Sourcebook*. LEC 4. Philadelphia: Westminster.

———. 1989. *Paul and the Popular Philosophers*. Philadelphia: Fortress.

Marcus, Ralph. 1956. "*Mebaqqer* and *Rabbim* in the Manual of Discipline vi.11–13." *JBL* 75: 298–302.

Markschies, C. 1994. "Die platonische Metapher vom 'inneren Menschen': eine Brücke zwischen antiker Philosophie und altchristlicher Theologie." *ZKG* 105: 1–17.

Marshall, I. Howard. 1999. "Romans 16:25–27—An Apt Conclusion." In *Romans and the People of God: Essays in Honor of Gordon D. Fee on the Occasion of His 65th Birthday*, edited by Sven K. Soderlund and N. T. Wright, 170–86. Grand Rapids: Eerdmans.

Marshall, Peter. 1987. *Enmity in Corinth: Social Conventions in Paul's Relations with the Corinthians*. WUNT, 2nd ser., 23. Tübingen: Mohr/Siebeck.

Martin, Dale B. 1990. *Slavery as Salvation: The Metaphor of Slavery in Pauline Christianity*. New Haven: Yale University Press.

Martin, R. A. 1965. "The Earliest Messianic Interpretation of Genesis 3:15." *JBL* 84: 425–27.

McNamara, Martin. 1972. *Targum and Testament*. Grand Rapids: Eerdmans.

Meeks, Wayne A., and Robert L. Wilken. 1978. *Jews and Christians in Antioch in the First Four Centuries of the Common Era.* SBLSBS 13. Missoula, MT: Scholars.

Meggitt, J. J. 1994. "Meat Consumption and Social Conflict in Corinth." *JTS* 45: 137–41.

———. 1996. "The Social Status of Erastus (Rom. 16:23)." *NovT* 38: 218–23.

Meinardus, Otto F. A. 1978. "Paul's Missionary Journey to Spain: Tradition and Folklore." *BA* 41: 61–63.

Menzies, Robert P. 1991. *The Development of Early Christian Pneumatology: With Special Reference to Luke-Acts.* JSNTSup 54. Sheffield: JSOT Press.

———. *Empowered for Witness: The Spirit in Luke-Acts.* Journal of Pentecostal Theology Supplement Series 6. London: T. & T. Clark.

Metzger, Bruce M. 1975. *A Textual Commentary on the Greek New Testament.* Corrected ed. New York: United Bible Societies.

Meyer, B. F. 1983. "The Pre-Pauline Formula in Rom. 3.25–26a." *NTS* 29:198–208.

Mitchell, Margaret M. 1991. *Paul and the Rhetoric of Reconciliation: An Exegetical Investigation of the Language and Composition of 1 Corinthians.* Louisville: Westminster John Knox.

Moo, Douglas J. 1986. "Israel and Paul in Romans 7:7–12." *NTS* 32:122–35.

———. 1996. *The Epistle to the Romans.* NICNT. Grand Rapids: Eerdmans.

Moore, George Foot. 1971. *Judaism in the First Centuries of the Christian Era, The Age of Tannaim.* 2 vols. New York: Schocken. Originally published Cambridge: Harvard University Press, 1927.

Morris, Leon. 1988. *The Epistle to the Romans.* Grand Rapids: Eerdmans.

Moses, A. D. A. 1996. *Matthew's Transfiguration Story and Jewish-Christian Controversy.* JSNTSup 122. Sheffield: Sheffield Academic.

Moyer, James C. 1969. "The Concept of Ritual Purity among the Hittites." Ph.D. diss., Brandeis University.

———. 1983. "Hittite and Israelite Cultic Practices: A Selected Comparison." In *Scripture in Context II: More Essays on the Comparative Method*, edited by William W. Hallo, James C. Moyer, and Leo G. Perdue, 9–38. Winona Lake, IN: Eisenbrauns.

Munck, Johannes. 1967. *Christ & Israel: An Interpretation of Romans 9–11.* Translated by Ingeborg Nixon. Philadelphia: Fortress.

Murray, Gilbert. 1915. *The Stoic Philosophy: Conway Memorial Lecture Delivered at South Place Institute on March 16, 1915.* New York: Putnam's.

Najman, Hindy. 2003. "A Written Copy of the Law of Nature: An Unthinkable Paradox?" *SPhilo* 15: 54–63.

Nanos, Mark D. 1996. *The Mystery of Romans: The Jewish Context of Paul's Letter.* Minneapolis: Fortress.

Neudecker, R. 1992. "'And You Shall Love Your Neighbor as Yourself—I Am the Lord' (Lev 19,18) in Jewish Interpretation." *Bib* 73: 496–517.

Nicholson, J. 1994. "The Delivery and Confidentiality of Cicero's Letters." *CJ* 90: 33–63.

Nickle, Keith F. 1966. *The Collection: A Study in Paul's Strategy.* SBT 48. Naperville, IL: Allenson.

Nock, Arthur Darby. 1964. *Early Gentile Christianity and Its Hellenistic Background.* New York: Harper & Row.

O'Brien, Peter Thomas. 1977. *Introductory Thanksgivings in the Letters of Paul.* NovTSup 49. Leiden: Brill.

Oeming, M. 1998. "Der Glaube Abrahams. Zur Rezeptionsgeschichte von Gen 15,6 in der Zeit des zweiten Tempels." *ZAW* 110: 16–33.

Olbricht, Thomas H., and Jerry L. Sumney, editors. 2001. *Paul and Pathos.* SBLSymS 16. Atlanta: SBL.

Olson, S. N. 1985. "Pauline Expressions of Confidence in His Addressees." *CBQ* 47: 282–95.

O'Neill, J. C. 2002. "How Early Is the Doctrine of *Creation ex Nihilo?*" *JTS* 53: 449–65.

Osiek, Carolyn, and Margaret Y. MacDonald, with Janet H. Tulloch. 2006. *A Woman's Place: House Churches in Earliest Christianity.* Minneapolis: Fortress.

Packer, J. E. 1967. "Housing and Population in Imperial Ostia and Rome." *JRS* 57: 80–95.

Padgett, Alan. 1987. "The Pauline Rationale for Submission: Biblical Feminism and the *hina* Clauses of Titus 2:1–10." *EvQ* 59: 39–52.

Park, Eung Chun. 2003. *Either Jew or Gentile: Paul's Unfolding Theology of Inclusivity.* Louisville: Westminster John Knox.

Parkes, James Williams. 1979. *The Conflict of the Church and the Synagogue: A Study in the Origins of Antisemitism.* New York: Atheneum.

Philip, Finny. 2005. *The Origins of Pauline Pneumatology: The Eschatological Bestowal of the Spirit upon Gentiles in Judaism and in the Early Development of Paul's Theology.* WUNT, 2nd ser., 194. Tübingen: Mohr/Siebeck.

Piper, John. 1983. *The Justification of God: An Exegetical and Theological Study of Romans 9:1–23.* Grand Rapids: Baker.

Pizzuto-Pomaco, Julia. 2003. "From Shame to Honour: Mediterranean Women in Romans 16." Ph.D. diss., University of St. Andrews.

Porter, Stanley E. 1997. "Paul of Tarsus and His Letters." In *Handbook of Classical Rhetoric in the Hellenistic Period 330 B.C.–A.D. 400,* edited by Stanley E. Porter, 533–85. Leiden: Brill.

Poythress, V. S. 1976. "Is Romans 1:3-4 a *Pauline* Confession After All?" *ExpTim* 87: 180–83.

Quarles, Charles L. 1996. "The Soteriology of R. Akiba and E. P. Sanders' *Paul and Palestinian Judaism.*" *NTS* 42: 185–95.

Raharimanantsoa, Mamy. 2006. *Mort et Espérance selon la Bible Hébraïque.* ConBOT 53. Stockholm: Almqvist & Wiksell.

Räisänen, Heikki. 1983. *Paul and the Law.* WUNT 29. Tübingen: Mohr/Siebeck.

Rajak, Tessa. 1995. "The Location of Cultures in Second Temple Palestine: The Evidence of Josephus." In *The Book of Acts in Its Palestinian Setting,* edited by Richard Bauckham, 1–14. Vol. 4 of *The Book of Acts in Its First Century Setting.* Grand Rapids: Eerdmans.

Ramirez, J. M. Casciaro. 1976. "El 'Misterio' divino en los escritos posteriores de Qumran." *ScrTh* 8: 445–75.

Ramsay, William M. 1904. "Roads and Travel (in NT)." In *Dictionary of the Bible,* edited by James Hastings, 5:375–402. Edinburgh: T. & T. Clark.

———. 1910. *Pictures of the Apostolic Church: Studies in the Book of Acts.* London: Hodder & Stoughton. Reprint, Grand Rapids: Baker, 1959.

Rapske, Brian. 1994. *The Book of Acts and Paul in Roman Custody.* Vol. 3 of *The Book of Acts in its First Century Setting,* edited by Bruce W. Winter. Grand Rapids: Eerdmans.

Reasoner, Mark. 2005. *Romans in Full Circle: A History of Interpretation.* Louisville: Westminster John Knox.

Reed, Jeffrey T. 1997. "The Epistle." In *Handbook of Classical Rhetoric in the Hellenistic Period 330 B.C.–A.D. 400,* edited by Stanley E. Porter, 171–93. Leiden: Brill.

Renehan, Robert. 1973. "Classical Greek Quotations in the New Testament." In *The Heritage of the Early Church: Essays in Honor of the Very Reverend Georges Vasilievich Florovsky on the Occasion of His Eightieth Birthday*, edited by David Neima and Margaret Schatkin, 17–46. OrChrAn 195. Rome: Pont. Institutum Studiorum Orientalium.

Rhodes, J. N. 2003. "Diet and Desire: The Logic of the Dietary Laws According to Philo." *ETL* 79: 122–33.

Rhyne, C. Thomas. 1981. *Faith Establishes the Law*. SBLDS 55. Chico, CA: Scholars.

Richards, E. Randolph. 2004. *Paul and First-Century Letter Writing: Secretaries, Composition and Collection*. Downers Grove, IL: InterVarsity.

Richardson, Alan. 1958. *An Introduction to the Theology of the New Testament*. New York: Harper.

Riesner, Rainer. 1998. *Paul's Early Period: Chronology, Mission Strategy, Theology*. Translated by Doug Stott. Grand Rapids: Eerdmans.

Robinson, John A. T. 1979. *Wrestling with Romans*. Philadelphia: Westminster.

Roetzel, Calvin J. 2003. *Paul: A Jew on the Margins*. Louisville: Westminster John Knox.

Rohrbaugh, Richard L. 1991. "The Pre-Industrial City in Luke-Acts: Urban Social Relations." In *The Social World of Luke-Acts: Models for Interpretation*, edited by Jerome H. Neyrey, 125–49. Peabody, MA: Hendrickson.

Rosner, Brian S. 1999. *Paul, Scripture and Ethics: A Study of 1 Corinthians 5–7*. Grand Rapids: Baker. Originally published Leiden: Brill, 1994.

Roth, S. John. 1997. *The Blind, the Lame, and the Poor: Character Types in Luke-Acts*. JSNTSup 144. Sheffield: Sheffield Academic.

Rothaus, Richard M. 2000. *Corinth: The First City of Greece, An Urban History of Late Antique Cult and Religion*. Religions in the Graeco-Roman World 139. Leiden: Brill.

Rowe, Galen O. 1997. "Style." In *Handbook of Classical Rhetoric in the Hellenistic Period 330 B.C.–A.D. 400*, edited by Stanley E. Porter, 121–57. Leiden: Brill.

Safrai, S. 1974–76. "Religion in Everyday Life." In *The Jewish People in the First Century: Historical Geography, Political History, Social, Cultural and Religious Life and Institutions*, edited by S. Safrai and M. Stern et al., 793–833. 2 vols. Compendia Rerum Iudaicarum ad Novum Testamentum 1. Vol. 1, Assen: Van Gorcum; Vol. 2, Philadelphia: Fortress.

Sanday, William, and Arthur C. Headlam. *A Critical and Exegetical Commentary on the Epistle to the Romans*. 5th ed. ICC. Edinburgh: T. & T. Clark, 1950.

Sanders, E. P. 1977. *Paul and Palestinian Judaism: A Comparison of Patterns of Religion*. Philadelphia: Fortress.

———. 1983a. *Paul, the Law, and the Jewish People*. Philadelphia: Fortress.

———. 1983b. "Romans 7 and the Purpose of the Law." *PIBA* 7: 44–59.

———. 1985. *Jesus and Judaism*. Philadelphia: Fortress.

———. 1990. *Jewish Law from Jesus to the Mishnah: Five Studies*. Philadelphia: Trinity.

———. 1992. *Judaism: Practice and Belief, 63 BCE–66 CE*. Philadelphia: Trinity.

———. 1993. *The Historical Figure of Jesus*. New York: Allen Lane, Penguin.

———. 2008. "Comparing Judaism and Christianity: An Academic Autobiography." In *Redefining First-Century Jewish and Christian Identities: Essays in Honor of Ed Parish Sanders*, edited by Fabian E. Udoh et al., 11–41. Christianity and Judaism in Antiquity 16. Notre Dame: University of Notre Dame Press.

———. 2009 (forthcoming). "Covenantal Nomism Revisited." *JSQ*.

Schechter, Solomon. 1961. *Aspects of Rabbinic Theology*. New York: Schocken. Originally published New York: Macmillan, 1909.

Schlatter, Adolf von. 1995. *Romans: The Righteousness of God*. Translated by Siegfried S. Schatzmann. Peabody: Hendrickson.

Schmidt, Peter Lebrecht. 2005. "Lector." In *Brill's New Pauly: Encyclopaedia of the Ancient World: Antiquity*, edited by Hubert Cancik and Helmuth Schneider, 7:345. Leiden: Brill.

Schnabel, Eckhard J. 2004. *Early Christian Mission*. 2 vols. Downers Grove, IL: InterVarsity.

Schoeps, Hans Joachim. 1961. *Paul: The Theology of the Apostle in the Light of Jewish Religious History*. Translated by Harold Knight. Philadelphia: Westminster.

Scholer, David M. 1980. "Paul's Women Co-Workers in the Ministry of the Church." *Daughters of Sarah* 6, no. 4: 3–6.

Schreiner, Thomas R. 1998. *Romans*. BECNT. Grand Rapids: Baker.

Schubert, P. 1939. *Form and Function of the Pauline Thanksgivings*. BZNW 20. Berlin: Töpelmann.

Schulz, R. R. 1987. "Romans 16:7: Junia or Junias?" *ExpTim* 98: 108–10.

Scott, James M. 1994. "Luke's Geographical Horizon." In *The Book of Acts in Its Graeco-Roman Setting*, edited by David W. J. Gill and Conrad Gempf, 483–544. The Book of Acts in Its First Century Setting 2. Grand Rapids: Eerdmans.

Scranton, Robert, Joseph W. Shaw, and Leila Ibrahim. 1978. *Topography and Architecture*. Leiden: Brill. Vol. 1 of *Kenchreai, Eastern Port of Corinth: Results of Investigations by The University of Chicago and Indiana University for The American School of Classical Studies at Athens*. Leiden: Brill.

Scroggs, Robin. 1966. *The Last Adam: A Study in Pauline Anthropology*. Philadelphia: Fortress.

———. 1983. *The New Testament and Homosexuality: Contextual Background for Contemporary Debate*. Philadelphia: Fortress.

Seifrid, Mark A. 1992. *Justification by Faith: The Origin and Development of a Central Pauline Theme*. NovTSup 68. Leiden: Brill.

Sevenster, J. N. 1975. *The Roots of Pagan Anti-Semitism in the Ancient World*. NovTSup 41. Leiden: Brill.

Shelton, Jo-Ann. 1998. *As the Romans Did: A Sourcebook in Roman Social History*. 2nd ed. New York: Oxford University Press.

Sherk, Robert K., editor and translator. 1988. *The Roman Empire: Augustus to Hadrian*. Translated Documents of Greece and Rome 6. New York: Cambridge University Press.

Shiell, William David. 2004. *Reading Acts: The Lector and the Early Christian Audience*. Biblical Interpretation Series 70. Leiden: Brill.

Sihvola, Juha, and Troels Engberg-Pedersen, editors. 1998. *The Emotions in Hellenistic Philosophy*. New Synthese Historical Library 46. Dordrecht: Kluwer.

Slater, H. T., Jr. 1969. "Does the Kiddush Precede Christianity?" *AUSS* 7, no. 1: 57–68.

Smith, Barry D. 2006. "'Spirit of Holiness' as Eschatological Principle of Obedience." In *Christian Beginnings and the Dead Sea Scrolls*, edited by John J. Collins and Craig A. Evans, 75–99. Acadia Studies in Bible and Theology. Grand Rapids: Baker Academic.

Söding, T. 1994–95. "Solidarität in der Diaspora. Das Liebesgebot nach den Testamenten der Zwölf Patriarchen im Vergleich mit dem Neuen Testament." *Kairos* 36–37: 1–19.

———. 1995. "Feindeshass und Bruderliebe. Beobachtungen zur essenischen Ethik." *RevQ* 16: 601–19.

———. 1998. "Nächstenliebe bei Jesus Sirach. Eine Notiz zur weisheitlichen Ethik." *BZ* 42: 239–47.

Spilsbury, P. 2003. "Flavius Josephus on the Rise and Fall of the Roman Empire." *JTS* 54: 1–24.

Stambaugh, John E. 1988. *The Ancient Roman City*. Ancient Society and History. Baltimore: Johns Hopkins University Press.

Stanley, Christopher D. 1992. *Paul and the language of Scripture: Citation Technique in the Pauline Epistles and Contemporary Literature*. SNTSMS 69. Cambridge: Cambridge University Press.

———. 1996. "'Neither Jew nor Greek': Ethnic conflict in Graeco-Roman Society." *JSNT* 64: 101–24.

Stendahl, Krister. 1962. "Hate, Non-Retaliation, and Love. 1QS x, 17–20 and Rom. 12:19–21." *HTR* 55: 343–55.

———. 1976. *Paul among Jews and Gentiles and Other Essays*. Philadelphia: Fortress.

Sterling, Gregory E. 1997. "Prepositional Metaphysics in Jewish Wisdom Speculation and Early Christian Liturgical Texts." *SPhilo* 9: 219–38.

Stowers, Stanley Kent. 1981. *The Diatribe and Paul's Letter to the Romans*. SBLDS 57. Chico, CA: Scholars.

———. 1984. "Paul's Dialogue with a Fellow Jew in Romans 3:1–9." *CBQ* 46: 707–22.

———. 1986. *Letter Writing in Greco-Roman Antiquity*. LEC 5. Philadelphia: Westminster.

———. 1994. *A Rereading of Romans: Justice, Jews, and Gentiles*. New Haven: Yale.

———. 2001. "Does Pauline Christianity Resemble a Hellenistic Philosophy?" In *Paul beyond the Judaism/Hellenism Divide*, edited by Troels Engberg-Pedersen, 81–102. Louisville: Westminster John Knox.

———. 2003. "Paul and Self-Mastery." In *Paul in the Greco-Roman World: A Handbook*, edited by J. Paul Sampley, 524–50. Harrisburg, PA: Trinity.

Stuhlmacher, Peter. 1991. "The Theme: The Gospel and the Gospels." In *The Gospel and the Gospels*, edited by Peter Stuhlmacher, 1–25. Grand Rapids: Eerdmans.

———. 1994. *Paul's Letter to the Romans: A Commentary*. Translated by Scott J. Hafemann. Louisville: Westminster/John Knox.

———. 2001. *Revisiting Paul's Doctrine of Justification: A Challenge to the New Perspective*. Downers Grove, IL: InterVarsity.

Talbert, Charles H. 1966. "A Non-Pauline Fragment at Romans 3:24–26?" *JBL* 85: 287–96.

———. 2001. "Paul, Judaism, and the Revisionists." *CBQ* 63: 1–22.

———. 2002. *Romans*. Smyth & Helwys Bible Commentary. Macon, GA: Smyth & Helwys.

Thielman, Frank. 1987. "From Plight to Solution: A Framework for Understanding Paul's View of the Law in Romans and Galatians against a Jewish Background." Ph.D. diss., Duke University.

———. 1994. *Paul and the Law: A Contextual Approach*. Downers Grove, IL: InterVarsity.

Thrall, Margaret E. 1994–2000. *A Critical and Exegetical Commentary on the Second Epistle to the Corinthians.* 2 vols. ICC. Edinburgh: T. & T. Clark.

Tiller, P. A. 1997. "The 'Eternal Planting' in the Dead Sea Scrolls." *DSD* 4: 312–35.

Tobin, Thomas H. 2004. *Paul's Rhetoric in Its Contexts: The Argument of Romans.* Peabody, MA: Hendrickson.

Trebilco, Paul R. 1991. *Jewish Communities in Asia Minor.* SNTSMS 69. Cambridge: Cambridge University Press.

Turner, Max. 1994. "The Spirit of Christ and 'Divine' Christology." In *Jesus of Nazareth: Lord and Christ, Essays on the Historical Jesus and New Testament Christology*, edited by Joel B. Green and Max Turner, 413–36. Grand Rapids: Eerdmans.

———. 1996. *Power from on High: The Spirit in Israel's Restoration and Witness in Luke-Acts.* Journal of Pentecostal Theology Supplement Series 9. Sheffield: Sheffield Academic.

———. 1998. *The Holy Spirit and Spiritual Gifts in the New Testament Church and Today.* Rev. ed. Peabody, MA: Hendrickson.

Urbach, Ephraim E. 1979. *The Sages: Their Concepts and Beliefs.* Translated by Israel Abrahams. 2 vols. 2nd ed. Jerusalem: Magnes, Hebrew University.

Venetz, H.-J. 2002. "Frauen von Rang und Namen. Ein anderer Blick in paulinische Gemeinden." *BK* 57:127–33.

Vermès, Géza. 1993. *The Religion of Jesus the Jew.* Minneapolis: Augsburg Fortress.

Vidler, Alec R. 1974. *The Church in an Age of Revolution: 1789 to the Present Day.* Penguin History of the Church 5. London: Penguin.

Wagner, Günter. 1967. *Pauline Baptism and the Pagan Mysteries: The Problem of the Pauline Doctrine of Baptism in Romans VI.1–11, in the Light of Its Religio-Historical "Parallels."* Translated by J. P. Smith. Edinburgh: Oliver & Boyd.

Wagner, J. Ross. 2002. *Heralds of the Good News: Isaiah and Paul "in Concert" in the Letter to the Romans.* NovTSup 101. Leiden: Brill.

Wallace-Hadrill, Andrew. 2003. "*Domus* and *Insulae* in Rome: Families and Housefuls." In *Early Christian Families in Context: An Interdisciplinary Dialogue*, edited by David L. Balch and Carolyn Osiek, 3–18. Grand Rapids: Eerdmans.

Wallis, Richard T. 1974–75. "The Idea of Conscience in Philo of Alexandria." *SPhilo* 3: 27–40.

———. 1975. "The Idea of Conscience in Philo of Alexandria." Center for Hermeneutical Studies in Hellenistic and Modern Culture Colloquy 13. Berkeley, CA: Center for Hermeneutical Studies in Hellenistic and Modern Culture.

Walters, James C. 2003. "Paul, Adoption, and Inheritance." In *Paul in the Greco-Roman World: A Handbook*, edited by J. Paul Sampley, 42–76. Harrisburg, PA: Trinity.

Watson, Deborah Elaine. 2006. "Paul's Collection in Light of Motivations and Mechanisms for Aid to the Poor in the First-Century World." Ph.D. diss., University of Durham.

Watson, Duane F. 2003. "Paul and Boasting." In *Paul in the Greco-Roman World: A Handbook*, edited by J. Paul Sampley, 77–100. Harrisburg, PA: Trinity.

Watson, Francis. 2007. *Paul, Judaism, and the Gentiles: Beyond the New Perspective.* Rev. ed. Grand Rapids: Eerdmans.

Weima, J. A. D. 1994. *Neglected Endings: The Significance of the Pauline Letter Closings.* JSNTSup 101. Sheffield: JSOT Press, Sheffield Academic.

———. 2000. "Epistolary Theory." In *DNTB*, 327–30.

Wenham, David. 1984. "Paul's Use of the Jesus Tradition: Three Samples." In *The Jesus Tradition Outside the Gospels*, edited by David Wenham, 7–37. Gospel Perspectives 5. Sheffield: JSOT Press.

White, L. Michael. 1996–97. *The Social Origins of Christian Architecture*. 2 vols. HTS 42. Valley Forge, PA: Trinity.

———. 2003. "Paul and *Pater Familias*." In *Paul in the Greco-Roman World: A Handbook*, edited by J. Paul Sampley, 457–87. Harrisburg, PA: Trinity.

Whittaker, Molly. 1984. *Jews and Christians: Graeco-Roman Views*. Cambridge Commentaries on Writings of the Jewish and Christian World, 200 BC to AD 200; 6. Cambridge: Cambridge University Press.

Wiles, Gordon P. 1974. *Paul's Intercessory Prayers: The Significance of the Intercessory Prayer Passages in the Letters of St Paul*. SNTSMS 24. Cambridge: Cambridge University Press.

Wilken, Robert Louis. 1998. "Roman Redux." *Christian History* 57: 42–44.

Williams, Margaret H. 2002. "*Alexander, bubularius de macello*: Humble Sausage-seller or Europe's First Identifiable Purveyor of Kosher Beef?" *Latomus* 61: 122–33.

Winter, Bruce W. 1994. *Seek the Welfare of the City: Christians as Benefactors and Citizens*. First-Century Christians in the Graeco-Roman World. Grand Rapids: Eerdmans.

———. 2001. *After Paul Left Corinth: The Influence of Secular Ethics and Social Change*. Grand Rapids: Eerdmans.

Wolfson, Harry Austryn. 1968. *Philo: Foundations of Religious Philosophy in Judaism, Christianity, and Islam*. 2 vols. Rev. ed. Cambridge: Harvard University Press.

Wright, N. T. 1999. "New Exodus, New Inheritance: The Narrative Structure of Romans 3–8." In *Romans and the People of God: Essays in Honor of Gordon D. Fee on the Occasion of His 65th Birthday*, edited by Sven K. Soderlund and N. T. Wright, 26–35. Grand Rapids: Eerdmans.

———. 2004. *Paul for Everyone: Romans*. Vol. 1. Louisville: Westminster John Knox.

Wuellner, Wilhelm. 1976. "Paul's Rhetoric of Argumentation in Romans: An Alternative to the Donfried-Karris Debate over Romans." *CBQ* 38: 330–51.

Yadin, Yigael. 1969. *Tefillin from Qumran (X Q Phyl 1–4)*. Jerusalem: Israel Exploration Society and the Shrine of the Book.

Young, N. H. 1974. "Did St. Paul Compose Romans iii.24f.?" *ABR* 22: 23–32.

Scripture Index

Romans (not including section and paragraph headings)

1 Corinthians

Ancient Sources Index

Josephus

Philo of Alexandria

Amoraic and Later Rabbinic Sources

Babylonian Talmud

INSCRIPTIONS AND PAPYRI

OTHER NON-MODERN SOURCES

Author Index

Subject Index